HUMAN RESOURCE MANAGEMENT

Issues, Challenges and Opportunities

HUMAN RESOURCE MANAGEMENT

Issues, Challenges and Opportunities

Rae Simons
Small-business owner and author,
Vestal, New York, U.S.A.

Apple Academic Press

Human Resource Management: Issues, Challenges and Opportunities

© Copyright 2011*
Apple Academic Press Inc.

This book contains information obtained from authentic and highly regarded sources. A wide variety of references are listed. Reasonable efforts have been made to publish reliable data and information, but the editors and the publisher cannot assume responsibility for the validity of all materials or for the consequences of their use.

First Published in the Canada, 2011
Apple Academic Press Inc.
3333 Mistwell Crescent
Oakville, ON L6L 0A2
Tel. : (888) 241-2035
Fax: (866) 222-9549
E-mail: info@appleacademicpress.com
www.appleacademicpress.com

> The full-color tables, figures, diagrams, and images in this book may be viewed at
> www.appleacademicpress.com

First issued in paperback 2021

ISBN 13: 978-1-77463-225-3 (pbk)
ISBN 13: 978-1-926692-89-0 (hbk)

Rae Simons

Cover Design: Psqua

Library and Archives Canada Cataloguing in Publication Data
CIP Data on file with the Library and Archives Canada

To the best of the publisher's knowledge, all articles in this book are copyrighted to the individual authors and are licensed and distributed under the Creative Commons Attribution License, which permits unrestricted use, distribution, and reproduction in any medium, provided the original work is properly cited.

CONTENTS

INTRODUCTION

Management in business pursuits and organizations can be defined as the process of coordinating people and processes in order to accomplish specific goals and objectives. Business management specifically includes planning, organizing, staffing, directing operations, and resourcing. Resourcing, furthermore, requires the strategic use of human, financial, technological, and natural resources in accomplishing the goals of a business entity. Because businesses can be usefully viewed as "systems," business management can be seen as human action designed to facilitate useful outcomes from that system. This view allows for the opportunity to "manage" oneself, an important factor to consider before managing operations and employees.

Business management is generally viewed as equivalent to "business administration". College and university departments that teach business management are often called "business schools", such as the Harvard Business School. Others use the broader term "schools of management" (such as the Yale School of Management), which by definition include the management of entities outside of commerce, such as in nonprofit organizations and in the public sector.

In this book, current research in human resources has been appropriately emphasized. Human resource management is the function within an organization that focuses on recruitment of, management of, and providing direction for the people who work in the organization. It is the organizational function that deals with issues related to people such as compensation, hiring, performance management, organization development, safety, wellness, benefits, employee motivation, communication, administration, and training.

Human resource management is the strategic approach to the management of an organization's most valuable asset—the people who work for that organization and who, individually and collectively, contribute to the achievement of the objectives of the business Simply put, human resource management means employing people, training them, developing their talents, and utilizing, maintaining and compensating them for their services as appropriate to the requirements of the organization.

The competitive nature of twenty-first-century global commerce requires that businesses be managed strategically by managers who are knowledgeable in the principles of the field. The efficient, nonexploitive use of human resources is essential to building successful businesses around the world.

— Rae Simons

Corporate Social Responsibility: The Key Role of Human Resource Management

Suparn Sharma, Joity Sharma and Arti Devi

ABSTRACT

Business organizations have waked up to the need for being committed towards Corporate Social Responsibility. But still majority have just been taking up some form of philanthropic activities for its stakeholders. Nurturing a strong corporate culture which emphasizes Corporate Social Responsibility (CSR) values and competencies is required to achieve the synergistic benefits. The employees of an organization occupy a central place in developing such a culture which underlines CSR values and competencies. The present study, therefore, is an attempt to explore the engagement of human resource management professionals in undertaking Corporate Social Responsibility. It also suggests Human Resource Management to take a leading role in encouraging

CSR activities at all levels. The combined impact of CSR and human resource activities, which reinforce desirable behavior, can make a major contribution in creating long term success in organizations.

Introduction

Business houses, right from the inception of human race, have been regarded as constructive partners in the communities in which they operate. Though they have been instrumental in creating employment, wealth, products and services, yet the pressure on business to play a role in social issues involving employees, stakeholders, society, environment, government etc. is continuously increasing. The society is questioning the existence of business houses, especially in the wake of the scandals and scams conducted by the business houses like UTI, Enron, and WorldCom. In response to it, the organizations around the globe are forced to wake up to the need for being committed towards Corporate Social Responsibility. Over the years this concept of Corporate Social Responsibility (CSR) has gained unprecedent momentum in business and public debate and has become a strategic issue crossing the departmental boundaries, and affecting the way in which a company does business. It has become so important that many organizations have rebranded their core values to include social responsibility. Almost all corporate websites/ policies/reports talk about their endeavors for CSR which has become a way of ensuring that the organization is fulfilling all the obligations towards society and thus is eligible for the license to operate. It assures that the organization can grow on sustainable basis.

These activities of CSR ranging from small donations to bigger projects for social welfare sustainable practices differ from organization to organization depending on the resources available to an organization for undertaking sustainable practices. Business practices of big and successful companies, with plenty of resources at their end, have set the trend for being committed to sustainable practices. Such business houses around the globe show their commitment to social responsibility. In India, the initiatives of Dabur India Limited, for example, which commenced 'Sundesh' in 1993, a non-profit organization, with an aim to promote research and welfare activities in rural areas are appreciable. On the same track to fulfill its urge to do something for community, Bharat Petroleum Corporation Limited has adopted 37 villages as their responsibility to develop in all walks of life. It has made efforts to make them self-reliant, provided them fresh drinking water, sanitation facilities, medical facilities, vocational training and literacy camps. Around its industrial facilities, Tata Group has created towns and cities like Jamshedpur, Mithapur, Babrala for the benefit of its employees. Cadbury India, Glaxo and Richardson Hindustan are some of the companies which are helping farmers to grow crops which in turn shall serve as raw materials for them (Tripathi & Reddy, 2006).

Although the implementation of such activities involves time, effort and resources yet the business houses have realized that it (CSR) is one of the important ways in which an organization can distinguish itself from its competitors. The tangible and intangible benefits associated with for organization are immense. A powerful tool like CSR not only enhances the brand image and reputation of the business but also leads to improvement in sales and customer loyalty, and increased ability to attract and retain employees. By capitalizing on it, the organizations can improve their financial performance and attract more investment with immense economic value. The word CSR has, as a result, occupied very important place in the plans and strategies of the organizations in the present era.

But still there are numerous organizations which understand CSR as undertaking some donations or philanthropic activities. Rather in its true sense CSR constitutes a strong commitment to social obligations and internalization throughout the organizational culture which lays emphasis on the execution of the obligations towards the employees and involving them in responsible endeavors. However from the very beginning the key player in undertaking such activities in the organizations has been top management and it has been the driving force in the area of social responsibility. Employees have been rarely covered under the ambit of CSR. To ensure organization-wide commitment, non-management workforce has to be involved in the process. This involvement of employees speaks of the strategic contribution of Human Resource Management (HRM) in CSR. In this context, the responsibility of human resource management department for encouraging sustainable practices that offer practically and theoretically new opportunities is very much.

So the present composition is an attempt to find out that how the staff can become the brand ambassadors of the organizations and that "feel good factor" can permeate out to others, especially customers and clients. To commensurate that it will try to suggest a plan of action by analyzing the CSR activities of various organizations to promote sound corporate citizenship which is necessary for the development of a culture for social responsibility. Divided into three sections, the present study shall put light on the studies emphasizing the involvement of human resources in socially responsible endeavors in Section I. Section II proposes suggestions on internalizing social responsibility by underlining the contribution of Human Resource (HR) and Section III concludes the study.

Literature Review

Different researchers at different points of time have emphasized the critical importance of HR for the proper implementation of CSR and the role that HR can play in developing the process where the business objectives are assessed and values re-aligned to match them with staff expectations.

Greening & Turban (2000) found that job applicant and employee perceptions of a firm's CSR determines their attractiveness towards the organizations. Moving on the same track Cropanzano et al. (2001) demonstrates that employee attitudes and behaviors are heavily influenced by fairness of organizational actions towards them. In a survey conducted by Cherenson group, a New Jersey based public relations and recruitment ad agency; in 2002 found that the most important factors affecting the reputation of an organization as a place to work in are the way the employees are treated and the quality of its products and services. Further Good relationships with employees also allows a company to gain additional benefits including improving their public image, increasing employee morale, and support from the community (Zappala and Cronin, 2002). Nancy (2004) while discussing the role of HR in developing CSR culture in organizations emphasized that with the growing importance of human capital as a success factor for today's organizations, the role of HR leadership has become more critical in leading and educating organizations on the value of CSR and how best to strategically implement CSR policies and programmes domestically and abroad. In view of this HR must be aware that effective CSR means respect for cultural and developmental differences and sensitivity to imposing values, ideas and beliefs when establishing global HR policies and programmes.

Redington (2005) with the help of twelve case studies, while underlining the HR professionals' key role in managing the changes required for CSR activities to succeed, stated that employees are the most neglected though most important stakeholder of the organization for conducting CSR activities. While accentuating on this issue he said that having a good reputation socially implies that a company's behaviour towards its people is consistent and is of a particular standard in which they are valued in as much as the external stakeholders. Rupp et. al. (2006) accentuated that CSR plays a role about fostering positive social relationships between organizations and communities. They highlighted that employees will turn to CSR to assess the extent to which their organization values such relationships and so high levels of CSR can meet employees' need for belongingness with the organization and the society. A survey by Sirota Survey Intelligence (2007) affirmed that employees who are satisfied with their organization's commitment to social and environmental responsibilities are likely to be more positive, more engaged and more productive than those working for less responsible employers and when employees are positive about their organizations' CSR commitment, their engagement rises to 86 per cent. On the other hand, when employees are negative about their employer's CSR activities, only 37 per cent are highly engaged.

Similarly, Murray (2008) on the basis of survey stated that more than one-third of respondents pointed that working for a caring and responsible employer was more important than the salary they earned and nearly half would turn away from an employer that lacked good corporate social responsibility policies.

However Fenwick & Bierema (2008) has pointed that HR department, which has the potential to play a significant role in developing CSR activities within the organization, found to be marginally involved or interested in CSR. Mehta (2003), in a survey, found that only 13 per cent of the companies involved their employees in undertaking the various CSR activities. Moreover, the employees have also been less likely to fully internalize the corporate culture (Rupp, et. al, 2006). The implementation of the CSR policy has also traditionally been in the hands of 'management' and 'employees' as the non-management workforce have been less likely to be involved in developing and implementing a policy on business responsibility towards society. There are large variations in the understanding of CSR in the head office and the local plant or sales office of an organization (Young, 2006). The perceptions of workers and management also differ about whether an organization is complying with such regulations as related to labour or working conditions (Mehta, 2003).

Agarwal (2007) stated that with the adoption of HR policies, such as, periodic review of employee performance, adequate training for the workforce and career advancement norms for its personnel, creating motivation, and commitment in the workforce the organization can reap the full business benefits and become successful to the great satisfaction of all its stakeholders. This is also reinforced by Malikarjunan (2006). Emphasizing upon such dimensions Krishnan & Balachandran (2004) pointed out the role of HRM in incorporating responsible practices within an organization. It is due to the lack of involvement of employees and failure to embed the socially responsible values into the organizational culture that many CSR initiatives inevitably fail and they just become an exercise in public relations (Mees & Bonham, 2004).

The above verdicts of different researchers at different points of time entail that no doubt they have underscored the role of employee involvement through HR in various socially responsible initiatives of organization. But they have paid little attention on this aspect that how the internalization of CSR culture can happen with the initiatives of HR department of organization. How the company's values and policies for corporate responsibility can be reflected through various HR functions and consequently how the HR function can be a powerful agent in effecting company-wide progress in its CSR performance. With this backdrop in mind present study has designed.

Internalizing CSR: Initiatives of HRM

The role of HR function in embedding the CSR values in the corporate culture is immense and has been underlined also. An organization can exhibit a better image in the minds of people by presenting itself as an excellent employer which cares for its people and involves them in the ambit of social responsibility. This involvement of employees indicates the strategic importance of HRM in the CSR initiatives of an organization. Human Resource policies, forming the framework for the culture in the business management, create awareness towards the need to achieve the business goals in the best possible and ethical manner (Agrawal, 2007). With the help of HR functions, the socially responsible values can be inculcated and sustained in the organizational culture through the following ways:

- The HR department should take the responsibility to develop a formal policy on sustainable practices involving employees. British gas, for example, used employee volunteering as a vehicle to achieve business-driven culture. The success of the initiative led to the development of a formal policy on employee volunteering. The company developed the 'Cardiff Cares' volunteering initiative with the purpose of encouraging employees to raise funds and donate some of their time to the local community (Redington, 2005). Employee fundraising was a way to show support for the local community, to build positive team spirit in the organization and to create a 'winning' environment at the workplace. The managing director and the HR team's strong commitment enabled the initiative to be a big success improving the employee retention levels and employee satisfaction.

- The orientation programme of newly recruited candidates should be designed in a manner that corporate philosophy about CSR gets highlighted. The commitment of top management towards CSR is very important which should be expressed in tangible terms to reinforce the right kind of behavior in the organization. Wipro, for example, inculcates CSR values amongst its workforce right at the beginning during the induction process. Corporate presentations, keeping employees updated through mails, regular newsletters are the instruments used to keep employees energized about the organization's socially responsible initiatives.

- The designing of Performance Management System should be done in such a manner that it measures the socially responsible initiatives taken by employees. This becomes important as the internalization of CSR in an organizational culture requires that appropriate behaviors get appraised, appreciated as well as rewarded. Otherwise, the organization might fail to inculcate it amongst all employees due to lack of positive reinforcement.

- The Training facilities may also be made available to instill the CSR culture among employees. This becomes necessary to make employees learn and practice CSR activities. The training of employees through "CSR Living Our Values Learning Tool" at Cadbury Schweppes (Young, 2006), the major global beverage and confectionary organization, has been a good example of partnership between HR and CSR. The company has also included social responsibility in the latest management development initiatives like the global "Passion for People" management skills programme.

- Empowerment of managers by giving them decision-making authority shall help in executing social responsibility at local level. It becomes important when an organization with plants or units at multiple locations around the world operate. Armed with decision making authority, the managers will be able to appreciate and assess the needs. Therefore, the employees may be appropriately authorized to encourage initiative in the area of social responsibility. Clear reporting and review mechanisms may be put in place in the organization which shall improve the focus and effectiveness of CSR (Mehta, 2003).

- Code of ethics of an organization can stimulate social responsibility to a great extent reinforcing amongst its employees the underlying values. Training on code of ethics should be undertaken by the organization. Best Buy, a fortune 100 company and the largest specialty retailer of consumer electronics in the United States and Canada, has initiated ethics training for its employees. Electronic Data Systems (EDS) has a global CSR strategy which is well supported by HR function and the employees (Redington, 2005). The HR department of the company has also developed an e-learning course for its employees built around the Department of Trade and Industry, CSR Competency framework.

- Responsible Human Resource Management practices on equal opportunities, diversity management, whistle blowing, redundancy, human rights, harrasment shall give credibility to the CSR initiatives of the organization. It is beyond doubt that protecting human rights such as denial or prevention of legal or social rights of workers is a very important issue under CSR. Companies like Wipro, Infosys, Dabur, and ICICI have even framed whistle blowing policy, providing protection to the employees who come to know about any unethical practice going on within the organization, covering a whole gamut of subjects and showing their positive approach towards unethical practices.

- The separation of employees during mergers, acquisitions, downsizing etc. should be strategically aligned with the business strategy as well as Corporate Social responsibility. Retraining, retention, redeployment of people can be worked out with aggressive communication, information campaigns and outplacement services in place to assist the transition of people from the organization. Hindustan Unilever Limited (HUL), for example, provided outplacement services to the employees of its foods division at Bangalore when they were unable to move to Mumbai in 2006. Over 60 firms and 25 placement agencies were contacted by the company to arrange for multiple job interviews for a number of employees.

- Social Reports or Sustainability Reports should be prepared to underline the organization's commitment to social or sustainable practices. In India, the top management, in their messages, speeches to shareholders and in annual reports has been resorting to social reporting but it should be made more formal in nature (Bhatia, 2005 & Raman, 2006). Tata Steel Limited, for example, has been preparing Sustainability Reports under the stringent guidelines of Global Reporting Initiatives, 2002 on economic, environment and social performance.

- The Human Resource department should effectively measure and evaluate CSR activities. The value added by CSR in the form of direct results, such as, economic savings and indirect results like increase in employee satisfaction, less employee turnover, measured by staff attitude surveys, shall indicate contribution to improved business performance. There is also a need to conduct periodic review of the CSR activities. CurAlea Management Consultants Pvt. Ltd. (2007) has suggested for conduction of periodically an independent internal review or audit of the effectiveness of CSR programmes.

Conclusion

Successful programmes on social responsibility rely heavily on enlightened people management practices. In this context HR department is assumed to be the co-ordinator of CSR activities in getting the employment relationship right which is a precondition for establishing effective relationships with external stakeholders and thus can orient the employees and the organization towards a socially responsible character. There is also an increasing trend in the corporate sector which has started leveraging upon employees and their management for exhibiting their commitment towards CSR. Armed with a strong and committed organizational culture reinforced by responsible Human Resource Management practices, the organizations can achieve heights of success by improved profitability, employee morale, customer satisfaction, legal compliance and societal approval for its existence. It is high time for all other organizations which have been paying only lip service to CSR that they must capitalize upon the existing Human Resource Department in framing such practices, procedures and policies that ensure the internalization of quality, ethics and excellence in the whole system. By doing this they can sensitize the employees and the whole organization towards CSR without adding any additional cost.

To recapitulate it can be said that companies have increasingly felt the need to co-ordinate their CSR activities and demonstrate their commitment to social responsibility. But delivery, not rhetoric, is the key in developing the trust of external stakeholders for any organisation and it cannot be done without beginning charity at home. To do that social responsibility needs to be embedded in an organisation's culture to bring change in actions and attitudes in which Human Resource can play a significant role. Otherwise, CSR may run the risk of being categorised as shallow 'window-dressing'.

References

Agrawal Kalpana (2007). Corporate Excellence as an Outcome of Corporate Governance: Rethinking the Role and Responsibility of HRM, the ICFAI Journal of Corporate Governance, Vol.VI (1): 6–16.

Bhatia S (2005). Business Ethics and Corporate Governance, Deep and Deep Publications Pvt. Ltd., New Delhi.

Cropanzano R, Byrne ZS, Bobocel DR, & Rupp D E (2001). Moral virtues, fairness heuristics, social entities, and other denizens of organizational justice, Journal of Vocational Behavior, 58: 164–209.

Fenwick Tara, Bierema Laura (2008). Corporate Social Responsibility: Issues for Human Resource Development Professionals, International Journal of training and Development, Vol. 12(1).

Greening DW, & Turban DB (2000). Corporate social Performance as a competitive advantage in attracting a quality workforce, Business and Society, 39: 254–280.

http://timesofindia.indiatimes.com/articleshow accessed on August 4th, 2008

http://www.curalea.com/pdffiles/CurAlea_ApproachPaperForAuditofCSR accessed on August 26th, 2008.

http://www.developednation.org/interviews accessed on May 8th, 2008

http://www.hrmguide.net/usa/commitment/employer_branding accessed on March 30th, 2008.

http://www.karmayog.org/csr500companies/ accessed on April 7th, 2008.

http://www.tatasteel.com/corporatesustainability accessed on April 25th, 2008

Krishnnan K, Sandeep & Balachandran Rakesh (2004). Corporate Social Responsibility as a determinant of Market Success: An Exploratory Analysis with Special Reference to MNCs in Emerging Markets, paper presented at IIM K- NASMEI International Conference.

Malikarjunan K (2006). Best of HRM Practices, HRM Review, Vol. VI (2): 33–34.

Mees Adine & Bonham Jamie (2004). Corporate Social Responsibility Belongs with HR, Canadian HR Reporter, Vol. 17(7): 11

Mehta Bindi (2003). Corporate Social Responsibility Initiatives of NSE NIFTY Companies: Content, Implementation, Strategies & Impact, retrieved on April 15th, 2008 from http://www.nseindia.com/content/research/res_papers.

Murray Norm E (2008). Corporate Social Responsibility is the Number One Criteria for Job Hunters Today, retrieved on March 30, 2008 from http://normmurray.org/2008/02/18/corporate-social-responsibility-is-the-number-one-criteria-for-job-hunters-today/

Nancy R Lockwood (2004). Corporate Social Responsibility: HR's Leadership Role December, retrieved on June 15th, 2008 from http://www.shrm.org/Research/quarterly/1204RQuart_essay.asp.

Raman S Raghu (2006). Corporate Social Reporting in India-A View from the Top, Global Business Review, Vol. 7(2): 313–24.

Redington Ian (2005). Making CSR Happen: The Contribution of People Management, Chartered Institute of Personnel and Development, retrieved on April 15, 2008 from www.bitc.org.uk/document.rm?id=5103.

Rupp Deborah E, Ganapathi Jyoti, Aguilera Ruth V, Williams Cynthia A (2006). Employee Reactions to Corporate Social Responsibility: An Organizational Justice Framework, Journal of Organizational Behavior, 27: 537–43.

Sirota Survey Intelligence (2007) quoted from CSR boosts employee engagement, Social responsibility boosts employee engagement 09 May, http://www.management-issues.com/2007/5/9/research/social-responsibility-boosts-employee-engagement.asp

Tripathi PC and Reddy PN (2006). Principles of Management, Tata McGraw Hill, New Delhi: 41.

Young Mark (2006). HR as the Guardian of Corporate Values at Cadbury Schweppes, Strategic HR Review, Vol.5 (2): 10–11.

Zappala Gianni and Cronin Caitlin (2002). The Employee Dimensions of Corporate Community Involvement in Australia: Trends and Prospects, Paper Presented at the 6th ANZTSR Conference; 27-29 November, Auckland, New Zealand, 1–24.

Assessment of Human Resources Management Practices in Lebanese Hospitals

Fadi El-Jardali, Victoria Tchaghchagian and Diana Jamal

ABSTRACT

Background

Sound human resources (HR) management practices are essential for retaining effective professionals in hospitals. Given the recruitment and retention reality of health workers in the twenty-first century, the role of HR managers in hospitals and those who combine the role of HR managers with other responsibilities should not be underestimated. The objective of this study is to assess the perception of HR managers about the challenges they face and the current strategies being adopted. The study also aims at assessing enabling factors including role, education, experience and HR training.

Methods

A cross-sectional survey design of HR managers (and those who combine their role as HR manager with other duties) in Lebanese hospitals was utilized. The survey included a combination of open- and close-ended questions. Questions included educational background, work experience, and demographics, in addition to questions about perceived challenges and key strategies being used. Quantitative data analysis included uni-variate analysis, whereas thematic analysis was used for open-ended questions.

Results

A total of 96 respondents from 61 hospitals responded. Respondents had varying levels of expertise in the realm of HR management. Thematic analysis revealed that challenges varied across respondents and participating hospitals. The most frequently reported challenge was poor employee retention (56.7%), lack of qualified personnel (35.1%), and lack of a system for performance evaluation (28.9%). Some of the strategies used to mitigate the above challenges included offering continuing education and training for employees (19.6%), improving salaries (14.4%), and developing retention strategies (10.3%). Mismatch between reported challenges and strategies were observed.

Conclusion

To enable hospitals to deliver good quality, safe healthcare, improving HR management is critical. There is a need for a cadre of competent HR managers who can fully assume these responsibilities and who can continuously improve the status of employees at their organizations. The upcoming accreditation survey of Lebanese hospitals (2010-2011) presents an opportunity to strengthen HR management and enhance competencies of existing HR managers. Recognizing HR challenges and the importance of effective HR strategies should become a priority to policy makers and top managers alike. Study findings may extend to other countries in the Eastern Mediterranean region.

Background

The 2006 World Health Report [1] launched the Health Workforce Decade (2006-2015), with high priority given to retaining high-quality health care workers. The Kampala Declaration (2008) stressed the crucial role of retaining an effective, responsive and equitably distributed health workforce [2]. Sound human resources (HR) management practices are a key strategy for retaining effective health professionals in health care organizations (HCOs). Given the recruitment and retention reality of the health workforce in the twenty-first century, the role of HR managers in health care organizations (HCOs) and those who combine the role of HR managers with other responsibilities should not be underestimated.

One of the biggest challenges for hospitals today is the availability of a strong, capable, and motivated workforce. Hospitals are 'people-driven' and their primary expenses are labour costs. As in many developed and developing countries, many hospitals in Middle Eastern countries have come to realize that the most important asset to their organization, besides physical capital and consumables, is their health human resources, without which they cannot properly function [3]. At the system level, evidence indicates a strong link between the availability of health care providers and population health outcomes [4].

Poor work environments and the absence of sound recruitment and retention practices are some of the key health human resources challenges that are facing many Middle Eastern hospitals. These obstacles have resulted in growing staff shortages, attrition and early retirement, poor staff satisfaction, high turnover, and emigration [5]. Many hospitals suffer from poor managerial and planning capacity in the area of health human resources, and lack recruitment and retention strategies. Such strategies are essential in terms of planning, job satisfaction, and intent to stay [6]. Few studies have been conducted to assess recruitment and retention practices and strategies in the Eastern Mediterranean Region (EMR). A study targeting nursing directors in Lebanon found that the majority of the sampled hospitals (88.2%) reported facing challenges in retaining their nurses due to unsatisfactory salary and benefits (80.8%); unsuitable shifts and working hours (38.4%); presence of better opportunities abroad (30.1%) and within the country (30.1%); workload (27.4%); and instability of the country (16.4%) [6]. Many hospitals reported engaging in strategies to mitigate the above challenges such as offering financial rewards and benefits (62.7%); implementing a salary scale (47.8%); flexible schedules (31.3%); staff development (29.9%); offering praise, incentives and motivation (19.4%); improving the relationship between nurses and management (19.4%); improving work environment (14.9%); and promotion opportunities (11.9%) [6]. One of the main findings of the study was the mismatch between reported challenges and implemented strategies which will probably lead to further challenges for Nursing Directors in Lebanese hospitals.

There is a need for sound and proven strategies developed by HR managers for recruiting and retaining HR in hospitals. Hospitals need effective Human Resources Management (HRM) to be able to deliver quality and safe care [7]. According to evidence in the literature, effective HRM practices lead to better health and well-being of workers, higher satisfaction, lower absenteeism and turnover, financial advantages (reduced costs, increased productivity), and better quality of care and patient outcomes. Thus effective HRM strategies practiced by HR managers are becoming critical to the success of hospitals [7]. The most prominent challenges to HRM include policies and procedures which hinder the process and delay recruitment and retention; very centralized and fragmented HR management systems; lack of incentives; poor utilization of current staff in addition to absence of proper leadership [8]. In spite of the fact that effective human resources management is essential for the success of organizations, limited knowledge is available about the challenges and the nature of interventions utilized by human resource managers in hospitals including enabling factors and the competences they have or require. In addition, limited knowledge is available on the number, qualifications, experience and competences of existing HR managers in hospitals. This is known in several East Mediterranean countries, and Lebanon is no exception.

To our knowledge, no study has been done in Lebanon and the region to survey HR managers in hospitals about their views on current HR challenges, strategies implemented, and enabling factors including role, education, experience and training.

Objective

The objective of this study is to assess the HR challenges and strategies as perceived by HR managers in Lebanese hospitals. Specifically, the study is aimed at assessing the perception of HR managers about the challenges they face and the current strategies being adopted. The study also aims at assessing enabling factors including role, education, experience and HR training.

Methods

A cross-sectional survey design of HR managers (and those who combine their role as HR manager with other duties) working in all Lebanese hospitals was developed. To ensure a balanced design with respect to service and care characteristics, the hospitals were stratified by size (number of beds) into the three categories defined by the Lebanese Ministry of Health as follows: small (≤ 100 beds), medium (101-200 beds) and large (>200 beds).

The survey targeted HR managers (and employees who combine the role of HR manager with other duties) in Lebanese hospitals and was designed based on an extensive literature review and discussions among the research group. The research team used a combination of open- and close-ended questions to allow the HR managers to better document their viewpoints regarding challenges and strategies. Questions included educational background, qualifications, work experience, gender, and age. The survey also included questions about perceived challenges facing the human resources component at hospitals and key strategies to mitigate these challenges. These were open-ended questions so that respondents could freely describe the specific issues pertaining to each question. The survey also addressed other issues such as the categories of human resources with whom HR managers were facing the most challenges in retention, frequency of conducting performance appraisal, trends in assessment of credentialing for medical and nursing staff, existing continuing education or development programs, in addition to the presence of recruitment and retention strategies being utilized by the hospital.

The questionnaire was originally developed in English and then translated to Arabic as it is the primary language of most HR managers in Lebanon. Back translation to English was conducted to validate the Arabic translation. After the questionnaire was finalized, it was pilot tested for both language versions after which minor changes were made to the wording of some questions.

HR managers (and those who combine the role of HR manager with other duties) in all Lebanese hospitals were contacted. Hospitals were asked to forward the survey to individuals in charge of the HR function. When contacted, the hospitals were informed about the purpose and significance of the study. Hospitals were assured that participation was voluntary in addition to the confidentiality and anonymity of their responses. After obtaining informed consent to participate in the study, the questionnaire was provided to HR managers. In some instances, hospitals did not have a designated HR manager, therefore, two or more employees often combined their primary role in the hospital (whether clinical or non-clinical) with the HR management function. In these cases, all employees affiliated with the HR department filled the survey.

All hospitals were sent a fax requesting their participation in the study. A total of 72 hospitals expressed their willingness to participate and 61 hospitals responded to the survey with a total of 97 respondents.

Data Analysis

Data was entered and analyzed using the Statistical Package for Social Sciences (SPSS) 16.0. The quantitative data analysis included uni-variate and bi-variate analysis. The qualitative data analysis comprised thematic analysis of open-ended questions to derive the main challenges and strategies adopted by hospitals as perceived by HR managers. Answers were thematically analyzed and coded. Similar codes were grouped under categories and related categories were then gathered under themes. Strategies were compared against reported challenges to assess whether the adopted strategies can serve to mitigate the impact of the reported challenges. Thematic analysis followed both an inductive and deductive approach whereby some themes were based on a search of the literature (inductive) and others emerged from findings (deductive). The predetermined HR challenges included financial constraints, employee shortages and lack of qualified personnel, migration, poor job satisfaction, recruitment challenges (or lack of such a system), and poor employee retention (incentive programs). As for proposed strategies, the predetermined themes included improving salaries and strengthening incentive plans, enhancing managerial support, developing recruitment and retention strategies, and offering continuing education to staff. Additional challenges and strategies were also derived from the deductive approach.

Analysis of quantitative data included questions on level of education, qualifications in HR management, experience and training in HR management, and plans for continuing education in the realm of HR management, in addition to other information about the hospital where respondents were employed.

Results

Characteristics of Respondents

When the respondents were asked whether they were in charge of the HR function at the hospital, 68% answered positively, and 42% of those held other jobs in the hospital (mainly administrative positions). The majority of respondents (40.2%) held a bachelors degree (Bachelors of Business Administration (BBA), Bachelors of Arts (BA) or Bachelors of Science (BS)), while 26.8% held a masters degree (Masters of Business Administration (MBA), Masters of Arts (MA) or Masters of Science (MS)), and 12.4% a Masters of Public Health (MPH) (See Table 1).

A total of 63.6% of respondents reported holding some qualifications in HRM and 72.2% reported currently pursuing education or training related to HRM. In addition, 82.5% reported being interested in pursuing education or training related to HR management. However, approximately half the respondents (47.4%) reported not having attended any HRM workshops over the past 3 years.

The question on years of experience had only a 24.7% response rate and thus may not represent the entire sample. Respondents who answered this question had an average experience of 7.56 (± 5.57) years. It is also worth noting that only 41.2% had previously worked in the field of HRM. Most respondents were female (74.2%) and 64.9% were between 30 and 45 years of age.

Table 1. Qualifications and description of respondents

	N (%)
Are you the individual in charge of HR department at your hospital?	
No	31 (31.9%)
Yes	66 (68.1%)
If yes, do you hold another position as well?	
No	38 (57.6%)
Yes	28 (42.4%)
Highest level of education	
High School	2 (2.1%)
BBA/BA/BS	39 (40.2%)
BSN	7 (7.2%)
BT/TS	12 (12.4%)
MBA/MA/MS	26 (26.8%)
MPH	5 (5.2%)
MD	4 (4.1%)
Other	2 (2.0%)
Qualifications in HRM	
No	41 (36.4%)
Yes	56 (63.6%)
Currently pursuing education or training related to HRM	
No	27 (27.8%)
Yes	70 (72.2%)
Interested in pursuing education or training related to HRM	
No	17 (17.5%)
Yes	80 (82.5%)
Previously attended workshops on HRM over the past 3 years	
No	46 (47.4%)
Yes	51 (52.6%)
How long have you been working in this hospital?	
< 5 years	10 (10.3%)
5.1 - 10 years	8 (8.2%)
10.1 - 15 years	3 (3.1%)
15.1 - 20 years	2 (2.1%)
> 20 years	1 (1%)
Missing	73 (75.3%)
Mean (Standard Deviation)	7.56 (5.57)
Have you previously worked in the field of HRM?	
No	57 (58.8%)
Yes	40 (41.2%)
Gender	
Male	25 (25.8%)
Female	72 (74.2%)
Age	
Below 30 yrs	19 (19.6%)
Between 30 and 45 yrs	63 (64.9%)
Between 46 and 55 yrs	11 (11.3%)
Over 55 yrs	4 (4.1%)

HR Challenges, Strategies and Enabling Factors

Thematic analysis revealed that challenges varied across respondents and participating hospitals. The most highly reported challenge by respondents was poor employee retention at hospitals (56.7%), particularly for nurses (see Table 2). Lack of qualified personnel (35.1%) ranked second whereby respondents reported that there are few candidates for specific positions in their hospitals. Moreover, some required specialties are not available in universities and schools (e.g. occupational health and safety officers, quality managers, etc.). This may cripple the hospitals' ability to provide quality care, as existing staff members cannot assume these roles. The lack of person/job fit may thus impede the hospitals' ability to provide certain services or meet national hospital accreditation requirements in Lebanon. The lack of a system for performance evaluation (28.9%) also emerged as a major challenge as it has reportedly limited the hospitals' ability to evaluate the competencies and performance of their staff, especially critical staff members. Financial constraints were also reported as a major challenge by 24.7% of respondents, as many staff members may value it more than other forms of incentives. Other less frequently reported challenges included overall employee shortages (10.3%), poor satisfaction (8.3%), competition with other hospitals (particularly governmental hospitals) (8.3%), and limited capacity and authority of the HR department (6.2%). The lack of an HR strategic plan also emerged as a challenge but was only reported by 6.2% of participants (see Table 2).

Table 2. Most commonly reported challenges and strategies

	N (%)
Challenges	
Poor employee retention	55 (56.7%)
Lack of qualified personnel	34 (35.1%)
Lack of a system for performance evaluation	28 (28.9%)
Challenges in recruitment system	26 (26.8%)
Financial constraints	24 (24.7%)
Employee shortages	10 (10.3%)
Poor satisfaction	8 (8.3%)
Competition by governmental hospitals	8 (8.3%)
No strategic planning	6 (6.2%)
Limited capacity of HR Department	6 (6.2%)
Strategies	
Offer continuing education and training for employees	19 (19.6%)
Improve salaries	14 (14.4%)
Develop retention strategies	10 (10.3%)
Develop incentives	8 (8.3%)
Managerial support	7 (7.2%)
Needs assessment of existing challenges	6 (6.2%)
Develop recruitment strategy	5 (5.2%)
Develop an HR strategic plan	5 (5.2%)
Improve overall environment in hospital	5 (5.2%)
Have strategies been successful? (based on 68 respondents who reported retention strategies)	
Yes	54 (79.4%)
No	14 (20.6%)

Respondents were asked to report on some strategies utilized by the hospital to mitigate the impact of the above-reported challenges. Although many respondents reported HRM challenges, a total of 68 respondents (70.1%) reported strategies to mitigate the effect of these challenges. Thematic analysis (reported in

Table 2) revealed that the most commonly reported strategy by respondents was offering continuing education and training for employees (19.6%). Hospitals often send some of their employees to workshops or short courses to improve their knowledge on certain aspects of their job. Some hospitals also use credits collected from attending such courses when considering promotion opportunities. Improving salaries ranked second (14.4%) among reported strategies, as many hospitals believe that this may be the only way they can keep their employees. Some hospitals also reported developing retention strategies (10.3%) to better retain their employees; but respondents did not specify exact strategies being utilized. Other hospitals have started developing incentive plans (8.3%), mainly through material rewards, to encourage staff members to remain employed. Managerial support (7.2%) also emerged as an HRM strategy, but was only reported by few respondents. Other strategies included but were not limited to needs assessment of existing challenges (6.2%), developing recruitment strategies (5.2%), developing an HR strategic plan for the hospital (5.2%), and improving overall work environment in the hospital (5.2%) (see Table 2).

It is worth noting that 79.4% of respondents reported that the adopted strategies were successful in improving the status of health workers in surveyed hospitals.

Respondents were asked about enabling factors that foster employee retention, such as conducting performance appraisal and evaluation, in addition to staff retention strategies. When asked about the frequency of conducting performance appraisal, 77.3% reported conducting annual performance appraisal for all of their employees in the hospital (see Table 3). Although conducting performance appraisals is a requirement of the Lebanese hospital accreditation program, our findings imply that not many hospitals recognize its importance for employee retention yet. The remaining hospitals did not report conducting performance appraisals. However, respondents indicated that some specific staff members are often appraised as needed, such as heads of departments, some members of the medical staff, and selected nurses and technicians.

Periodic assessment of credentialing for medical and nursing staff was reported by 62.9% of respondents. Furthermore, 54.6% of hospitals reported having a continuing education or career development programs in their hospitals. Most of the HR managers (85.6%) reported that they provided staff with ad-hoc training sessions both in and outside the hospital (89.2%). Moreover, over half the respondents (56.7%) reported a need for training in specific HR skills to help them in their role within this department in their hospital (see Table 3).

Only 26.8% of respondents reported that their hospital has a recruitment and retention strategy. The low percentage on this question may reflect a lack of awareness about the extent to which recruitment and retention strategies are effective HR management tools in Lebanese hospitals (see Table 3).

Table 3. HR Management trends in participating hospitals

	N (%)
Does the hospital conduct performance appraisal for all staff members on regular basis?	
Yes	75 (77.3%)
No	22 (22.7%)
Does the hospital conduct periodic assessment of credentialing of medical and nursing staff?	
Yes	61 (62.9%)
No	36 (37.1%)
Does the hospital have continuing education or career development program for employees?	
Yes	53 (54.6%)
No	44 (45.4%)
Does the hospital hold regular training sessions for staff?	
No	14 (14.4%)
Yes	83 (85.6%)
In the hospital	8 (9.6%)
Outside the hospital	0 (0.0%)
Both	74 (89.2%)
Missing	1 (1.2%)
Does the hospital require training on specific skills in HR management?	
Yes	55 (56.7%)
No	42 (43.3%)
Does the hospital have a recruitment and retention strategy?	
Yes	26 (26.8%)
No	71 (73.2%)

Respondents were finally asked to select the top three categories of health professionals facing the most challenges at their hospital. The majority of respondents reported that the staff categories facing the most challenges were registered nurses (78.4%), practical nurses (49.5%), and administrative staff (33.0%) (See Table 4). Respondents also reported that they are facing challenges with additional members of the hospital staff, including: housekeeping staff, technicians and casual employees (paid on a daily basis).

Table 4. Categories of health professionals facing most challenges

	N (%)
Registered nurse	76 (78.4%)
Practical nurse	48 (49.5%)
Administration	32 (33.0%)
Physicians	18 (18.6%)
Technician	16 (16.5%)
Dieticians	10 (10.3%)
Physical, occupational, or speech therapist	5 (5.2%)
Respiratory therapists	4 (4.1%)
Pharmacists	1 (1.0%)
Unit assistant	1 (1.0%)
Other	18 (18.6%)

Discussion

The results of this study indicate that HRM in Lebanese hospitals should be strengthened in order to build capacity to better manage and retain health workers. The findings showed that not all hospitals clearly delineate the departmental responsibilities for its HRM function. This can be demonstrated by the challenges and strategies that emerged from thematic analysis. The most striking observation is the mismatch between challenges and strategies in this study. This finding is similar to an earlier study targeting nursing directors [6], where retention strategies did not always correspond to the reported challenges. However, this does not necessarily imply that the HR managers are not aware of how to address the challenges they reported. On the contrary, it may reflect the limited capacity and authority they have to mitigate challenges that are hindering HR development at their institution. This was actually reported as a challenge by some of the respondents. Another challenge reported by some respondents was the lack of a strategic plan for HR in hospitals. It is worth noting that Lebanese hospitals are currently in the process of preparing for a new national accreditation survey, and the development of a HR strategic plan is a requirement in the Lebanese accreditation standards.

While many themes (related to challenges and strategies) derived from the results of this study correspond well with those derived from the literature, it should be noted that additional challenges and strategies emerged. The additional challenges include: lack of a strategic HR plan, competition with other hospitals (particularly governmental hospitals), limited capacity of the HR department, absenteeism, social constraints, poor communication across departments, hospital location, and lack of trust in hospital administration. As for retention strategies, the additional themes that emerged from the results are: needs assessment for existing challenges; improving work environment; communicating specialties needed at universities and schools; cooperating with other institutions on continuing education for staff members; and cross training to fill vacant positions (for promotion from within hospital). It is clear that many of these additional challenges and reported strategies are specific to the context of Lebanon.

As previously stated, many of the reported strategies deployed by HR managers did not exactly match the reported challenges. However, many of the proposed strategies can remedy to some extent the reported challenges. For instance, the most commonly reported strategy was offering continuing education and training for employees (19.6%). Moreover, 54.6% of respondents reported offering continuing education sessions to staff while 85.6% offer training sessions. Offering continuing education and implementing professional clinical/career ladders have been cited as effective strategies for improving employee retention [9-12] and improving health worker efficiency which is linked to the scaling up of pro-ductivity [13]. They are forms of non-financial incentive which allow employees the opportunity to advance in their careers. Further research is needed to asses whether continuing education at Lebanese hospitals is strategic and in line with training needs of staff.

Many respondents revealed that hospitals are engaging in financial incentives in an effort to retain their staff. Despite the attractiveness of financial rewards, it has a limited impact if not combined with improved working conditions, em-ployee motivation and linked to individual performance [14]. It should be noted that only 14.4% of hospitals are engaging in financial incentives, although 24.7% reported having financial constraints that did not allow them to compensate their staff as appropriately as desired. It is also worth noting that some respondents (8.3%) reported that hospitals are beginning to develop incentives without speci-fying whether they were financial or non-financial. More work is needed to un-derstand the types of incentives used by Lebanese hospitals and their level of success.

Managerial support has been cited as an effective mechanism to improve em-ployee motivation, job satisfaction and retention [15,16]. Managerial support in-cludes but is not limited to coaching and mentoring staff, supporting continuing education pursuits, staffing and scheduling, and mediation between staff and ad-ministration, among other responsibilities [15]. Managers also have a leadership role, which is as essential component of employee retention, particularly through encouraging an atmosphere of autonomy and shared governance, in addition to empowerment and group cohesion [16]. Despite the importance of managerial support, only 7.2% of respondents cited it as a retention strategy at their hospital. Furthermore, a mere 10.3% of respondents reported developing retention strate-gies to counter the HR challenges at their hospitals. However, this does not neces-sarily imply that hospitals do not recognize the importance of retention strategies. With regard to enabling factors for employee retention, many hospitals reported engaging in performance appraisals (77.3%) and assessment of staff credentials (62.9%). Such practices are now required in the Lebanese hospital accreditation program, and all hospitals are required to comply with standards relating to per-formance appraisals and credentialing. However, there is a lack of information on the degree of compliance of hospitals with this standard and the types of perfor-mance appraisals being used.

Many respondents reported that the strategies adopted by their hospitals were successful in mitigating existing challenges. It is not clear how success was assessed, particularly in that many of the reported strategies did not fully correspond to the reported challenges. This may be an indirect outcome of the qualifications of the respondents and their capacity to fill the position of HR managers. Although some respondents had a masters level degree, the majority reported that it was their working experience that qualified them to fill this role in their hospital. It is worth noting that many of the respondents had dual roles in the hospital which may have affected their perception of the existing challenges and limited their capacity to enforce proper strategies to counter their impact.

Conclusion

With the upcoming accreditation survey of Lebanese hospitals (2010-2011), there is an opportunity for hospitals to enhance competencies of existing HR managers, and strengthen the HR management component. There is a need to develop a competency framework for the knowledge, skills, attitudes and behavior required for various HR managers. Thorough assessment of what qualifications and experience HR managers have, including all those who work in health care organizations, is required. In this context, there is a need to maintain an adequate number of HR managers in health care organizations with clearly delineated roles, responsibilities and competencies. One of the major findings of this study was that many respondents combine their duties in the HR department with other roles in the hospital. This comes to exemplify the need for a cadre of competent and well-trained HR managers who can fully assume these roles in Lebanese hospitals and work to continuously improve the status of employees at their hospitals. In this context, middle managers (department heads) can play a vital role in HR management and provide supervisory support. These middle managers can participate in selection/recruitment processes of HR; and they can perform supervisory functions related to HR performance management and appraisal. With regard to retention strategies, proper assessment of the impact of current retention strategies in Lebanese hospitals is required. Such information will be crucial to improving HRM practices at the hospital level, and also in providing lessons for peer hospitals, particularly ones that are not currently implementing any retention initiatives.

HRM is a discipline which requires a distinct knowledge base and training. It is not common in certain areas in the health sector at the moment to find professional HR managers, as they are usually promoted from other disciplines. As a result, further education or training is generally required in order to have the necessary competencies to perform well. There is a need to expand HR professional knowledge and competencies for the effective management of human resources in HCOs. There is also a need to increase the pool of competent HR professionals. A new cadre of HR managers will need to be trained and enabled to have real input into operational and strategic decisions about HRM.

Our study findings may apply to other countries in the Eastern Mediterranean Region. Another recent study in nine countries found that health systems suffer from poor HRM, resulting in absence of effective recruitment and retention strategies, poor HR planning, lack of proper performance evaluation mechanisms, and absence of a policy for re-licensing of medical staff [5], and other negative consequences. HRM challenges in HCOs should be valued by policy makers and managers and developing effective HR strategies should become a priority.

Abbreviations

WHO: World Health Organization; HR: Human Resources; HCO: Health Care Organization; EMR: Eastern Mediterranean Region; HRM: Human Resources Management; SPSS: Statistical Package for Social Sciences; BBA: Bachelors of Business Administration; BA: Bachelors of Arts; MBA: Masters of Business Administration; MA: Masters of Arts; MS: Masters of Science; MPH: Masters of Public Health

Competing Interests

The authors declare that they have no competing interests.

Authors' Contributions

FE made substantial contributions to the conception, design, as well as analysis and interpretation of results. VT substantially assisted with the literature review, data analysis and write-up of the article. DJ made substantial contributions to analysis of data and interpretation of results. All authors read and approved the final manuscript.

Acknowledgements

Special thanks to Mr. Razmig Markarian for data entry.

References

1. Working Together for Health: The World Health Report 2006. Geneva, Switzerland: World Health Organization; 2006.

2. Global Health Workforce Alliance: [http://www.who.int/entity/workforceal-liance/forum/1_agenda4GAction_final.pdf] Health Workers for All and All for Health Workers, The Kampala Declaration and Agenda for Global Action. 2008.

3. Kabene SM, Orchard C, Howard JM, Soriano MA, Leduc R: The importance of human resource management in health care: a global context. Human Resources for Health 2006, 4:20.

4. El-Jardali F, Jamal D, Abdallah A, Kassak K: Human Resources for health planning and management in the Eastern Mediterranean Region: facts, gaps and forward thinking for Research and Policy. Human Resources for Health 2007, 5:9.

5. El-Jardali F, Makhoul J, Jamal D, Tchaghchaghian V: Identification of Priority Research Questions Related to Health Financing, Human Resources for Health, and the Role of the Non-State Sector in Low and Middle Income Countries of the Middle East and North Africa Region. Research Report Submitted to Alliance for Health Policy and Systems Research 2008.

6. El-Jardali F, Merhi M, Jamal D, Dumit N, Mouro G: Assessment of Nurse Retention Challenges and Practices in Lebanese Hospitals: The Perspective of Nursing Directors. Journal of Nursing Management 2009, 17:453–462.

7. Flynn W, Mathis R, Jackson J: Healthcare Human Resource Management. Second edition. Thomson South-Western; 2008.

8. O'Neil M: Human resource leadership: the key to improved results in health. Human Resources for Health 2008, 6:10.

9. Gullatte MM, Jirasakhiran EQ: Retention and Recruitment: Reversing the Order. Clinical Journal of Oncology Nursing 2005, 9(5):597–604.

10. Shields MA, Ward M: Improving nurse retention in the National Health Service in England: the impact of job satisfaction on intentions to quit. Journal of Health Economics 2001, 20(5):677–701.

11. O'Brien-Pallas L, Duffield C, Hayes L: Do we really understand how to retain nurses? Journal of Nursing Management 2006, 14:262–270.

12. Gould D: Locally targeted initiatives to recruit and retain nurses in England. Journal of Nursing Management 2006, 14:255–261.

13. Dussault G, Fronteira I, Prytherch H, Dal Poz M, Ngoma d, Lunguzi J, Wyss K: Scaling up the stock of health workers: A review. International Centre for Human Resources in Nursing, International Council of Nurses, Florence Nightingale International Foundation; 2009.

14. Dussault G, Dubois C: Human resources for health policies: a critical component in health policies. Human Resources for Health 2003, 1:1.

15. Anthony MK, Standing TS, Glick J, Duffy M, Paschall F, Sauer MR, Sweeney DK, Modic MB, Dumpe ML: Leadership and nurse retention: the pivotal role of nurse managers. Journal of Nursing Administration 2005, 35(3):146–155.

16. Force M: The Relationship Between Effective Nurse Managers and Nursing Retention. Journal of Nursing Administration 2005, 35(7-8):336–41.

Turnover and Heterogeneity in Top Management Networks: A Demographic Analysis of Two Swedish Business Groups

Sven-Olof Collin and Timurs Umans

ABSTRACT

A theory based on the demography of top management teams is used to explain membership turnover in two Swedish business groups, network analysis being used to define group membership. The results suggest these business groups possess a combination of financial and industrial experience as a group resource and the socialising strategy of control as a force counteracting the conflict-producing force of heterogeneity. An organisational demographic perspective focusing on opposing forces of heterogeneity and homogeneity is developed. It is shown that the perspective can be applied both to formal organisations and to informal ones such as networks.

Keywords: top management networks, turnover, heterogeneity, business groups

Introduction

Organisational demography (Pfeffer, 1983) involves measuring the individual characteristics of persons belonging to an organisation, using these to describe the organisation and explain organisational outcomes. A common issue involved is that of explaining turnover, i.e., the exit of members of an organisation, especially members of top management teams (TMT), on the basis of such heterogeneity-related variables as differences in age, culture, tenure, education and functional experience (Daily and Dalton, 1995; Elron, 1997; Hambrick and D'Aveni, 1992; Keck and Tushman, 1988; Keck and Tushman, 1993; Kirkman & Shapiro, 2001; McCain, O'Reilly III and Pfeffer, 1983; O'Reilly III, Caldwell and Barnett, 1989; Pelled, 1996; Wagner, Pfeffer and O'Reilly III, 1984; Wiersema and Bantel, 1993, and Wiersema and Bird, 1993). A basic hypothesis concerns the "similarity-attraction paradigm" (Tsui and O'Reilly, 1989) stating that persons prefer individuals who are similar to themselves, or more specifically that high heterogeneity triggers turnover.

A demographic perspective alone however, does not indicate which individual dimensions trigger turnover. While in some situations heterogeneity of branch, for example, can trigger turnover (Jackson, Brett, Sessa, Cooper, Julin and Peyronnin, 1991), it can, however, be expected to be negatively related to turnover in the case of business groups, as will be argued in this paper. There is thus the need for considering the context of the organisation when predicting the dimensions that are important in triggering turnover, as indeed has been argued by Alexander, Nuchols, Bloom and Lee (1995) and Milliken and Martins (1996). Additionally, the heterogeneity of even highly relevant dimensions does not necessarily influence turnover appreciably, since it is conceivable that countervailing forces of an integrative character may reduce the turnover effects of heterogeneity (Hambrick, 1994).

A demographic perspective has often been used to explain TMT processes and outcomes in formal organisations, and it has expanded to include boards of directors (Knippenberg et al., 2004; Schippers et al., 2003; Zajac and Westphal, 1996) and the relationships between the board and the TMT (Golden and Zajac, 2001; Daily and Schwenk, 1996; Kor, 2006). While Hambrick (1994), in an extensive review of the literature argues for studies focusing one level below the organisational edge, i.e., the business unit level, we contend that the level above the single organisation, when it exists, is as important to study as the other levels. Indeed, there are informal organisations such as business groups (Collin, 1998; cf.

Gerlach, 1992) consisting of separate corporations linked by flows of ownership, management, board members, board directors, capital, and the like. It is, therefor, likely that some teams are based within more than one formal organisation. These groups take on the form of conglomerates or spheres of influence (Levine, 1972) for example, in the US, of konzerns and bank groups in Germany, of Keiretsus in Japan (Aoki, 1990), of industrial groups in France (Encaoua and Jacquemin, 1982) and of financial groups in Sweden (Collin, 1990). Business groups seem to consist of elite individuals, quite similar to "the inner circle" in UK (Useem, 1984) and "upper echelons" in US (Hambrick and Mason, 1984). They can be seen as basically equivalent to the TMTs of formal organisations. Thus, the paper extends the notion of TMT turnover to include top management teams other than formal ones.

However, lacking formal status, the TMTs of business groups cannot be identified through methods such as those of letting the position in the formal hierarchy determine whether a manager belongs to the TMT of the corporation or not. The present paper proposes that a TMT can better be identified through network analysis in which such criteria as possibilities for interaction and frequency of interaction are used to identify those managers who belong to the TMT.

The paper's aim is to predict turnover in networks of elite individuals identified on the basis of interlocking directorship data (this study is based on the data from 1975, 1980 and 1986) from the two largest business groups in Sweden (the Wallenberg group and the Handelsbank group). The theory put forward to explain turnover here states that the TMT of a business group possesses a combination of financial and industrial experience, that this branch heterogeneity represents a resource, and that a socialising strategy of control serves to counteract the potential conflicts which this heterogeneity tends to produce. The major contributions of the paper are the idea of countervailing forces affecting turnover, the application of turnover to elite networks and use of an operational definition of the TMT based on explicit group considerations.

The paper is divided into five sections. The first section describes the demographic perspective and deals with questions of turnover, heterogeneity and the definition of TMT that the paper is addressing. The second section examines turnover in Swedish business groups, first introducing the two largest Swedish business groups, and then developing a theory to explain TMT turnover in these business groups. The third section takes up the method by which the members of the TMTs of the business groups were identified, the data that were obtained and the measures that were employed. The fourth section presents the results of the analysis. The last section concludes the paper and considers possible implications for research and offers a simple rule of thumb for management when composing a TMT.

The Perspective of Organisational Demography and its Application to TMT Turnover

A study of TMT composition using the perspective of demography has to be based on certain arguments concerning issues of both ontology and methodology. This section is devoted to the arguments a) that organisational demography should retain its objective character, b) that the study of TMT and its composition, i.e., turnover, is important since TMTs and the composition those have affect the organisation and can be regarded as a strategic resource for the organisation, c) that it is partly a substantive theoretical problem to determine which demographic dimensions that are relevant in predicting turnover, and finally d) that the operational definition of a TMT should be based on team characteristics, making it possible to study elite"s in non-formal organisations such as networks and the forces behind their compositional characteristics.

The Objective Character of Demography

Ever since the time of Malthus, researchers in economics have been interested in demographic variables. It was Pfeffer (1983) that has introduced demographic considerations into organisation theory as a perspective of its own after considering demographic variables in a number of empirical studies (McCain, O'Reilly and Pfeffer, 1983; Pfeffer and Leblebici, 1973; Pfeffer and Moore, 1980). Since Pfeffer"s (1983) classical work, demography of organisations became a rapidly expanding field that an organisational perspective focused on culture and organisational economics has been.

The rapid expansion of demographic studies in organisational science not only can be attributed to the long-established tradition, but also to the possible use of quantitative and objective measures well suited to statistical analysis, as well as to employable data with few problems of access (cf. Stewman, 1988). All this have fitted with the Anglo-American research tradition of explanation and prediction based on use of statistics and statistical techniques, finding strengths in the use of such clearly objective variables as tenure, age and gender. Pfeffer (1983, p. 301) indicates that, whereas organisation theory often employs variables that in a methodological sense are subjective—specifically such conceptual constructs as norms and roles—demographic variables are facts which it is therefore possible to observe. However, the shortcoming of the demographic perspective is a conception of the individual through the prism of the demographic characteristics the perspective takes into account, moreover the intervening variables—such as communication, social integration and conflict-the subjective ones are still concealed in the darkness of the black box (cf. Bacharach and Bamberger, 1992; Lawrence, 1997; Pettigrew, 1992; Priem, Lyon and Dess, 1999).

However, recent research has been concerned with opening up this black box through the study of the intervening processes, measuring both direct effects and indirect effects of a group's demography (Ancona and Caldwell, 1992; Ancona, 1990; Kirkman and Shapiro, 2001; O'Reilly, Caldwell and Barnett, 1989; Pelled, 1996; Simons, 1995; Smith et al., 1994; Umans, 2008). Pfeffer's (1983) contention that the variance explained by the intervening process variables should be small has received mixed support, Smith et al. (1994) obtaining negative support and Ancona and Caldwell (1992) positive. Yet the main objection that Pfeffer (1983) has against focusing on the process is both epistemological, involving the difficulties associated with observing subjective variables, and methodological, concerning the problem of accessibility. In the research referred to above, arguments for the possibility of observing intervening variables such as social integration (Smith et al., 1994), debate (Simons, 1995) and relative cohesiveness of groups (O'Reilly, Caldwell and Barnett, 1989) have largely been lacking. Despite this, the epistemological objection only casts doubt on the possibility of measuring the intervening variables, not on the impact these can have. In fact, it is impossible to comprehend the impact of demographics without theorising about the processes in which demographics are an input and turnover, for example, is an outcome. The present paper accepts the Pfeffer arguments for the strong rule of organisational demographics. The paper theorises about intervening variables generally and examines empirically the effect of demographic variables.

The Importance of TMT and its Composition

In the attempt to explain various organisational outcomes, organisational demographics could well concern itself with the demographic composition of the entire organisation. However, most of the efforts to explain organisational performance are focused on the top management team (Daily and Dalton, 1995; Elron, 1997; Ely and Thomas, 2001; Hambrick and Mason, 1984; Hambrick and D'Aveni, 1992; Heijltjes, Olie and Glunk, 2003; Murray, 1989; Norburn and Birley, 1988; Priem, 1990; Smith, et al., 1994; Wagner, Pfeffer and O'Reilly, 1984), on strategic change (Keck and Tushman, 1988; Wiersema and Bantel, 1992), on innovation (Ancona and Caldwell, 1992; Bantel and Jackson, 1989) and on board composition (Westpal and Zajac, 1995; Zajac and Westphal, 1996). The rational behind such a focus is that the TMT and its composition influence the organisation. At this stage of research, the idea that top management makes a difference is becoming less an assumption (Meindl, Ehrlich and Dukerich, 1985) than an empirical conclusion, one that a variety of empirical studies have supported (e.g.,

Kosnik, 1990; Norburn and Birley, 1988; Smith, Carson and Alexander, 1984; cf. Furtado and Karan, 1990), especially from a strategic choice perspective (Eisenhardt, 1989; Wiersema and Bantel, 1992). Such intriguing conclusions as the following have been drawn: "..it would appear that environmental determinism and strategic choice are not ends of a continuum but, rather, separate dimensions." (Eisenhardt and Schoonhoven, 1990, p. 525). In these terms, there are certain degrees of freedom that a TMT can access, making the quality of the TMT an important variable for the organisation.

Recognising the importance of the TMT to the outcome of an organisation makes it possible to treat the top management team as a definite resource for the firm involved. The composition of such a team in terms of age, tenure, social background, experience, network connections, education, and the like can be considered as a quality of the TMT as a whole. Not only the individual members, but also the overall composition of the TMT can thus be regarded as a valuable and scarce resource that would be hard for competitors to imitate (Barney, 1986, 1991; Castanias and Helfat, 1991). Consequently, the composition of a TMT can be considered a strategic variable.

However, treating the composition of a TMT as a strategic variable assumes a causal link between strategy and the composition of the TMT, a matter which can be questioned (cf. Mittman, 1992). For example, the strategy and structure of an organisation, together with the composition of its external and internal labour pools (Haveman, 1995), determine the organisation's demographic composition. The demographic composition of an organisation can in turn influence strategy and structure of the organisation. Thus, determining causality can be a definite problem present in demographic studies. Bantel and Jackson (1989), for example, found innovation and top management team composition, just as Keck and Tushman (1988) found strategic reorientation and top executive team composition, to be correlated. Is it this team composition, then, that determines innovation and reorientation, or is it the other way around? Or is it perhaps, as Michel and Hambrick (1992) assert, a reinforcing spiral? Keck and Tushman's (1993) findings can be interpreted as supporting the latter view, although they primarily concern the influence of reorientation upon changes in TMT. To make the argument short, a TMT and its composition—despite certain causality problems—can be considered as a strategic variable for the organisation, thus merit scientific concern.

Demographic Heterogeneity and Turnover

The composition of a TMT can be influenced by the TMT itself. Westphal and Zajac (1995), and Zajac and Westphal (1996), showed that powerful CEOs tend to influence the composition of the board through promoting directors that are demographical similar to them. This result is consistent with the hypothesis, which Tsui and O'Reilly (1989) call "the similarity-attraction paradigm," that persons prefer individuals who are similar to themselves. One can suppose that human groups generally have a tendency to become homogeneous and to regard heterogeneity as disturbing (Jackson et al., 1991). One explanation of this general tendency of similarity-attraction is contained in self-categorisation theory (Turner, 1987), which Tsui, Egan and O'Reilly (1992) and Westphal and Zajac (1995) have applied to demographic studies, arguing that individuals shape their self-identity through categorisation and that in the pursuit of high self-esteem they prefer individuals who are similar to them in terms of these categorises. Another explanation of similarity-attraction is that individuals minimise their transaction costs in relationships through interacting with similar individuals, thus reducing the efforts necessary for gaining understanding. This is expressed by Kanter (1977, p. 58) for example as follows: "Social certainty, at least, could compensate for some of the other sources of uncertainty in the tasks of management."

A central hypothesis in demographic studies of organisations is that homogeneity, i.e., sameness with respect to certain dimensions, creates stability and ease of communication (Priem, 1990; Smith et al., 1994; Zenger and Lawrence, 1989) due to individuals' involved sharing similar experiences (Blau, 1977). Heterogeneity, in contrast, appears to readily create conflicts, reducing the ability to interact (Kirchmeyer and Cohen, 1992; Kosnik, 1990; Sutcliffe, 1994), although at the same time it is often associated too with such forms of change as innovation (Bantel and Jackson, 1989; cf. Watson, Kumar and Michaelsen, 1993), strategic change (Keck and Tushman, 1988; Wiersema and Bantel, 1992) and turnover (Wagner et al., 1984).

According to "the similarity-attraction paradigm," as well, both strategic change and innovation are associated with heterogeneity. Keck and Tushman (1988) found support for the hypothesis that reorientation, representing a change in both strategy and structure, increases heterogeneity. The causality involved does not have to apply to both aspects of reorientation, however, since heterogeneity could well be caused, for example, by a change in the internal labour pool brought on by structural change. Such causality supports in any case there being a relationship between heterogeneity and change. In like manner, Bantel and Jackson (1989) obtained support for the hypothesis that innovativeness and functional heterogeneity are correlated. Their conclusion is as follows:

> On the one hand, heterogeneity has a positive effect on innovative and creative decision-making. On the other hand, heterogeneous (and thus, innovative) groups are subject to higher turnover, presumably because members find the increased conflict and decreased communication to be stressful. (1989, p. 118)

Turnover and heterogeneity have been hypothesised to be correlated as well, studies such as those of Godthelp and Glunk, 2003, McCain, O'Reilly and Pfeffer (1983), Wagner et al. (1984) and Wiersema and Bird (1993) being confirmative of this, whereas Wiersema and Bantel's (1993) study, for example, is disconfirmative. However, an important theoretical question concerns individual characteristics that tend to trigger turnover. Wagner et al. (1984) found that similarity in date of entry and age correlated positively with turnover, which has also been supported by the findings of Godthelp and Glink (2003). This is a cohort aspect of turnover that could be thought to apply to any type of organisation. As already indicated, a TMT composition characterised by heterogeneity, for example functional heterogeneity (Bantel and Jackson, 1989) or heterogeneity in years of education (Smith, et al., 1994), can be a valuable resource for a firm, partly due to the cognitive conflicts it produce (Amason, 1996). Countervailing forces of integration, i.e., of homogenisation, might likewise be found within the organisation. These could prevent the heterogeneity from triggering turnover and allow heterogeneity to be retained as a resource.

The homogeneity which groups tend to show have been suggested by Murray (1989) and Michel and Hambrick (1992) to be a phenomenon similar to that of the Ouchi'an clan. The broad and strong interaction within a clan and the long tenure of its members point towards group homogeneity, making homogeneity and clan membership, therefore, appear similar. Although such similarity can be considered to be basically valid, it can only be assumed to be found on those dimensions that constitute the clan. Obviously, clan members cannot be alike on all dimensions conceivable. The overriding problem is to identify those dimensions that are relevant when cohort similarity creates cohesion. Murray (1989) appears to conclude that it is not homogeneity per se, but functional homogeneity in particular, that explains the performance results obtained in his sample of oil companies. In another working group, in which functional heterogeneity was an imperative from the start, Murnighan and Conlon (1991) found for British String Quartets that homogeneity on dimensions such as age, sex and school background were positively correlated with success. Contrary to their prediction Alexander et al. (1995) found a downward curvilinear relationship between heterogeneity in employment status and turnover in a sample of US nursing staffs, concluding "... that demographic heterogeneity does not operate similarly across all demographic attributes." (p.1477) This indicate one possible explanation to the reported (West and Schwenk, 1996) nonfindings between an aggregate measure of 12 variables measuring demographic homogeneity and performance. Demographic variables probably need to be treated with more care than summed up into one single measurement. Thus, it can be asserted that a theory predicting a certain relationship between heterogeneity and turnover has to consider the organisation in question, i.e., it is partly a substantive theoretical problem to determine which dimensions that are relevant in predicting turnover.

To summarise, human groups have a tendency towards homogeneity due to the shaping of self-identity and ease of understanding, thus creating groups characterised by stability. As an opposite, heterogeneity creates conflict and stimulate turnover but tends to be correlated with innovation due to the diversity of perspectives in the group. However, we argue that the general tendency of heterogeneity triggering turnover has to consider the specific group and its context. It is conceivable that there exists groups such as TMTs were heterogeneity is a valuable resource that can be retained through countervailing forces of integration, i.e., of homogenisation, thus preventing heterogeneity from triggering turnover.

Operationalisations of TMTs

Finally, turning to a methodological problem with ontological implications in TMT studies, one can note that studies of the team demographics of top management have concentrated largely on formal organisational aspects (Pettigrew, 1992), with the consequence that non-formal organisations have been neglected and TMTs have in large been only formally defined. Since it is difficult to verify the existence of a team in the true sense in any organisation (Hambrick, 1994), it generally is assumed that top management represents a team. Empirically, three different methods have been used to identify teams. One has been to define the TMT in terms of members' formal titles, such as those of vice president or higher (Wagner, Pfeffer and O'Reilly, 1984), as well as secretary and treasurer (Keck and Tushman, 1993). Defining teams in this way is quite arbitrary, however. Eisenhardt and Schoonhoven (1990) adopted a more qualitative approach, defining as a founding team those persons who were founders or were working full-time as executives at the time of founding. Such a method has the weakness of neglecting the importance of informal organisations (Hambrick 1994). A second method of identifying the TMT is to simply transfer the problem from the researcher to the CEO, letting the latter identify the TMT given either more thorough instructions (Bantel and Jackson, 1989; Boeker, 1997) or more general ones (Amason, 1996; West and Schwenk, 1996; Amason and Sapienza, 1995; Smith et al., 1994). This method has the disadvantages of a person who is not trained scientifically making the observations, and of its being impossible to measure the reliability of the observations since independent observers are lacking. A third method, used by Weirsema and Bird (1993) and partly by Jackson et al. (1991) and Umans (2008), considers the frequency of meeting in executive committees to document the existence of a TMT. This method can be regarded as superior since group membership is determined by a dimension, i.e., frequency that is relevant in defining groups. It has the additional advantage of being consistent with the assumption of interaction that the similarity-attraction paradigm makes.

The focus on formal organisations has withheld attention from organisations that are not formal in character but have an elite group equivalent to a TMT, as exemplified by certain kinds of networks. In a pioneering paper, Pfeffer and Leblebici (1973) analysed the moving of executives to a new role or location as one form of interorganisational communication and coordination. Thus considered, there might appear to be no major ontological or methodological differences between analysing formal organisations and analysing informal organisations such as networks of organisations or persons. As Useem (1984), for example, has shown a network of organisations can be governed by an elite group of individuals, just as a formal organisation can be. To be sure, the top management that constitutes a team is as much a matter to be examined empirically as is a network of individuals that constitutes a team of a larger network. In examining non-formal organisations such as networks, however, the researcher cannot rely on formal positions or even on CEO opinions, but is forced to define a TMT theoretically.

In summary, based on the self-attraction paradigm, one of the relevant factors in identifying TMTs is frequency of interaction, which has the additional advantage of being possible to apply to non-formal organisations governed by an elite group equivalent to TMTs.

Concluding this section, we have argued for a demographic perspective using objective variables predicting turnover in TMTs on the general notion of heterogeneity, but with a consideration of the existence of countervailing forces in specific groups, such as elite groups of networks, and with the operational definition of a TMT being based on team characteristics. In the following, a specific type of network organisation that of business groups, is examined in this way.

Turnover in Swedish Business Groups

In contrast to the UK and the US, Sweden has constellations of corporations, quite similar in certain respects to the Keiretsus of Japan, in which several corporations are connected through relations of ownership, interlocking directorates and financial service. The individuals who interlock and connect the boards of the various corporations in the group represent the group's elite; an elite that can be regarded as equivalent to the TMT of a single corporation, and in a similar vein represents a valuable resource for the group. The composition of this elite group can thus be assumed to be of importance of the group. The aim in this section is to formulate predictions concerning turnover based on the assumption that business groups possess as a group resource a combination of financial and industrial experience and, as a force counteracting the conflict-producing force of this branch heterogeneity, a socialising strategy aimed at control. The section starts with a brief account of Swedish business groups, since the reader may not be acquainted with them. It concludes with the deducting of various hypotheses based on a demographic perspective, hypotheses predicting member turnover in the elite of the business groups involved.

A Digest on Swedish Business Groups

The Swedish industrial economy is dominated by some few business groups, each consisting of industrial and/or financial corporations connected through relations of ownership, interlocking directorates and financial service. Two groups of this sort, the Wallenberg-group (W-group) and the Svenska Handelsbank-group (SHB-group), are of special importance in Sweden since they in some sense controlled corporations that represented roughly 50 per cent of the stock value of all the corporations listed on the Stockholm stock exchange in the 90s and still dominate the Swedish economy.

Both groups are very old, having been created during the depressed years in the 1920s and 1930s (Sjögren, 1991). Their evolution has been viewed as a corporate response to financial problems and to problems of ownership (Berglöv, 1994; Collin, 1998). The groups have been centred around two large banks, Stockholms Enskilda Bank (the W-group) and Svenska Handelsbanken (the SHB-group). Although Swedish banks, as opposed to their German counterparts, have never been allowed to possess shares in industrial corporations, much of the early history of the two Swedish business groups is similar to that of their German counterparts (Chandler, 1990). Typically the groups contain multinational corporations, exploiting raw materials from Sweden, such as iron and wood, and utilising technical innovations. For example, in the year of 1986, the groups contained two similar corporations, Stora (belonging to the W-group) and SCA (belonging to the SHB-group), which utilised raw material from the large forests in the northern and central parts of Sweden. Others utilised technical innovations, for example Aga (gas, belonging to the SHB-group) and Astra (pharmaceuticals, belonging to the W-group). The corporations tend to be highly internationalised. For the year 1990, the non-domestic sales of the 20 largest corporations in the two groups were found to be 78 percent (median: 82) and their non-domestic employees to represent 48 percent (median: 57) of their working force.

The strong ties the member companies once had to the two banks have in large part been replaced by strong ties to two investment corporations: Investor (W-group) and Industrivärden (SHB-group). The W-group has been managed through control of "Investor" by the family heads of the Wallenberg clan, who until the 80s were Jacob and Marcus Wallenberg, then being governed by the new family head, Peter Wallenberg, son of Marcus Wallenberg, and recently a fourth generation assumed the power. The SHB-group has no such ultimate capitalists as the clan Wallenberg. Rather, it is much more nebulously based, cross owner-ship and historical relations playing a major role. In both groups interlocking directorates form a closely knit network linking all the corporations involved. The members of the boards are generally not employed by the corporation in question, the distinction between insider and outsider, so important in UK and US, being a non-issue in these groups, and in Sweden at large. The two business groups are very distinct, being clearly separated. There has only been one corporation, name-ly Ericsson, that has been shared by the two groups, each of which has an equal share of the votes and an equal number of directors on the board of that company. Each of the other corporations in the two groups belongs to either the one group or the other but not to both. In a manner similar to the inclusion of the member corporations within a single group, those persons linking the corporations of the one business group through interlocking directorships do not have extensive rela-tions with persons or corporations belonging to the other group. Thus, the two business groups are quite distinct from each other, with very few overlaps. As op-posed to the Japanese Keiretsu, the intercorporate trade is very slight.

The groups have been very stable in their structure during the whole 1900 and they appear rather similar today (cf. Collin, 2007), having the characteristics of highly international corporations controlled by a financial centre, utilising inter-locks and ownership as control devices. The changes over the years consist mainly in some corporations being divested and some being added to the structure.

In sum, the two business groups, although lacking legal identity, build strongly on ownership ties and interlocking directorates, the investment corporations serv-ing as centres. They divide a considerable part of the Swedish industrial economy into two separate camps. The elite of the interlocking directorates of these two groups can be regarded as conceptually closely comparable to the top manage-ment teams (TMTs) of formal organisations, making it only confusing to invent a new term for them, such as e.g., Top Directors Team (TDT). Both can be seen as being subjected to the same forces of inclusion and exclusion in connection with demographic composition.

A Demographic Explanation of Membership Turnover in Business Groups

In terms of the "similarity-attraction paradigm," turnover can be explained on the basis of heterogeneity, and is treated as an attribute of the TMT (McCain, O'Reilly and Pfeffer, 1983). The heterogeneity possibly found in the original or the earlier composition of a group tends to decline through members who are dissimilar to the majority being separated from the group. Nevertheless, those dimensions with heterogeneity that trigger separation, i.e., the turnover of group members, should be identified. In this section, identification of the dimensions triggering turnover in the TMTs of the two Swedish business groups is dealt with, eight hypotheses being considered.

An obvious cause of turnover in elite networks is that of individuals' leaving the TMT due to retirement. The general tendency of elderly employees to have lower voluntary turnover compared to younger ones is thus not applicable on elite networks since they can be assumed to consist of rather old people. Additionally, younger members of the elite network presumably have no incentive to leave since there are no real alternatives to the group due to the fact that they are on the edge of the society. Accordingly, considering the specific group in question, the first hypothesis expresses the expectation that an increase in age will increase a person's probability of leaving the team.

H_1: Age is positively related to turnover.

The second hypothesis is the general cohort argument that the individuals belonging to a given generation tend to share similar norms and similar perceptions of reality (Wiersema and Bantel, 1992; Wiersama and Bird, 1993), this fostering cooperation. Differences in age imply difficulties in communication and understanding, leading to turnover of individuals who are dissimilar.

H_2: Age heterogeneity is positively related to turnover.

However, as previously argued, one has to consider the specific organisation. For one of the two Swedish business groups, the Wallenberg group, the fact that a capitalist family is the controlling principal creates a dynastic pattern which could be expected to result in a heterogeneity of age. Indeed, the age distribution in the sample that is to be analysed is skewed, the heterogeneity of age being greater for the W-group than for the Handelsbank group. If the most deviant values on the age variable for the Wallenberg group are deleted, the difference in heterogeneity between the groups disappears almost entirely. This can be attributed to the Wallenberg group's being a family group in which one or two family members are installed early and leave late. In 1975 the third and fourth generations of the Wallenberg family belonged to the group. In 1980 the oldest brother in the third generation had died, and in 1986 the entire third generation was deceased. The first individuals from the fifth generation were recruited after the death of those in the third generation. Such patterns are presumably common in dynastic groups. One obvious explanation of this dynastic pattern is the family's need to educate the coming generations for the possible role of assuming the function of family head. Another explanation, based on the "similarity-attraction paradigm" and analogous to the socialising strategy of control through rotation (Edström and Galbraith, 1977), is that an early recruitment to the group has the function of bridging the generation gap. Generational identity, just as is the case of cultural identity in international organisations, needs to be replaced by an organisational one, i.e., by family identity that fosters cooperation and control of the group. This serves to explain why one person tends to stay so long in the position of being family head. This reflects not only his being the pater of the family, which seems the most obvious explanation, but also the need of socialising younger generations so as to reduce generational discrepancies. The skewed age pattern makes it unwise to consider only persons below the age of 65, as Wiersema and Bantel (1992, 1993) did, for example, since here it excludes several of the most important persons in one of the groups. Thus, we expect that family membership resists turnover.

H_3: Family membership is negatively related to turnover.

Returning to demographic aspects, the fourth hypothesis relates to differences in professional outlooks. Similar to the turnover effect of functional heterogeneity (Bantel and Jackson, 1989), experiences from different branches can be assumed to create different attitudes, norms and perspectives (Jackson et al., 1991). Since individuals according to the similarity-attraction paradigm can be expected to recruit similar individuals and to expel dissimilar, one could readily hypothesise that turnover would be triggered by heterogeneity in branch experience. In terms of strategy, there are definite arguments for there being an effect of this sort. The origin and survival of Swedish business groups have been viewed as being partly based on the success of such groups in finding solutions to corporate problems of credit supply and ownership control which would call for particular communality in matters of financial strategy. The organisational structure of the two groups considered is indeed more similar to that of the financial holding company form (H-form), consisting of loosely coupled corporations whose major inter-transactions are the transfer of capital and of top management, than to that of the industrial functional form (F-form) or of the multi-divisional form (M-form), which both involve operations as a whole being more closely linked. Through particular emphasis being placed on the financial experience of their members, the selection of members of the TMT in Swedish business groups could, according to this line of reasoning, be expected to reflect a desire for a branch homogeneity directed towards the financial part of the economy, i.e., banks and investment corporations. The dominance of financial experience in the TMT that the branch homogeneity creates would in turn enforce the group's financial strategy.

However, there is a rather different logic that might be expected to apply to business groups, thus emphasising the need of considering the organisation in question when deducing predictions on demography. Ever since Hilferding (1910) wrote of the growing enterprises in Germany in which banks and industrial corporations were intertwined, the finance capital to which he referred has been regarded as a form of cooperation between industrial and financial corporations, something much resembling what is found in the two groups under consideration. If, as already indicated, these business groups represent a solution not only to financial problems but also to corporate governance problems, then it can be regarded as rational for industrial and financial experience to be mixed.

The TMT of a business group can be expected to represent the whole group, both internally and externally, and has therefore to reflect the cooperative trait between industrial and financial corporations. Due to this symbolic consequence of diversity (Hambrick, 1994; Ely, 1995; Milliken and Martins, 1996) heterogeneity in branch experience cannot be expected to trigger turnover. On the contrary, a decrease in heterogeneity in branch experience would insipid the symbolic impression of cooperation, and would therefore be avoided through selection and turnover.

Another consideration suggesting that branch heterogeneity does not trigger turnover involves the dynamics that heterogeneity creates. The business groups and their corporations, having been in business for at least 60 years, could be expected to have brought competitive advantage to the corporations of which they are comprised. According to studies of the relation between heterogeneity and performance, heterogeneity is related to innovation, high performance, high turnover (Murray, 1989) and growth (Eisenhardt and Schoonhoven, 1990). In the business groups in question, branch heterogeneity might therefore be expected not only to reflect the composition of financial and industrial capital, but also to be a competitive resource providing a balance between a financial and an industrial orientation to corporate governance. Thus, branch heterogeneity might best be seen as a coveted quality of the group and not something that would trigger turnover. In fact, if branch heterogeneity is indeed that which is desired, one would expect that a person with a similar branch experience as others who were in the group would be avoided as a member or be considered for replacement. In these terms, branch heterogeneity would be expected to have a negative triggering effect on turnover.

H$_4$: Branch heterogeneity is negatively related to turnover.

Functional heterogeneity has been shown to readily lead to conflict (Kosnik, 1990), reducing possibilities for communicating and interacting (Sutcliffe, 1994). The business groups can be thought to possess a centripetal force in the sense of homogenisation occurring in the sense of socialisation counteracting and thus reducing the conflicting and centrifugal force of branch heterogeneity. Accordingly, the fifth hypothesis concerns tenure, operationally defined as the proportion of one's career spent within the group. An integrating mechanism within a business group is the learning and transmission over time of norms and values, i.e., the indoctrination of ideology. One way of operationalising such a concept is by the use of the variable "Tenure," measuring the length of exposure (Wiersema and Bird, 1993). However, such an operationalisation cannot separate age and indoctrination. Two persons, each with 10 years of tenure, but one of them with 20 years of additional experience from another organisation, and the other with the 10 years of experience in the group and nothing more, differ in their degree of involvement in the organisation. It could be expected that the one with experience only from the current corporation would be more aligned to the corporate norms than the one having only one third of the corporate experience gained in the corporation under consideration. Thus, the transmission of norms and values is not simply a matter of length of service, but also of the proportion of the individual's career spent in the group. Focusing on socialisation thus rules out the alternative explanation, offered by Jackson et al. (1991), that the members of the group are highly paid for performance and therefore are induced to tolerate conflict. The heterogeneity argument states here that individuals with a similar socialisation history in terms of having spent a similar proportion of their career within the group, tend to stay.

H_5: Heterogeneity in the proportion of one's career spent in the group is positively related to turnover.

Turning to those individual characteristics of earlier origin, one might well expect such factors as class origin and education to influence turnover. Differences in the social origin of an individual lead not only to different experiences a person has had but also in different behaviour and manner of communicating. Thus, one might well expect a higher turnover for those most dissimilar in origin.

H_6: Heterogeneity in class origin is positively related to turnover.

In Japan, education measured in terms of the prestige of the university attended has been shown to have impact on turnover (Wiersema and Bird, 1993). One might well have similar expectations for Sweden. Persons who have been educated at the same university tend to have had similar experiences and constitute according to self-categorisation theory an easily knowledgeable category in which people can be classified. Sweden also does have one prestigious private business school and one prestigious institute of technology, former students there presumably easily feeling an affiliation with the elite of Swedish society. Educational level could have a similar influence, making those educated at the university level dissimilar in experience and attitudes to those of lower educational level.

H₇: Having attended a prestigious business school or institute of technology is negatively related to turnover.

H₈: Heterogeneity in educational level is positively related to turnover.

Turnover in what amounts to the top management team in both of the Swedish business groups is thus predicted here to be influenced by the general factors of demography such as age, heterogeneity of age, the heterogeneity in the proportion of one"s career spent in the group, and heterogeneity in social origin and educational characteristics. Turnover was also predicted to be influenced by organisational specific factors such as family membership and branch heterogeneity.

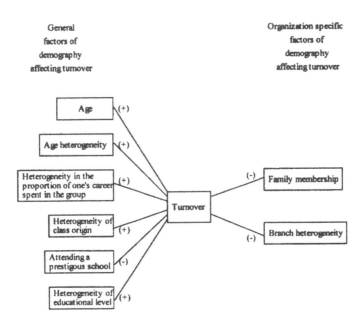

Figure 1: Eight hypothesis on turnover

Method

The TMT-equivalent for a Swedish business group can be constructed by the use of network analysis. The method section begins with a discussion of this and ends with an account of how the variables were constructed and how the data were collected.

The Construction of a 'Network' TMT

The two business groups in question, although frequently referred to in the Swedish press, do not exist as formally established entities. Before a business group and the equivalent to a TMT within it could be analysed, they had to first be identified. An initial step to doing this empirically was to select, from Sundqvist's (1986) systematic account of ownership links between corporations in Sweden, a total of 38 corporations listed on the Stockholm stock exchange that appeared on the basis of having large voting shares to belong to one or the other of the two groups.

Data on the persons elected as board members at the annual meetings of shareholders of the corporations selected was obtained for the years 1975, 1980 and 1986. There are other persons on Swedish boards of directors, but they are excluded in this data set since they are elected by the white and blue collar unions or the government, thus not being representatives for the owners. The reason for selection to the board being used as a criterion for identifying TMT members is that the board of directors is considered to be one of the most important arenas for influencing a corporation (Tricker, 1993). Other important arenas, in particular industry-wide organisations and other pressure group providing political representation, would have been inferior alternatives due to the strategic importance that boards of directors have (cf. Stockman, Ziegler, and Scott, 1985; Useem, 1984). A rather long time interval between the measurement points was selected since the groups and their members seem rather stable. The networks were originally constructed to show the stability of the two business groups (as reported in Collin, 1990). The differing periods of time between the successive measurement points, 5 years and 6, can be assumed to not have had an appreciable impact on the results. Since neither the network analysis nor the descriptive statistics indicate any radical change in the groups over time, this difference appears to have had no disruptive effect.

From the sample of individuals who for the years 1975, 1980 and 1986 were on the boards of directors of the 38 corporations selected (n=237, 224, 205 respectively), the set of those persons who had positions on two or more boards was drawn (n=56, 73, 71) so as to provide a means of examining the interconnections between the corporations. A network analysis (not reported here, but available upon request), with hierarchical clustering using lamda sets (Borgatti, Everett and Freeman, 1992), confirmed there being clusters of two distinct sets of individuals, taken to represent the upper-echelon individuals of the two business groups.

Identification of the equivalent of a top management team in each was carried out using two criteria so as to construct a core set of persons from the sample of interlocking directors of the 38 corporations. The first criterion was that these company board members were all to have connections with each other, such that each of them met with each of the others on at least one board. Formally, it meant that the network had a density of one (1). The second criterion was that, under the restriction of density = 1, the frequency of connections inside the core network was to be maximised. The rationale for use of these two criteria was that a TMT was assumed to be a closely knit network of high density in which there were as many opportunities as possible for interaction. Other clustering techniques that were possible were unable to produce networks with high frequency of member contact under the restriction of the density equalling one (cf. Borgatti, Everett and Shirey, 1990). The density criterion was crucial since it is hard to imagine a genuine team in which some of the members never meet. The frequency criterion was based on the assumption that the team identity of the individuals depends to a large extent on the number of interactions (cf. Weirsema and Bird, 1993). This clustering procedure, reported in Collin (1990), created networks consisting of 4, 8, and 11 individuals for the Wallenberg group, and 6, 11 and 13 individuals for the Svenska Handelsbank group for the years 1975, 1980 and 1986, respectively. These two groups of individuals are distinct and separate from each other. Only a few members of the respective groups met with members of the other group. There were some few corporate boards where this could occur, for example on the board of Ericsson, the ownership of which is divided equally between the two business groups.

Data and Measurements

The dependent variable "Turnover" was registered in 1980 and in 1986 as having either occurred or not occurred. In the present context, turnover signifies that an individual, even if excluded on the basis of the two criteria employed, may nevertheless have been present in the network of interlocking directors and be a member of one or several of the boards. Turnover thus represents not absence from the network but absence from frequent interaction with those members who are characterised by a high frequency of interaction, i.e., with those members belonging to the core network that constitutes the business group's TMT. This is a less rigorous indication of turnover than that which applies to a formal organisation in which absence means that the individual has left some formal position, even though one may still be present within the organisation. Yet, as Tsui, Egan and O'Reilly (1992) argue, turnover is a radical change in an individual's attachment to the organisation, psychological disattachment being less dramatic. Thus, turnover in an elite network falls in between these two extremes.

However, a more important point is that within the network the criteria of turnover are relational, exclusion of an individual from the TMT changing the network characteristics of all the individuals still included, as well as the possibilities for additional individuals being included. This means that turnover in terms of exclusion from the network is an empirical representation of there being lesser possibilities of interacting with the closely knit members of the top management team. An alternative to this dichotomous approach is to use the concept of team involvement, as measured for example by distance from the network centre. Although it is tempting to avoid the difficulties connected with dichotomous variables through use of continuous variables, the conceptual gain is small. Both logically and methodologically, team involvement requires the concept of a centre to which the individual's involvement can be related. The creation of a centre of this sort requires somewhat different assumptions and calls for clustering techniques, of which the one described below represents one possibility.

The selection of 1986 as the last year was due to its being the first year for which extended ownership data was available, making selection of the corporations to be studied a better informed one than it would otherwise have been. It would have been wise to take five-year steps backwards. However, the magic of the decade seems to have been the reason for selecting the years 1975 and 1980. A rational argument is that my data and results were easier to relate to other investigations of the Swedish economy since they too are restricted to the "decade magic."

Demographic data on the individuals was collected from the annual reports of the corporations and from a Swedish publication "Who Is That?" (Vem är det?, 1981; Vem är det?, 1985). The data concerns those individuals present in the business groups in 1975 and in 1980, respectively. Since some of the individuals were present both in 1975 and in 1980, the population tested (N=29) is larger than the sum of the individuals involved (S=23).

Branch experience was divided into financial, industrial and other experience. The category "Other experience" consisted of governmental service in different forms, research appointments and working in private organisations supporting trade and industry such as the Swedish Employers' Confederation. Functional heterogeneity, being the equivalent to branch heterogeneity, is seldom defined theoretically but arbitrary divided into traditional functions such as marketing, production, etc. The distinction between financial and industrial experience is conform to the theory and sufficient for the purpose of the theory of financial capital (Hilferding, 1910). It implies that financial experience is gained in financial organisations and industrial in industrial corporations. A person working in a financial department of an industrial corporation is considered as gaining industrial experience, whereas a person working in an investment corporation, mainly on the board of directors some one of the corporations it owns, is considered as gaining financial experience. Although such a categorisation is becoming less and less adequate due to increasing separation between the financial and the industrial operations of large corporations, e.g., through the creation of internal banks, it was still a feasible categorisation in the 70s. Since nearly all the persons in the sample gained the major part of their experience prior to the 80s, this categorisation was regarded as relevant. As a proxy for branch heterogeneity, financial experience measured as Financial experience/(Financial + Industrial + Other experience), that is, as the proportion of working-life experience gained in financial corporations, was selected. One could equally well have taken "Industrial" experience in place of "Financial" experience in the above ratio since industrial and financial are almost mutually exclusive, the category "other", representing basically governmental or scientific service, being only a small category.

Tenure was measured by the variable "Years Spent in the Group" (YSG), defined as the number of years the individual had been employed by one or more of the corporations belonging to the business group. In both groups the individuals in question had been in the group for some 20-25 years. As already indicated, such a measure has a serious deficiency in its reflecting both group indoctrination and age (the Pearson coefficient being 0.66, p <.000 for "Age" and YSG). One way of removing the age component is to divide YSG by the variable "Years of Working Life," defined as the difference between the present age and the age at first employment. This procedure creates the variable "Proportion of one's Career Spent in the Group" (PCL), measuring the proportion of the individual's working life spent in corporations belonging to the business group (where the Pearson coefficient for "Age" and PCL is 0.02, p=0.902).

Heterogeneity on the individual level was assessed by a network-equivalent measure of similarity, involving each individual's distance to the others in the network, a measure proposed by Wagner et al. (1984). The following expression defines the i-individual's distance:

$$D_i = \min_s \left[\frac{1}{n} \sum_{j \in S} (x_i - x_j)^2 \right]^{1/2}$$

where i and j belongs to a subgroup S, defined as all subsets with a largest integer size of (n+1)/2. An advantage of this measure is that it considers the structure of the whole group. As an example in the Wagner et al. article indicates, a five-person group with years of entry of 1, 1, 3, 5, and 5 involves a lesser distance for the first and the second person than if they had been in a group with 1, 1, 5, 5, and 5 years of entry. The first-year-entry persons have a distance of 1.155 in the first group and one of 2.309 in the other.

Due to the Wallenberg-group having a dynastic pattern involving family members, a dummy was created with 1 for individuals with close kinship, i.e., related by blood, and 0 for those not belonging to the family or only related by marriage.

Class origin classified according to the father's occupation was the variable expressing class position. The classificatory scheme was a socioeconomic classification (Socioekonomisk indelning) used quite commonly in Sweden, defined by a governmental bureau with responsibility for statistics made available to public authorities (SCB, 1982). The prestigious-school variable was coded 1 if the individual had more than a year of education at the Stockholm School of Economics or at the Royal Institute of Technology, both schools without doubt the most prestigious in Sweden. Educational level was divided into four levels, the first three of these corresponding roughly to the North American levels: university level, senior high school, grade school, and a fourth level for those with only six years school, as was once possible.

It has been argued (Pelled, 1996) that the visibility of a demographic dimension influences the triggering effect of the dimension, clearly visible dimensions such as gender, race and age being most conflicting and thus stronger predictor of turnover. Gender and ethnical origin are highly visible dimensions and could be expected to be of some importance since, concerning gender, women have a high involvement in the wage labour force of Sweden and, concerning ethnical origin, most of the corporations in the business groups are highly internationalised in terms of sales and production. However, none of these variables was included due to lack of variance. All members in the business groups were simply Swedish men.

Results

Table 1 summarise the descriptive statistics. During the 16 years, 10 persons were subject to turnover, whereas 19 persons were still in the TMT of the group in question, suggesting Swedish business groups to be fairly stable. Turnover is strongly correlated with age and age heterogeneity, and is only slightly correlated with distance in proportion of one's career spent in the group (p=.15). The age variable indicates these persons to be relatively old, varying between 43 years and 83 years of age. The two distance measures, concerning heterogeneity of financial experience and proportion of the career spent in group, are comparable in the sense of the variable underlying each having a range of 0 to 1. On the average, distance is larger for financial experience than for proportion of one's career spent in the group. The same is true for the variation involved. Heterogeneity seems to be less for the proportion of one's career spent in the group than for financial experience, providing support for our proposed theory that branch heterogeneity is a coveted resource. However, one should observe that some of the individuals are ones who show low branch heterogeneity and high heterogeneity in the proportion of their career spent in the group and who thus, according to the theory presented, could be strongly expected to experience turnover.

Since the other measures of distance differ from these and from another in the range of the underlying variables, no direct comparisons between them are possible. However, one can note the small differences found in educational level, reflecting the fact that the majority of the individuals have university or business school education. Almost half of them attended the two highly prestigious schools, but as can be seen in the correlation matrix, attendance is not correlated with turnover, which is in accordance with the expectations here.

Table 1: Mean Standard Deviation and Correlation Coefficients for Dependent and Independent Variables (N=29)

	M	SD	2.	3.	4.	5.	6.	7.	8.	9.
1. Turnover	0.34	0.48	.51*	.39*	-.14	.27	.05	-.14	.24	.02
2. Age of individual	58.7	10.1		.30	.02	-.14	.46*	-.21	.21	.11
3. Distance in age	4.63	2.71			.19	.10	.30	-.35†	.04	.06
4. Distance in the proportion of financial experience	16.1	18.5				-.08	.29	.20	-.23	-.29
5. Distance in the proportion of one's career spent in the group	11.8	11.6					-.45*	.10	.11	-.19
6. Family membership	0.17	0.38						-.44*	-.15	.11
7. Distance in class	.31	.33							-.07	-.22
8. Distance in educational level	.09	.27								-.33†
9. Prestigious school attendance	.48	.51								

†$p<.1$; *$p<.05$; **$p<.01$; ***$p<.001$

Table 2 presents the logistic regression equation in which the eight hypotheses are tested.5 The model is significant at the 0.01-level and correctly classifies 86% of the cases, or 25 out of the 29. The age effect, as expected, is highly significant in predicting turnover, and contributes most to the model, as the R-statistics in the right-hand column of the table indicate. These R-measures, which range from—1 and +1, and are based on the Wald statistics, can be interpreted as the partial contribution of the variable in question to the model. Three other variables contribute to the model at a significance level of between .05 and .1. One of these is heterogeneity of age, a slight cohort influence on turnover being evident. Another is heterogeneity in the proportion of one's career spent in the group, likewise found to affect the probability of turnover. In addition, family relationship can be seen to have a negative influence on the probability of turnover, as predicted.

Table 2: Result of logit regression analysis (N=29)

	Turnover	Stand Errors	R
2. Age of individual	.41*	.19	.28
3. Distance in age	.73†	.38	.21
4. Distance in the proportion of financial experience	-.12	.07	-.12
5. Distance in the proportion of one's career spent in the group	.15†	.08	.19
6. Family membership	-8.2†	4.74	-.16
7. Distance in class	-.45	3.18	0
8. Distance in educational level	-.68	3.66	0
9. Prestigious school attendance	.69	2.03	0
Constant	-28.3*	11.8	
Model chi-square	20,88**		
Percent correct predicted	86.21		

†$p<.1$; *$p<.05$; **$p<.01$; ***$p<.001$

Branch heterogeneity, measured as distance in terms of financial experience, has the expected sign but is not even significant at a .1-level. However, the support for hypothesis here concerning the impact of branch heterogeneity upon turnover can be regarded as slightly stronger than the test involved indicates. In the regression presented here, heterogeneity of financial experience is used as a proxy for branch experience. A slightly different result would appear if one used industrial experience as the proxy for branch experience. Remember that three categories of branch experience were distinguished: "financial," "industrial" and "others." Accordingly, correlation between financial and industrial heterogeneity is extremely high (.87) but not equal to one, since there is a third category, "others." With the use of industrial experience as the measure of branch heterogeneity, the results are similar, the same number of cases being correctly classified and the chi-square of the model improving to 24.7, with an accompanying lowering of the significance level to .002. The significance levels and relative impact of the variables other than branch heterogeneity are not changed, branch heterogeneity being significant at a .1-level. Although there is only weak significance, the results can be interpreted as suggesting that branch experience can influence turnover in such a way as heterogeneity decreases, the probability of turnover becomes higher.

The social background variable and the educational variables had no significant impact on turnover. This supports the contention that, although these variables can surely have an impact on a person's possibility of starting the journey to the top, the social forces at the top within an organisation, such as those relating to branch heterogeneity, commitment and heterogeneity of the proportion of one's time spent within the group, and of age, are more narrow in time in the influence they have.

It can be concluded that the theory of TMT turnover presented here, based on a demographic perspective, received a slight support from the TMT constructed here through network analysis. Although support for the model as a whole was found to be significant, the effects for most of the variables were only found to be significant at the 0.1 level. The results should be treated with caution since a logit regression requires larger sample size than n=29 in order for the findings to be considered robust. However, one should note that demographic studies employ rough variables such as age and functional heterogeneity in attempting to represent complicated social processes. As a result, such studies typically have a low capacity to explain the variance of the dependent variable.

Discussion and Conclusion

A demographic perspective can reveal important aspects of the functioning of organisations, aspects otherwise not easily detected, due partly to data access problems. This is true regardless of whether the organisations are formal ones or networks. Here it has been demonstrated that network organisations of a certain kind have counterbalancing forces. The business groups and their TMTs that were investigated as constructed networks were branch heterogeneous and characterised by long tenure. Age, heterogeneity of age and heterogeneity of group investment influenced turnover, whereas family membership and branch heterogeneity had only a slight and uncertain influence, although in the predicted direction of restraining turnover. These results can be interpreted as indicating that the business groups possess a combination of financial and industrial experience as a group resource and that the socialising strategy of control serves to counteract the conflict-producing influence of branch heterogeneity.

The empirical results were weak and have therefore to be regarded as preliminary. Nevertheless the result obtained imply the need for distinguishing theoretically between those dimensions characterised by heterogeneity, which is presumed to be conducive to turnover, and those characterised by homogeneity, which is seen as facilitating integration. Dimensions of these two opposing types may both be active and yet counterbalance each other. In taking account of forces of both an integrative and a separative type simultaneously, a demographic perspective can make a contribution to the science of organisations, where the latter tends to focus on integrative forces alone (Perrow, 1986). However, there is nothing in the demographic perspective itself that can distinguish which type of dimensions is involved. In the contribution to organisational demography by Pelled (1996), it is argued that job-relatedness and visibility relevant dimensions here, triggering conflicts and thus affecting turnover. Since the only means of identifying job-relatedness that is available is to have a substantive theory about the empirical phenomenon in question, a demographic perspective must rely on a theory that in relation to the empirical object can predict what dimensions are relevant. The present paper has emphasised this point by making a prediction of branch heterogeneity on the basis of a substantive theory of business groups, a prediction that is in opposition to predictions of many demographic studies using functional heterogeneity in a organisation as an equivalent. Heterogeneity was predicted to hamper turnover instead of promoting it due to branch heterogeneity being a resource valuable to the group. Accordingly, propositions in organisational demography has to consider the organisation in question

The model was significant, but except for the age variable, the significance of the individual variables was rather weak. There are at least two possible causes of this one could suggest: the small sample size and inadequate determination of the TMT's. The sample size was indeed quite small (N=29), making the influence of each of the observations on the results rather strong. Thus, outliers and misinterpreted observations of even a rather small magnitude can clearly influence the results. This can only be compensated for by increasing the sample size. Since Sweden only had, and still has two business groups of any particular importance, no other groups than these could be included. The sample size could be increased through use of the time trick as already used here, the size of the sample having been extended in the present case through observations of turnover not in one but in two different time periods (ending in 1980 and 1986, respectively). Thus, one method of enlarging the sample size would be to include a greater number of time periods. Another method would be to include business groups from other countries such as bank groups from Germany, Keiretsus from Japan and holding groups from Belgium. This would be possible now since business groups have been given more attention in research (cf. Yiu, Lu, Bruton & Hoskisson, 2007) thus making it possible to share data from different countries. As will be argued below, the fear of a strong cultural influence distorting the results appreciable when three or four countries that are culturally different are included is probably unfounded.

The definition of a TMT employed here, i.e., density being equal to one and frequency being maximised, might conceivably create a group lacking in empirical reality, making the correlation's random and meaningless. However, the problem of defining the top group is present in every TMT study. In fact, as the paper argues, a network definition of a TMT ought to be a superior method for defining it since such a construction is based on such relevant group dimensions as density and frequency, no attention being directed at comparatively inferior dimensions as formal positions in the firm or CEO opinions. Despite the weak results, it can be concluded that the model offered has a bearing for predicting turnover in business groups but that the empirical test could be improved through increasing the sample size by including business groups from other countries.

The latter step would raise the question of whether the results obtained reflect primarily cultural factors. Since Sweden is known to be a collectivist society (Triandis, 1995), forces towards conformity should be strong, at least if one accept analogous arguments that Wiersema and Bird (1993) have put forward concerning Japan. Although the present sample, to be sure, is very small and Sweden did not have any other business groups similar to the ones studied, it does not appear that the results simply reflect Swedish conformity. If there are strong forces towards conformity in Swedish society generally, then forces of conformity that might be quite special for particular organisations such as those of group investment would not be expected to influence turnover since conformity is created in and by society. Put simply, there is no need of creating organisational conformity in a highly conforming society. Indeed, one can argue as we do here that the dynamic power which extreme heterogeneity provides is made possible by the countervailing force of homogeneity which the business groups endeavour to achieve. The cultural traits which are relevant here may not be those of either heterogeneity or homogeneity, but rather of other dimensions, the impact of each being a function of the cultural context. Heterogeneity of class, for example, could be expected to have a rather different impact in a more class-conscious society such as England. Similarly the prestige of a particular university could well have a protracted effect in a less informal society such as that of Germany, of France or, as Wiersema and Bird (1993) found, of Japan. In the Scandinavian countries, and possibly in other informal countries such as the US, the impact of having attended a prestigious university or business school can be expected to diminish quickly with age. Thus, the generalisability of results here is probably not appreciably hampered by culture.

The generalisability of the results is limited, especially by the gender invariance that was present. The sample consisted exclusively of men, making heterogeneity of gender a meaningless variable. This seems to be quite common in demographic studies of TMTs. The exclusion of gender in TMT studies is probably caused in part by the low variance of the gender variable. For example, Zenger and Lawrence (1989) excluded gender since only 4.3% in the sample were women, and Tsui and O'Reilly (1989) reported that in a group higher than middle management only 4% were women. The effect of the gender variable having been excluded due to low variance is that most results cannot be generalised to TMTs in general, but to the most frequent type of TMT, that consisting of males only. It is quite conceivable that groups in general and TMTs in particular could display other outcomes if faced with high heterogeneity of gender or if populated only by females. In fact, Tsui, Egan and O'Reilly (1992) found that men's attachment to an organisation diminished to a great extent when a mixed-gender group was involved than women's did. An interesting question is whether the hypothesised causal link between heterogeneity and turnover is as valid in female as in male groups. Even in Sweden, where the say of women is particular strong, e.g., with roughly 50% women in the parliament, such an investigation of TMT groups must await the advent of a greater number of women on the scene, recent data on the TMTs of the listed Swedish corporations having shown that only 18% were women (Berg, 2003).

One of the major contributions by this paper would appear to be the determination of a TMT through network analysis, allowing it to be defined on the basis of such team characteristics as frequency of contacts and density, instead of formal positions. Demography appears to be a viable concept for explaining outcomes and processes not only in formal positions and in formal organisations, but also in certain non-formal organisations such as the business groups considered here. The latter are elite groups basically similar to the TMTs of formal organisations. Not only can the network approach to assessing membership taken here be applied to formal organisations as well, but there are also phenomena somewhat similar to what was studied here which could be examined in a similar way, such as the cooperation, for example, between companies in science parks. The latter represent the assembling of different research organisations at a given geographical site, where service, support and other types of resources are exchanged. An interesting question is whether interactions of this type are based primarily on functional, personal or demographical considerations. Considering networks highlights certain problems concerned with the makeup of teams. Whereas one can reasonably assume that there are persons in the upper echelons of formal organisations who constitute a TMT, its being an empirical question who these persons are, the same assumption cannot be made for non-formal organisations without the help of empirical data. Data on cooperation and team-like characteristics is indeed found in the case of Swedish business groups. For science parks, no such data has as yet to our knowledge been assembled. This emphasises the importance of regarding membership in a TMT as an empirical question that only can be answered after the analysis of patterns of interaction.

A limitation of the present study, that of its particular focus on networks, should be noted. An important difference between a formal organisation such as a corporation and an informal organisation such as a business group is that in the latter case the environmental forces influencing turnover are much more difficult to comprehend. This is particularly apparent when one considers performance, an important variable in TMT research (Keck and Tushman, 1993; Priem, 1990; Dess and Priem, 1995; West and Schwenk, 1996). Whereas the performance of a corporation can indeed be measured, certain difficulties notwithstanding (Murray, 1989), it is extremely difficult or even impossible to measure the performance of an informal organisation. The present paper has focused on group factors that influence turnover there. This leaves to further research the intriguing question of the effects of environmental forces on networks and on their upper echelons.

TMT demographics focuses on the composition of the TMT but generally considering only one of two compositional events, the turnover (Daily and Dalton, 1995; Hambrick and D'Aveni, 1992; Keck and Tushman, 1988; Keck and Tushman, 1993; McCain, O'Reilly III and Pfeffer, 1983; O'Reilly III, Caldwell and Barnett, 1989; Pelled, 1996; Wagner, Pfeffer and O'Reilly III, 1984; Wiersema and Bantel, 1993, and Wiersema and Bird, 1993). The other event which influences the composition of a TMT is the inclusion of a new member. Whereas decisions of hiring are often scrutinised in social psychological studies (Westpahal and Zajac, 1995), selection processes in the internal managerial labor market that create a pool of would-be TMT-members are an almost virgin area for demographic research. Few studies have concentrated on the inclusion of new members in TMTs it has been empirically researched by those concerned with board composition (e.g. Furtado and Karan, 1990; Westphal and Zajac, 1995) and have been highlighted by the innovative paper by Pfeffer and Leblebici (1973). Thus, although turnover is a rather well covered aspect of TMT composition, it is time to focus on the "turn-in" or selection of TMT-members.

The balancing of integrative forces of homogenisation that create stability and of the separative forces of heterogenisation that create change is of genuine managerial concern. The functioning of a group, for example its capacity to process information (Thomas and McDaniel, 1990) and its performance in an ultimate sense, depends not only on the competencies of the individuals involved, but also on the group's composition. It is highly tempting to consider the possibility, however trivial it may appear, of recruiting for such business groups as the Swedish ones examined, a greater number of financially oriented individuals at times when the companies involved are under financial stress. The present results emphasise the importance of considering the total effects of recruitment and dismissal. The manager and the researcher face the same basic difficulty of distinguishing those dimensions for which heterogeneity has a noticeable effect on the group or company from those for which it has little or no effect. One possible rule of thumb could be one based on the idea of countervailing forces considered in this paper, i.e., the idea that in stable environments TMTs can be functionally and branch homogeneous without much effort needing to be spent on socialising the members, whereas in complex and turbulent environments diversity in branch experience and functional heterogeneity creates the need of homogenising through socialisation the individuals involved. Simply put, playing golf and holding dinners for the TMT are a necessary investment in homogenisation for corporations in medicine, for example, but a waste of money for corporations in the oil business.

Acknowledgements

The order of authors reflects their contributions. The work this paper represents was funded by The Swedish Council for Research in Humanities and Social Sciences, and The Bank of Sweden Tercentenary Foundation. Lars Bengtsson and Michael Lubatkin provided helpful comments. Robert Goldsmith provided language editing.

Appendix

The Wallenberg Group and the Handelsbank Group in 1986

Only the largest corporations are included. The arrows indicate share ownership. Similarities between the groups are stressed at the expense of such dissimilarities as the fact that the Wallenberg group depends ultimately on non-contestable control of a few, large foundations, while the Handelsbank group has smaller foundations making the group slightly more vulnerable for control contests.

References

Afifi, A., and V. Clark (1990). Computer-Aided Multivariate Analysis (2d ed.), New York: Van Nostrand Reinhold.

Alexander, J., B. Nuchols, J. Bloom and S.-Y. Lee (1995), "Organisational Demography and turnover: An examination of multiform and nonlinear heterogeneity," Human Relations, 48,12, pp. 14551480.

Allison, P. D. (1978), "Measures of inequality," American Sociological Review, 43, pp. 865–879.

Amason, A. C. (1996), "Distinguising the effects of functional and dysfunctional conflict on strategic decision making: Resolving a paradox for top management teams," Academy of Management Journal, 39, pp. 123–148.

Amason, A. C. and H. J. Sapienza (1995), "The Effects of Top Management Team Size and Interaction Norms on Cognitive and Affective Conflict," Academy of Management Meeting at Vancouver.

Ancona, D. G. (1990), "Outward Bound: Strategies for Team Survival in an Organisation," Academy of Management Journal, 33, pp. 334–365.

Ancona, D. G. and D. F. Caldwell, (1992), "Demography and Design: Predictors of New Product Team Performance," Organisation Science, 3, pp. 321–341.

Aoki, M. (1990), "Toward an Economic Model of the Japanese Firm," Journal of Economic Literature, 28, pp. 1–27.

Bacharach, S. B., and P. A. Bamberger (1992), "Alternative Approaches to the Examination of Demography in Organisations," In Tolbert, P., and Bacharach, S.B. (eds.), Research in the Sociology of Organisations, 10, Greenwich, CT:JAI Press, pp. 885–111.

Bantel, K. A., and S. E. Jackson (1989), "Top Management and Innovations in Banking: Does the Composition of the Top Team Make a Difference?" Strategic Management Journal, 10, pp. 107–124.

Barney, J. (1991), "Firm Resources and Sustained Competitive Advantage," Journal of Management, 17, pp. 99–120.

Barney, J. B. (1986), "Organisational Culture: Can It Be a Source of Sustained Competitive Advantage?" Academy of Management Review, 11, pp. 656–665.

Berg, A. (2003), "Women's representation in leading business positions increases" European Industrial Relations Observatory Online, April 29th, 2003.

Berglöv, E. (1994), "Ownership of equity and corporate governance—The case of Sweden," in Institutional Investors and Corporate Governance, Baums, T.; Buxbaum, R. M. and Hopt, K. J. (Eds), Berlin: Walter de Gruyter, pp. 311–327.

Blau, P. M. (1977), Inequality and Heterogeneity—A Primitive Theory of Social Structure. NY: The Free Press.

Boeker, W. (1997), "Strategic change: the influence of managerial characteristics and organizational growth," Academy of Management Journa,l 40, pp. 152–170.

Borgatti, S. P., M. G. Everett and Freeman (1992), UCINET IV Version 1.0. Analytical Technologies, Columbia.

Borgatti, S. P., M. G. Everett and P. R. Shirey (1990), "LS Sets, Lamda Sets and other Cohesive Subsets," Social Networks, 12, pp. 337–357.

Castanias, R. P. and C. E. Helfat (1991), "Managerial Resources and Rents," Journal of Management, 17, pp. 155–171.

Chandler Jr, A. D. (1990), Scale and Scope. Cambridge Mass: Harvard University Press.

Collin, S.-O. (1990), Aktiebolagets Kontroll—ett Transaktionskostnadsteoretiskt Inlägg i Debatten om Ägande och Kontroll av Aktiebolag och Storföretag. (The Control of the Corporation—a Transaction Cost Approach to Ownership and Control of Large Joint Stock Companies), Lund Studies in Economics and Management 9, Lund, Sweden: Lund University Press.

Collin, S.-O. (1998), "Why are there these islands of conscious power found in the ocean of ownership? Institutional and governance hypotheses explaining the existence of business groups in Sweden," Journal of Management Studies, 35, 6, pp. 719–746.

Collin, S.-O. (2007), "Governance strategy: a property right approach turning governance into action." Journal of Management & Governance, 11, pp.215–237.

Daily, C. M. and D. R. Dalton (1995), "CEO and Director Turnover in Failing Firms: An Illusion of Change," Strategic Management Journal, 16, pp. 393–400.

Dess, G. and R. L. Priem (1995), "Consensus-performance research: Theoretical and empirical extensions," Journal of Management Studies, 32, 4, pp. 401–417

Edström, A. and J. R. Galbraith (1977), "Transfer of managers as a coordination and control strategy in multinational organisations," Administrative Science Quarterly, 22, pp. 248–263.

Eisenhardt, K. M. (1989), "Making Fast strategic decisions in high-velocity environments," Academy of Management Journal, 32, pp. 543–576.

Eisenhardt, K. M. and C. B. Schoonhoven (1990), "Organisational Growth: Linking founding team, strategy, environment, and growth among U.S. semiconductor ventures, 1978–1988," Administrative Science Quarterly, 33, pp. 504–529.

Elron, E. (1997). Top Management Teams Within Multinational Corporations: Effects of Cultural Heterogeneity. Leadership Quarterly, 8, pp. 393–412

Ely, R. J. (1995), "The Power in Demography: Women's Social Constructions of Gender Identity at Work," Academy of Management Journal, 38, pp. 589–634.

Ely, R. J., and D. A. Thomas (2001), "Cultural diversity at work: The effects of diversity perspectives on work group processes and outcomes," Administrative Science Quarterly, 46, pp. 229–273.

Encaoua, D. and A. Jacquemin (1982), "Organisational efficiency and monopoly power—the case of French industrial groups," European Economic Review, 19, pp. 25–51.

Furtado, E. P.H. and V. Karan (1990), "Causes, Consequences, and Shareholder Wealth Effects of Management Turnover: A Review of the Empirical Evidence," Financial Management, 19, pp. 60–75.

Gerlach, M. L. (1992), Alliance Capitalism. Berkley and LA, Ca: University of California Press.

Godthelp, M., and U. Glunk (2003), "Turnover at the top: demographic diversity as a determinant of executive turnover in the Netherlands," European Management Journal, 21, pp. 614–625.

Golden B.R., and E. J. Zajac (2001), "When will boards influence strategy? Inclination • power = strategic change," Strategic Management Journal, 22: pp. 1087–1111.

Hambrick, D. C. (1994), "Top Management groups: A conceptual integration and reconsideration of the "team" label," In B. M. Staw and L. L. Cummings (eds.), Research in organisational behavior, 16, pp. 171–214. Greenwich, CT:JAI Press.

Hambrick, D. C., and R. A. D'Aveni (1992), "Top Team Deterioration as Part of the Downward Spiral of Large Corporate Bankruptcies," Management Studies, 38, pp. 1445–1466.

Hambrick, D. C., and P. A. Mason (1984), "Upper Echelons: The Organisation as a Reflection of Its Top Managers," Academy of Management Review, 9, pp. 193–206.

Haveman, H. A. (1995), "The demographic metabolism of organisations: Industry dynamics, Turnover, and tenure distributions," Administrative Science Quarterly, 40, pp. 586–618.

Heijltjes, M., R. Olie, and U. Glunk (2003), "Internationalization of Top management Teams in Europe," European Management Journal, 21, pp. 89–97.

Hilferding, R. (1910), Finance Capital. London: Routledge and Kegan Paul (1985)

Jackson, S. E., J. F. Brett, V. I. Sessa, D. M. Cooper, J. A. Julin and K. Peyronnin (1991), "Some differences make a difference: Individual dissimilarity and group heterogeneity as correlates of recruitment, promotions, and turnover," Journal of Applied Psychology, 76, pp. 675–689.

Kanter, R. M. (1977), Men and Women of the Corporation. NY: Basic Books.

Keck, S. L. and M. L. Tushman, (1988), "A Longitudinal Study of the Change in Group Demographics," In Academy of Management Proceedings 1988, Hoy, F. (Ed), pp. 175–179.

Keck, S. L. and M. L. Tushman (1993), "Environmental and Organisational Context and Executive Team Structure," Academy of Management Journal, 36, pp. 1314–1344.

Kennedy, P. (1984), A Guide to Econometrics (5e ed.), Cambridge, Mass.: The MIT Press.

Kirchmeyer, C., and A. Cohen (1992), "Multicultural Groups: Their performance and reactions with constructive conflict," Group and Organization Management, 2, pp. 153–171

Kirkman, B. L., and D.L. Shapiro (2001), "The impact of cultural values on job

satisfaction and organizational commitment in self-managing work teams: The mediating role of employee resistance," Academy of Management Journal, 44, pp. 557–569.

Knippenberg, D., C. De Dreu and A. Homan (2004) "Work Group Diversity and Group Performance: an integrative model and research agenda," Journal of Applied Psychology, 89 pp. 1008–1022.

Kor, Y.Y. (2006). "Direcrt and interaction effects of top management team and board compositions on R&D investment strategy," Strategic Management Journal, 27, pp. 1081—1099.

Kosnik, R. D. (1990), "Effects of board demography and directors" incentives on corporate greenmail decisions," Academy of Management Journal, 33, pp. 129–150

Lawrence, B. M. 1997, "The black box of organisational demography," Organisation Science, 8, pp. 1–22.

Levine, J. H. (1972), "The Sphere of Influence," American Sociological Review, 37, pp. 14–27.

McCain, B. E., C. O'Reilly. and J. Pfeffer (1983), "The Effects of Departmental Demography on Turnover: The Case of a University," Academy of Management Journal, 26, pp. 626–641.

Meindl, J. R., S. B. Ehrlich and J. M. Dukerich (1985), "The romance of leadership," Administrative Science Quarterly, 30, pp. 78–102.

Michel, J. G. and D. C. Hambrick (1992), "Diversification Posture and Top Management Team Characteristics," Academy of Management Journal, 35, pp. 9–37.

Milliken, F. J. and L. L. Martins (1996), "Searching for common threads: Understanding the multiple effects of diversity in organisational groups," Academy of Management Review, 21, 2, pp. 402–433.

Mittman, B. S. (1992), "Theoretical and Methodological Issues in the Study of Organisational Demography and Demographic Change," In Tolbert, P., and Bacharach, S.B. (Eds.) Research in the Sociology of Organisations. 10, London: JAI Press, pp. 3–54.

Montgomery, D. C. and E. A. Peck (1982), Introduction to Linear Regression Analysis. NY: John Wiley and Sons.

Morita, J. G., T. W. Lee and R. T. Mowday (1993), "The Regression-Analog to Survival Analysis: A Selected Application to Turnover Research," Academy of Management Journal, 36, pp. 1430–1464.

Murnighan, J. K. and D. E. Conlon (1991), "The Dynamics of Intense Work Groups: A Study of British String Quartets," Administrative Science Quarterly, 36, pp. 165-186. Murray, A. I. (1989), "Top Management Group Heterogeneity and Firm Performance," Strategic Management Journal, 10, pp. 125–141. Norburn, D. and S. Birley (1988), "The Top Management Team and Corporate Performance," Strategic Management Journal, 9, pp. 225–237.

O'Reilly III, C. A., D. F. Caldwell and W. P. Barnett (1989), "Work Group Demography, Social Integration, and Turnover," Administrative Science Quarterly, 34, pp. 21–37. Pelled, L. H. (1996), "Demographic Diversity, Conflict, and Work Group Outcomes: An Intervening Process Theory," Organisation Science, 7, pp. 615–631.

Perrow, C. (1986), Complex Organisations—A Critical Essay. Random House, NY.

Pettigrew, A. M. (1992), "On Studying Managerial Elites," Strategic Management Journal, 13, pp. 163–182.

Pfeffer, J. (1983), "Organisational Demography," In Cummings, L.L., and Staw, B.M. (Eds.), Research in Organisational Behavior, 5, Greenwich, Conn: JAI Press, pp. 299–357.

Pfeffer, J. and W. L. Moore (1980), "Average Tenure of Academic Department Heads: The Effects of Paradigm, Size, and Departemental Demography," Administrative Science Quarterly, 25, pp. 387–406.

Pfeffer, J. and H. Leblebici (1973), "Executive Recruitment and the Development of Interfirm Organisations," Administrative Science Quarterly, 18, pp. 449–461.

Priem, R. L. (1990), "Top Management Team Group Factors, Consensus, and Firm Performance," Strategic Management Journal, 11, pp. 469–478.

Priem, R. L., Lyon, D. W., and Dess, G. G. 1999, "Inherent limitations of demographic proxies in top management team heterogeneity research," Journal of Management, 25, pp. 935–954. SCB, (1982), "Socioekonomisk indelning," Meddelande i samordningsfrågor, 1982:4, Stockholm:SCB.

Simons, T. (1995), "Top Management Team Consensus, Heterogeneity, and Debate as Contingent Predictors of Company Performance: The Complimentarity of Group Structure and Process," Academy of Management Best Papers Proceedings 1995, pp. 62–66.

Schippers, M., Hartog, D., Koopman, P. and Wienk,J. (2003) Diversity and Team Outcomes: the moderating effects of outcome interdependence and group longevity and the mediating effect of reflexivity, Journal of Organizational Behaviour, 24, pp. 779–802.

Sjögren, H. (1991), "Long-term Contracts in the Swedish Bank-Oriented Financial System during the Inter-War Period," Business History, 33.

Smith, J. E.; K. P. Carson and R. A. Alexander (1984), "Leadership: It can make a difference," Academy of Management Journal, 27, pp. 765–776.

Smith, K. G., K. A. Smith, J. D. Olian, H. P. Sims Jr, D. P. O"Bannon and J. A. Scully (1994), "Top Management Team Demography and Process: The Role of Social Integration and Communication," Administrative Science Quarterly, 39, pp. 412–438.

Stewman, S. (1988), "Organisational Demography,," Annual Review of Sociology, 14, pp. 173–202.

Stockman, F., R. Ziegler, and J. Scott, J. (Eds) (1985), Networks of Corporate Power. Glasgow: Polity Press.

Sundqvist, S.-I. (1986), Ägarna och Makten i Sveriges Börsbolag 1986. (Owners and Power 1986), Stockholm:Dagens Nyheters Förlag.

Sutcliffe, K. M. 1994. "What Executives notice: Accurate Perceptions in Top Management Teams," Academy of Management Journal, 37, 5, pp. 1360–1378.

Thomas, J. B. and R. R. McDaniel Jr (1990) "Interpreting strategic issues: Effects of strategy and the information-processing structure of top management teams," Academy of Management Journal, 33, pp. 286–306.

Triandis, H. C. (1995). Individualism & Collectivism. Boulder:Westview Press.

Tricker, B. (1993), "Corporate Governance—the new focus of interest," Corporate Governance 1 pp. 1–4.

Tsui, A. S., T. D. Egan and C. A. O'Reilly III (1992), "Being Different: Relational Demography and Organisational Attachment," Administrative Science Quarterly, 37, pp. 549–579.

Tsui, A.S. and C. A. O'Reilly III (1989), "Beyond Simple Demographic Effects: The Importance of Relational Demography in Superior-Subordinate Dyads," Academy of Management Journal, 32, pp. 402–423.

Turner, J. C. (1987), Rediscovering the Social Group: A Self-categorization Theory. Oxford:Basil Blackwell.

Umans, T (2008), " Ethnic identity, power, and communication in top management teams," Baltic Management Journal, 3, pp. 159–173.

Useem, M. (1984), The Inner Circle. NY:Oxford Univeristy Press.

Vem är det, 1981. (1981), Stockholm:Norstedt.

Vem är det, 1985. (1985), Stockholm:Norstedt.

Wagner, W. G., J. Pfeffer, and C. A. O'Reilly III (1984), "Organisational Demography and Turnover in Top-Management Groups," Administrative Science Quarterly, 29, pp. 74–92.

Watson, W. E., K. Kumar and L. K. Michaelsen (1993), "Cultural Diversity's Impact on Interaction Process and Performance: Comparing Homogeneous and Diverse Task Groups," Academy of Management Journal, 36, pp. 590–602.

West Jr, C. T., and C. R. Schwenk (1996), "Top management team strategic consensus, demographic homogeneity and firm performance: A report of resounding nonfindings," Strategic Management Journal, 17, pp. 571–576.

Westphal, J. D., and E. J. Zajac (1995), "Who Shall Govern? CEO/Board Power, Demographic Similarity, and New Director Selection," Administrative Science Quarterly, 40, pp. 60–83.

Wiersema, M. F. and K. A. Bantel (1992), "Top Management Team Demography and Corporate Strategic Change," Academy of Management Journal, 35, pp. 91–121.

Wiersema, M. F. and K. A. Bantel (1993), "Top Management Team Turnover as an Adaption Mechanism: The Role of the Environment," Strategic Management Journal, 14, pp. 485–504

Wiersema, M. F. and A. Bird (1993), "Organisational Demography in Japanese Firms: Group Heterogeneity, Individual Dissimilarity, and Top Management Team Turnover," Academy of Management Journal, 36, pp. 996–1025.

Yiu. D. W., Lu Y., Bruton, G. D., and R. E. Hoskisson (2007), "Business Groups: An Integrated Model to Focus Research," Journal of Management Studies," 44:8, pp. 1551–1579.

Zajac, E. J. and J. D. Westphal (1995), "Accounting for the Explanations of CEO Compensation: Substance and Symbolism," Administrative Science Quarterly, 40, pp. 283–308.

Zajac, E. J., and J. D. Westphal (1996), "Who shall succeed? How CEO/Board preferences and power affect the choice of new CEOs," Academy of Management Journal, 39, pp. 64–90

Zenger, T. R., and B. S. Lawrence (1989), "Organisational Demography: The Differential Effects of Age and Tenure Distributions on Technical Communication," Academy of Management Journal, 32, pp. 353–376.

Ziegler, R., D. Bender and H. Biehler (1985), "Industry and Banking in the German Corporate Network," in Stokman, F., Ziegler, R., and Scott, J. (Eds.) Networks of Corporate Power. Glasgow:Polity Press.

Change Management: Getting a Tuned Up Organization

Robert E. Ledez

ABSTRACT

Organizations as a whole and people specifically do not like to hear the word change. "Change" has a myriad of dreadful meanings in organizations such as, layoffs, downsizing, relocation and pay cuts. Employees have learned that when the word "change" is spoken to expect the bad but plan for the worst. For many people the prospect of change produces stress or tension in the work-place and on the employees that have to deal with the emerging process. The emergence of new technology, products and increased global competition will only facilitate the change that will be needed in order to compete. One cannot manage the past but can sure take charge of the future.

Introduction

"During this decade, American corporations will face a variety of developments. They will continue to experience the issues associated with globalization and new technological development. In domestic markets, they will encounter the expanding number of people riding the crest of the "Age Wave" and a variety of lifestyles. They will have to cope with baby boomers facing the issues of mid life changes with their interests turning towards family and quality of life. They will have to devote more attention to social and environmental issues and cope with a labor shortage. These trends will provide opportunities and require ongoing innovation in products and services. They will also require changes in organizational systems. Leaders of excellent firms are exploring the implications of these trends. They are developing innovations. They are transforming their firms to a new organizational form." (Holder, 2002, p. 1)

The third college edition of the Webster's New World Dictionary defines change as: to put or take (a thing) in place of something else, to make an exchange, a substitution. Another definition of change is: the letting go of the old and making strides toward obtaining the new or the end result, the journey in between is the transition. (M.A. Petrosky, personal communication, October 3, 2002). Fred Nickols, of the Distance Consulting Company, sums change up as "a matter of moving from one state to another, specifically from the problem state to the solved state." Change is one variable that can humble the bravest and the brightest and completely terrorize others. This leads to the matter of Change Management.

Change Management

"The first and foremost obvious definition of change management refers to the making of changes in a planned and managed or systematic fashion." (Nickols, 2002, p. 1) Change Management is the art or science of making changes to a certain method or system in an orderly, systematic fashion, to make sense out of the organizational chaos that is permeating the company, its employees, its suppliers and vendors and most importantly its customers. The "change" that will take place to the organization is internal. This means that the change will take place within the confines of the company and not outside the "walls" of the organization. The reason for the change however might be completely externally oriented. For example, many companies might have to adjust their pricing or changes in their products, react to a large cut in funding, the need to attract new customers and business, the changing of their current customer base due to external conditions, (i.e. economy, aging, etc.), the increased need for productivity and the hiring or laying off of large quantities of employees and managers. Some changes take place when the new "Boss" or Chief Executive Officer takes over the company and their personal interaction or philosophies slowly but surely change the culture of the company or organization.

The backbone of Change Management is composed of a variety of hard and soft sciences drawn upon psychology, sociology, business administration, economics, industrial engineering, systems engineering and the study of human and organizational behavior. (Nickols, 2002, p. 2)

Finally, yet importantly, Change Management theory includes a series of models, beliefs, concepts and principles known as the General Systems Theory (Nickols, 2002, p. 2). It has not yet been determined whether Change Management is an art, science, a profession or a discipline. It is more likely composed of a little of each and a totally separate entity in itself.

How "Change" Affects the Company

A little known writer by the name of Mark Twain summed it up eloquently by saying "You know, I'm all for progress. It's change that I object to."(Pieterson, 2002, p. 32) Organizations as a whole and people specifically do not like to hear the word change. "Change" has a myriad of dreadful meanings in organizations such as, layoffs, downsizing, relocation and pay cuts. Employees have learned that when the word "change" is spoken to expect the bad but plan for the worst.

For many people the prospect of change produces stress or tension in the workplace and on the employees that have to deal with the emerging process. Willie Pietersen, of the Journal of Business Strategy, has this perception on the change process. "For many people the specter of change produces what's sometimes called the FUD Factor—Fear, Uncertainty and Doubt." The psychology works like this:

- To change is to suffer loss of several kinds. We lose certainty, the comfort of the known and the familiar. We lose the sense of competency, the financial security and the status we enjoy in the existing order. And when change is being imposed upon us (as is often the case in a corporate setting), we lose the sense of control.

- Because change involves the loss, people must be persuaded that the gains will be greater than the losses if they are to embrace change.

- To succeed, therefore, the driving forces in support of change must be greater than the restraining forces of Fear, Uncertainty and Doubt.

There are many differing opinions about the actual systematic process of implementing change in the prototypical workplace. The number of steps ranges from three to thirteen depending on the individual and their overall opinion and beliefs. John P. Kotter in his book, The Heart of Change, Real Life Stories of how People Changed Their Organization, defines eight steps that will drastically enhance the change in the organization and help limit or lower the amount of stress or tension in the change model. They are as follows:

1. Increase Urgency

The figurehead of the organization or company must constantly stress the urgency for the change. This will help focus the employees on the change at hand and leave little time to look back at the "old way." This first step, though important, must not be rushed upon the employees. However, the change must proceed at a brisk but well organized pace. This will quickly entrench the employees in the new beliefs and processes of the change and allow the old corporate beliefs to fade away quickly.

2. Build the Guiding Team

Management must be well informed and have the mental and technical capabilities to enact the change. They must be able to see the grand scheme while at the same time defining the individual employee's responsibility to the overall structure. They must be perceived as capable leaders who can answer most questions and if not can adequately respond to the employees in a timely manner.

3. Get the Vision Right

They must be able to define the company vision form the top level down to the grass roots level. They must define their vision and not deviate from it in midstream. This will only present the perception that management does not know what it is doing.

4. Communicate for Buy-In

They must be able to sell the workers and fellow employees of the need for change. Some change managers like to stress the good side of the change while putting down the old system as inadequate. Anyway, they must be able to sell the product to the line workers and managers as well as the shareholders if necessary.

5. Create Short-Term Wins

Management must set small goals that that can realistically be met. This will increase employee moral, show that the end is possible, and hopefully distract from the long and often difficult haul of the change.

6. Empower Action

They must allow their managers the power to take the reins and run with it. The managers must have the capabilities to guide the ship without constant fear of repercussions.

7. Do Not Let Up

The act of the change must constantly be pressed onward, do not slow in your plan. Follow the guideline and press on ahead if things are working as planned. To stop in midstream would only jeopardize the power of the new "way" since the employees or line workers would be stuck in the transition period.

8. Make Change Stick

You must live the new process. You cannot fall back to the old way once the change is made. To do this would only jeopardize confidence in management and their overall ability to lead the company into the future.

Change in any organization is one of the most, if not the most, stressful situations that a company will have to deal with. How a company deals with change can, in extreme cases, decides whether the company will continue to be profitable and forge ahead with new ideas and products and continue to renew their organizational life cycle or start the descent of the business. Most companies that have continued to stay in business and stay profitable have continually added, renewed and changed their product line, their customer base and the general way that they do business.

Change Management and the Employees

"Gaining employee support and buy in is a critical first step in managing change, but leaders can't stop there. Employees have to continually be motivated to change their behaviors throughout the change. To use the diet analogy once more, people may understand all the reasons why the have to lose weight, but without proper support and motivation, they might never muster the energy required to do so."(Caudron, 2002, p. 3)

The first and most important step in initiating any change or massive reengineering project upon the company, certain departments or functional areas is to clearly and easily define the need for change and why it will only help not hinder the organization. Management must define all the points and benefits for the change. They must communicate endlessly and tirelessly about the changes needed. Management can never communicate enough with their employees, the grass roots level where the change will have the most drastic effect.

Second, management must adequately train and prepare for the implementation. The employees or individuals that will be affected by the transformation must not only understand the reason for the change but must be able to implement the new technique, style or dynamic that the company or organization is changing over to.

They must be more than ready for the change when the time for change occurs. The company can provide mandatory training on or off premises. They can offer after hours training to individuals that want to ensure that they are proficient in the new system or dynamic.

Third, the management must have certain allotted time to help implement the change. As the old saying goes, you cannot run before you walk. The management must be allowed the time and resources to train their employees, to answer all questions and to address issues of problems that might be the result of the change. They must be allowed to let some other areas suffer while they address the most important issue, change. They must have certain target objectives and goals that can be obtained. To assign goals that are not obtainable and impossible will only hurt the change. The period in between the change from point A to point B is the transition. This transition period must contain obtainable goals in order for the employees and management to see the light at the end of the tunnel. To deny this will cause negative repercussions on the reason for change and further cause employee and management resistance.

Fourth, the most important aspect for change is the constant recognition and praise for obtaining goals and to individuals that are embracing and supporting the change effort. Some studies have found that this non-monetary compensation is as good if not better than monetary compensation in some environments. The change manager must keep the group dynamics focused on the task at hand and not allow distractions from outside competitors to take away from their focus on the change.

Ten Ways to Fail at Change

There are certain procedures and steps that must be implemented to enforce change in the environment. Dr. Terry Paulson, of Paulson and Associates, has come up with ten ways that management can take to make sure that the change fails and does not happen. This is a summary of those ten points with a brief explanation:

1. Never give in to selling any change when you can exercise your power by demanding it. Tact and communication does to authority what sugar does to teeth. After all if your people or team had any ideas worth listening to they would be the boss.

2. Develop a varied arsenal of looks to master the put down. A well-placed sigh and a "that was dumb" stare can work wonders in silencing your people. Add verbal clinchers: "Are you kidding?" Try well placed sarcasm: "Yeah, I knew I would have this problem when I put a woman in charge!"

3. When providing performance feedback do not let them find their own solution when you can reinforce your position of authority by telling them what they obviously should have done. Be ready to use the Harvard Business review, your MBA notes or Dilbert cartoons to identify how defective they really are.

4. Never deal with the issues when you can attack the person. When they criticize your ideas, question their attitude and commitment to the team. When they miss a deadline question their ability to handle responsibility. If they persist in making their point, keep them in place by saying, "If I wanted your opinion I would give it to you!"

5. Keep harping on the phrase, "More with less" to explain your downsizing, re-organizations and cost containment initiatives. Busy people are happy people whether they want to admit it or not. Don't let your need to hold the line on wages to impress stockholders, stop you from taking the wage increases and bonuses you deserve for leading your team through such perilous times.

6. Never give information or strategic direction until you have to. Once you do, never change your position. Now, if there idea is really better, just wait a few weeks, make some slight adjustments, and then claim it as your idea. They will squawk in the restroom and lounges, but they will know what it is to respect authority.

7. When things go wrong, you know whom to sacrifice. If by chance your team does succeed on their own, take the credit. After all, with effective leadership even turkeys can fly in unison for 50 feet.

8. Build your own corporate torture chamber. Know how to schedule hours to produce maximum aggravation. Keep the pressure on my making them work with team members they hate and projects they have no skills to draw on.

9. Never give recognition: it sets the stage for complacency. After all, they are lucky they have a job. If you thank them, all they do is ask for more money.

10. Bark is as only good as a bite. Fear is a great motivator. Do not waste your time with petty, lengthy documentation with your tough employees; make a scene by threatening them with their job on the spot.

To summarize what Dr. Paulson (2002) listed above, management cannot over communicate change. Employees and managers must know in advance of the situation at hand. They must be allocated the resources to succeed. To with-hold any type of information or due process is a recipe for failure. The managers must have the power to make decisions on the spot based on the information that they have available. They must have obtainable and realistic goals. Managers and employees must be allowed the freedom to make mistakes and to learn from them without fear of repercussion or public embarrassment. Most major solutions to change problems have come about by someone making a mistake and then later finding a better way to resolve the situation.

Does Change Management Really Work?

Change Management involves a huge amount of resources monetarily and physically. Organizations must spend millions of dollars to upgrade their facilities, their computer networks, new product lines, to retrain new employees in the new systems and beliefs. This does not include the thousands of hours that employees must spend on their own to learn the new way of doing things. They must let go of the "old way" and all of the comfort and familiarity that went with it and embrace the "new" and extremely stressful way. They have to let go of their day-to-day confidence in their ability to handle problems the old way and learn to react in the new way. This causes tension in most employees whether visible or unseen. Management must spend countless hours in dealing with the emotional side of the change as well.

Richard Axelrod in his new book, Terms of Engagement, Changing the Way We Change Organizations, says that it just does not work. According to Axelrod (2002), "Traditional change management designed to infuse new life, creativity and innovation into an organization—instead breeds increased resistance and cynicism. Instead of synergy it creates polarization, with members of the change management team dictating strategy on once side and the remainder of the organization hovering fearfully on the other."

He continues by claiming that the bureaucracy becomes even more layered than the change management intentions of flattening out the corporate structure. This creates more headaches and levels of management that must be worked through to resolve common issues and complaints that were easier done before the change.

This new change also creates a new autocratic style. The management is from the top down, the individuals that are demanding the change force their views upon the lower level employees. This often causes resentment of the change, anger and sometimes complete refusal to change. This filters down to productivity problems, attendance problems and in some extreme cases a strike of union workers.

Mr. Axelrod favors a disbanding of the change paradigm and implementing a new structure called the engagement paradigm. (2002) He invokes making the entire organization responsible for the change not a management team or outside consulting company that comes in and run the change process. He argues that this will only increase employee responsibility and thus enhance the change process. His logic is that no one employee will feel left out and they will understand the whole picture of the change. They will no longer have the few deciding for the many.

The main theory behind this new paradigm is that everyone is included. No one, not even the lowest person on the organizational structure, will be left out. They will be informed of the real reason for the change. They will understand how the change affects the company as a whole and each individual department. It will allow employees to buy into the change process. It is no longer seen as an abstract beast but a viable, living entity that can and must be embraced in order to change successfully the organization.

The Future of Change Management

The first misconception that any company or individual must come to terms with is that change will never end. No longer can an organization or companies afford to be placated in their current way of doing business. Companies must always be looking for new and improved ways to enhance their productivity, their customer service and their sales goals. They must weigh the cost both cognitively and financially to the organization and the employees. What type of mental and financial strain will take place from the change and is it worth it?

Change will never stop, change is always happening. It is the natural life cycle of man, nature and business. A company cannot be afraid to implement change. They must understand that change is not always successful and must embrace the unknown in the change process. Too many companies settle for the outdated processes that are tried and true and familiar. They do not want to embrace change, they are afraid of failure. Nevertheless, without some failure any organization cannot grow. The sooner any company makes their error the sooner they can turn it into a useful learning experience.

To sum it up in one quote by Norman R. Augustine, President of Lockheed Martin, "The thing that we did that was most helpful was to visit seven or eight companies…. That had done a lot of mergers and acquisitions. We sat down with their CEOs, COOs and CFOs and asked them to share with us the things they'd done right and wrong to see what advice they would give us. We learned a lot of lessons. One that it is much better than to be eighty percent right fast than a hundred percent right slow; make the tough decisions and get them over with. Be very honest, candid and open, and don't try to sugarcoat the bad news; take the short term hits to do what's best for the long term." (Paulson, 2002, p. 5)

Conclusion

Change Management is a topic that will evoke more continued debate as the current economic and global climate demands constant evolution if companies want to succeed. The emergence of new technology, products and increased global competition will only facilitate the change that will be needed in order to compete. One cannot manage the past but can sure take charge of the future.

References

Axelrod, R. (2000). Terms of Engagement, Changing the Way We Change Organizations. San Fransico: Berret-Koehler Publisher

Caudron, S. (1996, November). Managing the Pain and Gain of Radical Change. BusinessFinanceMag.com. Retrieved October 9, 2002, from http://www.businessfinancemag.com/archi ves/appfiles

Caudron, S.. Taking Charge of Change. (1999, January) BusinessFinanceMag.com. Retrieved October 9, 2002, from http://www.businessfinancemag.com

Clemmer, J.. Growing with Change. The Clemmer Group, 1(1).

Decker, K., Engleman, S., Petrucci, T., & Robinson, S. (1999). United Parcel Service and the Management of Change. Retrieved October 9, 2002, from http://cbpa.louisville.edu/bruce/cases/ups.h tm/ups.htm

FitzGerald, T.. Corporate Superman—The Blue Caped CEO. The CEO Refresher. Abstract retrieved October 9, 2002, from http://www.refresher.com/!superman.html

Holder, B. J.. Executive Development: The Personal Aspect of Organizational Change. The CEO Refresher. Abstract retrieved October 9, 2002, from http://www.refresher.com/!holder2.html

Hoppe, D. (2001). Darwin did it. The Review.

HRnext.com Editorial Team.. Fed up With Change in Your Organization. AllBiz.com. Retrieved October, 2002, from http://all-biz.com/newroot/zoom.asp

Kotter, J. P. (2002). The Heart of Change, Real Life Stories of how People Changed Their Organization. Boston: Harvard Business School.

McNamara, C. (1999). Basic Context for Organizational Change. Organizational Change. Abstract retrieved October 9, 2002, from http://www.mapnp.org/library/mgmnt/orgc hnge.htm

Nickols, F. (2002, February 7). Change Management 101—A Primer. Abstract retrieved October 9, 2002, from http://home.att.net/~nickols/change.htm

Paulson, T.. Driving a Focused but Flexible Vision. Terry Paulson.com. Retrieved October 15, 2002, from http://www.terrypaulson.com/driving.html

Pietersen, W. (2002). The Mark Twain Dilemma. Journal of Business Strategy, 23(5), 32–38.

Riches, A.. Culture—Are you dancing with the devil. anneriches.com. Retrieved October 9, 2002, from http://www.anneriches.com.au/devil.htm

Simmerman, S. J.. Teaching the Caterpillar to Fly—Some Ideas on Managing Change. Retrieved October 9, 2002, from http://www.squarewheels.com/content/teaching.html

Tichy, N. (1997, April). Bob Knowlings Change Manual. Fast Company, 76. Abstract retrieved October 9, 2002, from http://www.fastcompany.com

Challenges at Work and Financial Rewards to Stimulate Longer Workforce Participation

Karin I. Proper, Dorly J. H. Deeg and Allard J. van der Beek

ABSTRACT

Background

Because of the demographic changes, appropriate measures are needed to prevent early exit from work and to encourage workers to prolong their working life. To date, few studies have been performed on the factors motivating continuing to work after the official age of retirement. In addition, most of those studies were based on quantitative data. The aims of this study were to examine, using both quantitative and qualitative data: (1) the reasons for voluntary early retirement; (2) the reasons for continuing working life after the official retirement age; and (3) the predictive value of the reasons mentioned.

Methods

Quantitative data analyses were performed with a prospective cohort among persons aged 55 years and older. Moreover, qualitative data were derived from interviews with workers together with discussions from a workshop among occupational physicians and employers.

Results

Results showed that the presence of challenging work was among the most important reasons for not taking early retirement. In addition, this motive appeared to positively predict working status after three years. The financial advantages of working and the maintenance of social contacts were the reasons reported most frequently for not taking full retirement, with the financial aspect being a reasonably good predictor for working status after three years. From the interviews and the workshop, five themes were identified as important motives to prolong working life: challenges at work, social contacts, reward and appreciation, health, and competencies and skills. Further, it was brought forward that each stakeholder can and should contribute to the maintenance of a healthy and motivated ageing workforce.

Conclusion

Based on the findings, it was concluded that measures that promote challenges at work, together with financial stimuli, seem to be promising in order to prolong workforce participation.

Background

One of the most notable changes in the working population is its ageing. The baby boom cohorts born after the Second World War (born between 1945 and 1965) are now middle-aged; the oldest of them have already started retiring. At the same time, lower birth rates in the past few decades imply that fewer young people will be entering the labour market [1]. These demographic changes are bringing about a shift in the ratio of workers to retirees that will lead to a relative shortage of active workers.

Of the major regions of the world, the process of population ageing is most advanced in Europe [2]. The median age of European Union (EU) citizens will increase between 2004 and 2050 from 39 to 49 years [3]. After 2010, the year that will mark the greatest number of members of the potential working population (i.e. those between 15 and 64 years), the population of working age will decline from 331 million to 268 million in 2050 [3]. In contrast, the proportion of people 65 years and older will increase.

These two demographic changes will result in an increase in the old-age dependency ratio (i.e. the number of people over 65 divided by the number of working-age people) from 25% today to about 53% in 2050 for the 25 EU countries [3]. At the same time, the share of older workers (i.e. those between 55 and 64 years) in the total potential workforce will logically increase. It is estimated that by the year 2025, between one in five and one in three workers will be an older worker [2].

It is clear that the demographic shift has serious economic and social implications, among others the financing of the social security systems, in that a shrinking number of economically active people (i.e. workers) will have to pay for the national pensions of an increasing number of retired persons. The ageing of the workforce also implies a change in the human resources (HR) strategies to manage age in the workplace. Thus, both government and private companies face the challenge of finding means to prolong the labour participation of (older) workers. This is especially true since, to date, many older people have left their jobs either voluntarily (i.e. because of early retirement) or involuntarily (i.e. because of work disability or unemployment) much earlier than the official age of retirement [4].

As in many countries, the social security system in The Netherlands used to offer the opportunity of retiring with a pension before the official retirement age of 65. This so-called early retirement pension (ERP) was implemented during a period of widespread unemployment, with the intention of providing better opportunities for the younger generation to find jobs. However, due to the population's ageing and its consequences, these early exits from work are no longer affordable from an economic point of view. Instead, appropriate measures are needed to prevent early exit from work and to encourage workers to prolong their working life.

During the last few years, measures discouraging early retirement have been implemented in many countries worldwide. For example, since 2006, ERP is no longer supported fiscally in the Netherlands, so that voluntary early exit from work has become more expensive. In other countries, raising the mandatory retirement age is one of the measures implemented. It may, however, be questioned whether such measures imposed by the government or the employer are effective. Commitment from the target group, i.e. the (ageing) workforce, is an important aspect for successful implementation.

To date, most of the research has focused on the determinants of early exit from work [5,6]. As far as the authors are aware, there are only limited data as to the motives of employees for prolonging working life. For example, a study of Lund and Borg [7] showed that very good self-rated health and high development possibilities were independent predictors for remaining at work among males. Among females, the same two predictors were found in addition to high decision authority, medium-level social support and absence of musculoskeletal problems in the knees [7].

In addition, some other recent studies showed that retirement decisions are influenced not only by the worker's health status, but also by income levels and pension rights [8,9]. Those aged 50 and over with poor health, high income or accumulated wealth and access to occupational pensions are more likely to retire at the normal retirement age or retire early [8,9]. Another study showed domestic and family considerations to be important influences of retirement behaviour [10]. In contrast, the evidence about the determinants of involuntary exit from work due to work disability shows occupational factors to be among the most important determinants [11,12].

However, the evidence as to the reasons for voluntary early exit from work is more scarce. From the few previous studies, it can be concluded that retirement decisions on a voluntary basis are multidimensional and not driven by any one single factor. In addition, the little available evidence as to the reasons for voluntary early retirement as well as for continuing working life is based mostly on quantitative data. There have been only a few attempts that involved qualitative data incorporating the worker's opinions about the factors that motivate them to prolong their work career after the official age of retirement.

For example, a semistructured interview study among persons who chose early retirement and those who did not, supported the quantitative finding that decisions about retirement are not made in a vacuum, but have to do with diverse types of possible routes into retirement [13]. These dealt with organisational restructuring, financial offers and opportunities for leisure and self-fulfilment that early retirement offers [13].

From a second qualitative study, it appeared that the way of conceiving work and retirement varied among persons from different socioeconomic backgrounds [14]. The conclusion was that various factors, including financial imperatives and HR practices, intersect at state pension age to shape people's routes into retirement and their options for continuing in work [14].

Finally, most of the previous studies have used cross-sectional data. Hence, the predictive value of the motives to retire early mentioned by those still working remains unclear.

Based on the limited literature on the determinants for prolonging working life, and the scarcity of qualitative data, the aims of the present study were: (1) to examine the reasons for voluntary early retirement; (2) to examine the motives for continuing working life after the official retirement age; and (3) to examine the predictive value of the reasons mentioned. A mixed-methods approach was applied, with quantitative and qualitative data.

Methods

This article describes the results of three studies. The first study includes data analyses of a prospective study among persons aged 55 years and older. The second study is based on qualitative data from interviews with workers, while the third study includes a workshop among occupational physicians (OPs) and employers.

Study 1. Quantitative Study (LASA)

The aim of this quantitative study was to examine the reasons for voluntary early retirement (first study aim) as well as the reasons not to voluntarily retire early. Moreover, with the data of both baseline and follow-up (i.e. three years later), the predictive value of the motives stated at baseline was determined (third aim).

Study Sample

The first study sample consisted of participants of the Longitudinal Aging Study Amsterdam (LASA). LASA is an ongoing, multidisciplinary, cohort study among persons aged 55 and over. It focuses primarily on the predictors and consequences of changes in older persons' physical, cognitive, emotional and social functioning.

The sampling and data collection procedures and the response rates were described in detail elsewhere [15,16]. In summary, LASA started with data collection in 1992–1993. A random sample of persons aged 55 years and over (birth years between 1908 and 1937), stratified by age, sex, urbanisation grade and expected five-year mortality was drawn from the population registers of 11 municipalities in three regions in The Netherlands. This procedure led to a representative sample of the Dutch older population, reflecting the national distribution of urbanisation and population density.

In 2002–2003, a second sample of men and women aged 55 to 64 years was drawn with the same sampling frame as the original cohort. The 2002–2003 sample is the sample for the current study, comprising 1002 participants aged 55–64 years (response rate 57%). In 2005–2006, a follow-up measurement of the second cohort took place (n = 908).

Written informed consent was obtained from all participants. The study was approved by the Medical Ethics Committee of the VU University Medical Centre.

Interviews

The interviews were held at the respondents' residences and were conducted by trained interviewers, who used laptop computers for data entry. The structured interview covered a wide range of topics related to physical and cognitive health and social and psychological functioning. For the purpose of the present study, the interview also included questions on reasons for considering early retirement.

The respondents were asked several questions as to their working status. Questions relevant to this study were: (1) Are you currently working in a paid job? (yes; no); (2) Are you currently (partially) work-disabled? (yes; no); (3) Have you already taken (partial) early retirement? (yes, completely; yes, in part; no); and (4) Would you consider taking (partial) early retirement if financially possible? (yes; no). Partial early retirement refers to working fewer hours in the main occupation.

To get insight into the reasons for voluntary early retirement as well as the reasons not to voluntarily retire early, respondents were asked their most important reason: (1) to take (partial) early retirement; (2) not to take full early retirement; (3) not to take early retirement at all; and (4) (among those who had already taken (partial) early retirement) to have taken (partial) early retirement. All four questions included branching questions that were asked to subgroups according to the working status and the consideration to take (partial) early retirement (Figure 1). The first two questions were asked of those with a paid job, who had not already taken early retirement, but who were considering taking early retirement, whereas the third question was asked of those with a paid job, who had not already taken full retirement and who were not considering taking early retirement. For each of these questions, the last of the five or seven answer categories included "another reason" than mentioned, leaving respondents space to fill in their own reason.

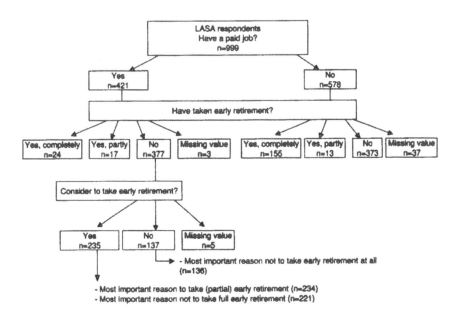

Figure 1. Flow diagram of the LASA respondents regarding working and retirement status.

Analysis

For the purposes of this study, descriptive analyses were conducted. A frequency table was produced for each of the four questions (see above) indicating the percentage of each reason specified. The "other reason" category was analysed in more detail; answers that could be clustered were grouped. The predictive value of the reasons reported was determined by a frequency table of the working status (i.e. working or having retired) at follow-up per reason mentioned at baseline. Analyses were performed using SPSS software, version 14.0 for Windows.

Both Study 2 and Study 3 were performed to get insight into the motivating factors for continuing to work and the measures that can be taken to stimulate prolonging working life.

Study 2. Interviews with Workers

Study Sample

Workers were recruited by the occupational health service (OHS) that participated in this study. By means of its customer database, the OHS approached 12 companies that differed in sector and size. Four companies agreed to participate. These four companies were from different sectors and included: (1) local government, (2) youth- and health care, (3) outdoor advertising and (4) an OHS, located in another city than the one involved in the recruitment in this study. The companies also varied in size (from approximately 60 to 700 workers), job characteristics and workers' educational level.

Within each company, the aim was to interview two workers individually and to hold one focus group interview with approximately five to 10 workers. Selection of the workers was done by a member of the HR staff or the head of the department, and was based on socioeconomic factors (e.g. sex, age, job position), availability and willingness to volunteer, to capture a broad range of characteristics. The workers were approached primarily face-to-face by their HR staff or supervisor to participate in the interviews. After agreement, the researcher arranged a specific date and time for the interviews.

Interviews

For the purposes of this study, semistructured interviews were held. Semistructured interviews define the area to be explored, at least initially, and allow the interviewer or the interviewee to diverge in order to pursue an idea in more detail [17]. This strategy encourages open answers, thereby eliciting new, additional information. During the interview, the interviewer tried to be interactive and to uncover factors that were not anticipated at the outset of the interview.

After briefly introducing the study and asking a few general questions, the interview guide posed the following questions: (1) "Are you willing to continue working until or after the age of 65?" (2) "What are factors that motivate you to continue working?" (3) "What measures can or should be taken to prolong your work career?"

All interviews took place face-to-face and were recorded on a digital voice recorder. The focus group interviews lasted approximately 50 minutes; the duration of the individual interviews varied from 24 to 42 minutes. During the interviews, the interviewer took field notes. The interviews were held in a meeting room at the company and were conducted by the principal researcher (KP).

Analysis

The interviews were fully transcribed by an assistant. Subsequently, content analysis was conducted by the principal researcher to analyse the transcripts. First, the transcripts were read and reread to become familiar with the text. Next, the text was marked with codes indicating the content of the response. The codes were then grouped together into key themes. In the Results section, interviewees' quotations that were considered representative for the theme are reported in order to illustrate the meaning of the themes.

Study 3. Workshop with Occupational Physicians (OP) and Employers

OPs and Employers

To compare the views of the workers with the opinions of important stakeholders, a two-hour workshop among OPs and employers was held. The workshop was organised within a general course for OPs by their occupational health service (OHS). As the workshop fit well in the programme, it was decided to incorporate the workshop in the OHS's OP course. In total, 20 OPs participated in the course, including the workshop. In addition, five representatives (human resource management (HRM) staff) of the four participating companies joined during the workshop.

Workshop

The workshop started with a 30-minute presentation by the principal researcher about the study and the results of the interviews among the workers. Subsequently, four working groups were formed, each consisting of one or two representatives of each company and five OPs.

For one hour, each working group discussed two issues. First, they discussed the motivating factors mentioned by the workers. In their discussion, the OPs and employers were encouraged to add motivating factors. The second issue discussed in the working group concerned the measures to be taken by the employer or the OHS that might stimulate workers to prolong their participation in the workforce. Each working group was asked to write down its views, and one person within each group was asked to report on these in the plenary session. In the plenary session, per working group, the workshop leader (KP) wrote down all views of each working group on a flip chart and gathered the papers of each working group.

Analysis

After the workshop, the views reported on the flip chart and the working groups' papers were copied by the researcher in an electronic form on a computer. The workshop notes were coded according to the themes identified by the interviews with workers. Similar to the analysis of the interviews (Study 2), the text was marked with codes and then grouped together into themes.

Results

Study 1

Table 1 shows the working status of the study population at baseline. A small majority (57.9%) did not have a paid job (any longer) at the moment of baseline measurement, and about a quarter of the respondents (23%) were work-disabled. The large majority (78.2%) had not taken early retirement. Of those currently working (n = 421), almost two thirds (63.2%) reported they were considering taking (partial) early retirement (Table 1). Further, among those with a paid job, n = 377 were not yet partially retired early (Figure 1).

Table 2 presents the frequencies of the workers' most important reasons not to take (full) early retirement. From this table, it can be concluded that the reasons for not taking early retirement at all are different from the reasons for not taking full early retirement. Having sufficient challenges at work appeared to be by far (59.6%) the most important reason for workers not to take early retirement, whereas the financial aspect (32.6%) and the social contacts (25.3%) were reported most frequently as the most important reasons not to take full early retirement (Table 2).

Table 1. Working status of the study sample (LASA cohort 2002–2003) at baseline

	% (n)
Have a paid job	n = 999
No	57.9% (578)
Yes	42.1% (421)
Have a (partly) work disability	n = 961[1]
No	77% (740)
Yes	23% (221)
Have taken early retirement	n = 960[1]
No	78.2% (751)
Yes, partly	3.1% (30)
Yes, completely	18.6% (179)
Consider taking early retirement	n = 372[2]
No	36.8% (137)
Yes	63.2% (235)

[1]Due to missing values, the number of respondents is not equal to 999.
[2]This question was asked of those currently working and not having taken early retirement.

Table 2. Frequency of most important reason not to take (full) early retirement

Most important reason reported at baseline	Most important reason not to take early retirement[1] % (n)	Most important reason not to take full early retirement[2] % (n)
Sufficient challenges at work	59.6 (81)	18.1 (40)
Maintain social contacts	17.6 (24)	25.3 (56)
Other pastime less pleasant	0.7 (1)	1.8 (4)
Financially more favourable	5.9 (8)	32.6 (72)
Other reason	16.2 (22)	22.2 (49)
	100% (136)	100% (221)

[1]This question was asked of those with a paid job, who had not taken early retirement, and who were not considering taking early retirement.
[2]This question was asked of those with a paid job, who had not taken early retirement, but who were considering taking early retirement.

Table 3 presents the predictive value of the reasons mentioned for work status at three-year follow-up. It appeared that the majority of those who reported challenges at work as the most important reason not to take (full) early retirement, were indeed still working three years later (84.4% and 66.7%) (Table 3). With respect to the financial advantages as the most important reason not to take full early retirement, it appeared that three years later, 68.3% were indeed still working or partly retired, but a quarter (24.2%) had taken full retirement. The maintenance of social contacts had less predictive value, since one third (35.4%) of those who reported social contacts as the most important reason not to take full retirement, had taken full retirement in the meantime.

Table 3. Working status at follow-up per reason not to take (full) early retirement as reported at baseline

Reason reported at baseline	Working status at follow-up per reason not to take early retirement			Working status at follow-up per reason not to take full early retirement			
	working % (n)	partly/fully retired early % (n)	disabled % (n)	working % (n)	partly retired early % (n)	fully retired early % (n)	disabled % (n)
Enough challenges at work	84.8 (56)	7.6 (5)	7.6 (5)	66.7 (20)	5.9 (2)	11.8 (4)	13.1 (4)
Maintain social contacts	80 (12)	0 (0)	20 (3)	32.5 (13)	10.4 (5)	35.4 (17)	17.5 (7)
Other pastime less pleasant	100 (1)	0 (0)	0 (0)	66.7 (2)	0 (0)	25 (1)	33.3 (1)
Financially more favourable	66.7 (4)	16.6 (1)	16.6 (1)	63.8 (37)	4.5 (3)	24.2 (16)	8.6 (5)
Other reason	84.6 (11)	7.7 (1)	7.7 (1)	46.3 (19)	8.9 (4)	33.3 (15)	9.8 (4)
Total	n = 84	n = 7	n = 10	n = 91	n = 14	n = 53	n = 21

Table 4 describes the most important reasons for taking early retirement among workers as well as among those who had retired early. Among the workers, the pleasure of spending more time on private concerns was by far the most important reason to take early retirement (59.4%). This reason was also reported most frequently by those who had already taken (partial) early retirement (27.3%) (Table 4). Further, among those who had taken early retirement, external factors, such as arrangements that made early retirement attractive and organisational changes, were also reported frequently as the most important reason to have taken early retirement. Health complaints as well as (physical or mental) workload were reported by a only small minority of the workers and retirees (<10%) (Table 4). Although the pleasure of spending more time on private pursuits was reported frequently as the most important reason to take early retirement, the majority (65.7%) were still working at follow-up (data not shown).

Table 4. Frequency table of most important reason to take (full or partial) early retirement

	Workers[1]	Early retirees[2]
Most important reason reported at baseline	% (n)	% (n)
Stress and pressure of work too high	9.8 (23)	6.3 (13)
Physically too heavy	6.8 (16)	5.4 (11)
Health complaints too limiting	6.8 (16)	6.3 (13)
Not motivated anymore	2.1 (5)	5.9 (12)
Nicer to spend more time on private life	59.4 (139)	27.3 (56)
Not possible anymore in the future	1.7 (4)	5.4 (11)
Having worked for many years[3]	2.1 (5)	-
Organisational changes in company[3]	2.6 (6)	9.8 (20)
Arrangements that made early retirement attractive[3]	-	14.6 (30)
Other reason	8.5 (20)	19.0 (39)
	100% (234)	100% (205)

[1]This group included those with a paid job, who had not taken early retirement, but who were considering taking early retirement.
[2]This group included those who have already taken (partial) early retirement.
[3]This category was formed after clustering the answers of "other".

Study 2

Interviews with Workers

Thirty workers were interviewed, either individually or in focus groups. With the exception of the local authority, within each company two interviews were held, each with one worker, as well as one focus group interview with five to eight workers. At the local authority, it was not possible to hold a focus group interview; instead, five workers were interviewed individually. Thus, a total of 11 individual interviews (six men, five women) and three focus group interviews were held among 19 workers (nine men, 10 women) aged 30 to 59 years.

Although the questions in Study 1 differ from those in the qualitative study (i.e. questions related to the reasons either to take or not to take early retirement versus the motivating factors to continue working), the results were rather similar. In line with the LASA results, where only about one third of those currently working were not considering taking early retirement, it appeared from the interviews that most workers were not willing to continue working after the age of 65 years. Although the majority of the interviewees indicated that they were still motivated to work, that they liked their job and that they (still) were healthy enough to perform their job, they did not intend to prolong their working life.

Furthermore, the major reasons (i.e. sufficient challenges at work, maintenance of social contacts and the financial aspect) reported by the LASA respondents for not taking (full) early retirement were also expressed by the interviewees as motivating factors to continue working. From the responses of the interviews, five key themes were identified: (1) challenges at work, (2) social contacts, (3) reward and appreciation, (4) health and (5) competencies and skills (Table 5). The themes include predominantly motivating factors, but also point to measures that can be taken to stimulate a sustained employability.

Table 5. Working status at follow-up per reason not to take (full) early retirement as reported at baseline

Themes	Motivating factors
Challenges at work	- Work climate is important - Being needed, feel oneself useful - Commitment to work and company - Work should be challenging and give satisfaction - Deliver a quality product
Social contacts	- Social contacts - Socially active
Reward and appreciation	- Financial compensation or reward at the sort term - Appreciation for the work done (by giving compliments)
Health	- Prevention of work strain (physically and mentally) - Healthy lifestyle - Optimal balance between work load and capacity
Competencies and skills	- Moving possibilities within company (horizontal and vertical) - Variation in tasks - Career support - Education and training - Coaching role for older worker - Retraining, occupational resettlement

Challenges at Work

Most of the interviewees considered the content of their job of importance to continuing to work. They indicated that they liked their job, were motivated by their work and that they needed their work. With the exception of the workers who performed a physically heavy job, which included routine, it was frequently indicated that they perceived a feeling of satisfaction and motivation when they were being challenged.

By nature, I am rather lazy, but I am challenged by my work. Being at work, I become challenged intellectually; without work, there is no interesting life for me."

"So far, I am not ready to stop. I am motivated to work, to continue work, because the job is challenging enough."

Social Contacts

Without exception, all workers interviewed appeared to set great store on the contact with colleagues and the associated work climate. One worker, for example, expressed this motive as: "Work is both intellectual and social food." Another worker reported: "It can be that your 'world will become so narrow' ... yes, the contact with colleagues and clients is very important."

Reward and appreciationMost of the interviewees highly valued appreciation from others for the work they did, and considered it as an important factor in continuing. This motive referred to both the financial aspect and reward expressed in words by the supervisor or colleagues. Although none of the interviewees indicated the financial reward as the most important reason to continue working, they agreed that "it definitely plays a role." One worker said: "Respect and appreciation, that's what I think is important."

As to the pat on the back (by the boss) as a motivating factor, they valued receiving a compliment from either the supervisor or colleagues. For example, one worker said:

"I absolutely think reward is essential in remaining motivated to perform the job. This can be through a bonus, but also by your colleagues who say to you how well you performed the task, or by having a dinner together, or something like that."

Health

In the company providing outdoor advertising, the interviewees performed heavy, physical jobs. These workers generally had a negative attitude about prolonged participation in the workforce. One reason for this negative attitude was associated with the total years of having worked when they reached the age of 65 years, since they had started working when quite young. Another reason for their negative attitude concerned the expectation that they would not be able to continue their (current) work, due to the heavy physical workload. Because of their workload, these workers suggested using tools that would reduce the physical work in order to be able to prolong participation in the workforce.

In the remaining three companies, physical workload was not the issue, in contrast to mental workload. Especially in the OHS, workers experienced (too) high work demands. To reduce or cope with work-related stress, some workers suggested implementing a relaxation programme or creating possibilities for relaxation, e.g. by means of a room where workers could rest, or through implementation of a yoga programme.

The promotion of a healthy lifestyle, including physical activity and diet, was also mentioned frequently as being an important factor for increasing the capacity and motivation to prolong a healthy working life. Although they generally agreed that a healthy lifestyle was the worker's own responsibility, they also agreed on the role of the employer in stimulating as well as facilitating such a lifestyle.

"I need to take care that I stay healthy; that's my own responsibility."

Competences and Skills

Finally, the interviewees agreed on the value of education and training of (older) workers to be able to keep up with technological developments. They also reported that training or education was valuable and should be offered by the employer in order to grow (personally), to stimulate challenges at work and to avoid routine work.

"One needs to develop oneself; as soon as the job becomes a routine, it's not good, and one will not remain motivated."

It was further suggested to include the competences and personal development in the functioning discussions:

"In my opinion, the personal development should be included in the yearly functioning discussion."

There were no substantial differences in factors stated by younger and older workers. It appeared only that younger workers had difficulties in describing factors that would motivate them to prolong their working life, as "it is such a long way off."

Study 3

Workshop with OPs and Employers

The OPs and employers generally agreed with the workers' opinions expressed in the interviews. No additional factors were mentioned by them.

As to possible measures to be taken by the employer or the OHS to prolong workers' participation in the workforce, the working groups generally agreed with each other and reported more or less the same measures. From the notes, the following main themes were identified: (1) health promotion, (2) education and training and (3) financial stimuli.

Health Promotion

Each working group independently reported factors that involved promoting the balance between workload and individual capacity, the latter receiving a notable amount of emphasis. The workshop participants not only referred to the promotion of physical activity and exercise, but also emphasised the role of a healthy diet, quitting smoking, a moderate consumption of alcohol and relaxation. Similar to the workers, they agreed on the responsibility of the worker, but also considered the role of the OP and the employer. One working group said, for example:

> "It is of importance to stay fit and healthy; this is the responsibility of the worker. The employer, on the other hand, should give the good example. There should be attention for a healthy lifestyle within the organisation."

Another working group expressed its opinion about this issue as follows:

> "The employer will do right if he implements a 'vitality policy' including physical activity, fitness, walking in lunchtime or walking during meetings. In most cases, the corporate culture needs to be changed in that it promotes health management with even more stringent measures when neglecting certain activities."

In addition to offering lifestyle programmes and providing information, they considered a periodic health screening to be a useful OHS tool, since the results of such a screening can give direct cause to providing (lifestyle) counselling. With respect to the other side of the balance, i.e. the workload, all agreed that this should be tuned to individual capacity.

Education and Training

The working groups stated that work should be fun and offer sufficient challenges. This could, for example, be achieved by making plans about the work career and education needed and to be followed. Education and training should also be promoted, as it created variation in work, the latter being an important boost to taking pleasure in work. To achieve variation in work, some in the working groups suggested exchanging workers from different companies, or to give older workers a coaching or mentor task in orienting new colleagues.

To illustrate, one working group indicated:

"It is of crucial importance that one enjoys the job! This can be realised by several measures—among others, by giving older workers a coaching task in which they train young workers; the employer can also make agreements with the (older) worker about career planning."

Financial Stimuli

Consistent with the interviews among the workers, attention was paid to the financial aspect. The OPs and employers agreed on the desirability of having both the employer and the government provide financial stimuli to workers who prolonged their working life. Moreover, they advocated maintaining the same net salary when demoting workers because of a (age-related) reduction in work ability.

Discussion

The aim of this study was to examine the reasons for voluntary early retirement as well as for prolonging working life after the official retirement age. Insight into these motives is useful, among other reasons, as input to the HRM policy to retain healthy (older) workers who are able and willing to prolong their labour force participation. Despite the need to tailor the HRM policy to the needs and preferences of older workers [18], it should be kept in mind that older workers are a heterogeneous group in that differences exist in personal characteristics, needs and work ability between individual workers. This was confirmed by the OPs and employers in the present qualitative study, in that they stated that the workload should be tuned to individual capacity.

From the LASA analyses, it was shown that, of those currently working, about two thirds were considering taking early retirement. In view of the economic need to prevent early exit from work, this proportion is substantial. As mentioned before, it is important to encourage workers not to take early retirement, but to prolong working life instead. In order to achieve this, workers should be able as well as be motivated to continue working.

Indeed, the most important reason given by the LASA respondents currently working for not taking early retirement appeared to be the motivation to perform the job, i.e. the presence of challenge at work. This was supported by the interviews among the workers, where pleasure at work was mentioned frequently as a motive to prolong working life. Based on the LASA follow-up data, it appeared that the presence of sufficient challenges at work positively predicted the working status three years later. That is, the majority of workers who found their work challenging, and indicated this was an important reason not to take early retirement, actually remained in the workforce.

Another notable result of this study concerned the fact that the reasons for not taking full early retirement differed from the reasons not to take early retirement (at all). Based on the LASA analyses, the main reasons for the former were the financial aspect of working and the maintenance of social contacts. The social aspects, but particularly the financial advantages of working, thus seemed to play an important role in the decision to either fully retire or to cut down work gradually by partial early retirement.

Again, these results were confirmed by the qualitative study. The large majority of the workers interviewed said the social contacts with colleagues and others at work were of great importance to work motivation. However, based on the LASA follow-up data, it appeared that the maintenance of social contacts had a weak predictive value for the working status three years later. A substantial part of those who had reported social contacts being the most important reason not to take full retirement, did take full retirement in the meantime.

As to the financial aspect, both the workers interviewed and the OPs and employers agreed on its significance. In addition, the financial advantage of not taking retirement appeared to reasonably predict the working status three years later.

Based on these findings, including the desire of the majority of workers to take early retirement, it seems sensible to aim for a gradual exit from work through a period of working fewer hours in order to prevent full early retirement. In this way, the workers benefit financially and moreover can spend some more time on private pursuits, this being the most important reason to take early retirement, as shown by the LASA analyses. This was confirmed by a recent study by Cebulla et al. [19], which stated that there is broad consensus that older workers should be given the opportunity to retire gradually.

Another study found control over the retirement decision to be an important factor in retirement well-being, which persisted three years after retirement [20]. They also found that gradual retirement was followed by a positive change in health. Gradual retirement was linked to an improvement in health. According to the authors of that study, those findings suggest that HR practices that promote employees' control of their retirement decisions will enhance well-being in later life and facilitate prolonged workforce participation [20].

As mentioned in the introduction, not much literature has been published as to the reasons for voluntary early exit from work or for an enduring working life. However, the few previous studies performed in different countries support our results.

For example, Armstrong-Stassen (2006) investigated the importance of six HRM strategies relevant in the retention of older workers [21]. These six factors were: (1) flexible working options, (2) training and development, (3) job design (e.g. reduce workload), (4) recognition and respect, (5) performance evaluation and (6) compensation (e.g. financial, incentives). Although different terms have been used in Table 5, most of the five strategies, if not all, are reflected.

From Armstrong-Stassen's study, it appeared that both retired and employed men rated three HRM practices the same as to their influence on the decision to remain in the workforce: (1) providing challenging and meaningful job tasks; (2) recognising experience, knowledge and skills; and (3) showing appreciation for doing a good job [21]. Further, data from a representative sample of the household population aged 50 and over in England, the English Longitudinal Study of Ageing (ELSA), confirm that influences on retirement are multidimensional, with economic incentives being an important, if not the most important, determinant for continuing working life [22].

Two other factors of influence appeared to be health and social issues. As to the financial aspect as a determinant of retirement behaviour, the literature is consistent [23]. Using ELSA data, Banks et al. (2007) found that both pension accrual and pension wealth are important determinants of the retirement behaviour of men aged 50 to 59. This was also valid among women of the same age, although it was somewhat weaker [24]. It further appeared that there was a U-shaped pattern of being in paid work by quintile of the wealth distribution, with those at the bottom and the top of the wealth distribution being less likely to be in paid work than those in the middle of the wealth distribution, but for different stated reasons: those with relatively low levels of wealth were most likely to stop working due to ill health [24]. Thus, ELSA showed that financial need may act as an incentive to continue working life, but that this varies with wealth, income and education levels [25].

Strengths and Limitations of the Study

As mentioned before, the few previous studies regarding the reasons for early retirement and prolonging working life have mostly used quantitative research methods. One of the strengths of the present study is that it is based on mixed methods, with both quantitative and qualitative data. Such a triangulation method is useful as it approaches the same phenomenon by using different methods, each having its own value. Qualitative research techniques add vast amounts of relevant data [26].

There were, however, some limitations in our qualitative study. Although the transcripts were made by an assistant, the interviews were performed by one researcher, as were the analyses of the responses into codes and themes. Further, despite our not believing that it introduces bias, we did not use a computer software programme in which each item is compared with the rest of the data to establish analytical categories [26]. Instead, the interviewer herself read and reread the recordings, identified the codes and grouped the codes together into key themes. The analyses were performed manually, which was feasible and acceptable, instead of by means of a software package specifically designed for qualitative data management. Although the latter would have made the process easier, we assumed the chance to be small that the manual process would have yielded substantially different clusters. However, as is the case in all qualitative studies, the categorisation of the themes depended on the human factor (i.e. the researcher), and might well have resulted in different clusters if the process had been performed by another researcher.

Another strength of this study is that the quantitative study involved a longitudinal study among a representative sample of older adults in The Netherlands. The LASA follow-up data were useful to provide information about the predictive value of the motives reported at baseline to take (or not) early retirement. Overall, results indicated that the motives reported did not have a high predictive value. However, considering the small number of follow-up data used, prudence is needed for the conclusions as to the predictive value of the reasons mentioned. In this respect, it is also worthwhile to mention that the present study can be considered as a pilot study in that it is based on data of Dutch workers only. As the topic of ageing workers is of worldwide interest, a future study involving diverse countries with diverse policies to encourage a sustained participation in the workforce would be valuable.

Finally, although the involvement of different stakeholders in the qualitative study added value to the study in that extra input could be generated instead of involving only one target group, the number of the representatives of companies was low. Nevertheless, the inclusion of the four companies, which included different in type of workers and work activities, yielded useful information about the organisation of the (HRM) policy with respect to the promotion of an enduring participation in the workforce of older workers.

Conclusion

Taken together, findings suggest that each stakeholder (i.e. the worker, the employer, the OHS and the government) should contribute to the maintenance of a healthy and motivated ageing workforce. In doing so, one should take into account the differences in strategies for different groups, such as different socio-economic status groups or those at different ages. Due to the small size of the study, and especially the qualitative study, the present study could not draw such conclusions for different subgroups. So, further research examining the motivating factors to prolong working life among different groups is recommended.

In addition to their ability to work, workers' motivation is considered to be crucial in sustaining participation in the workforce. Workers who lack pleasure at work and are not motivated to prolong their working life, probably confirm the negative image of some employers about older workers, i.e. lower productivity and "waiting out one's time." There are still some employers for whom the negative effects of ageing prevail over the value of older workers, in that older workers are less productive or resist change or innovations. In order to oppose this view, the employer can and should implement simple measures, such as offering education and expressing appreciation to the personnel. Finally, measures that promote challenges at work, together with financial stimuli, seem to be promising in keeping older workers in the workforce.

Competing Interests

The authors declare that they have no competing interests.

Authors' Contributions

All three authors made a substantial contribution in the design of this specific study. DD was (and still is) involved and responsible for the design and data collection of the quantitative study (Study 1). KP and AvdB were involved in the design and the acquisition of the qualitative data (Study 2). KP performed the statistical analyses. All three authors read and approved the final manuscript for submission to this journal.

References

1. Griffiths A: Ageing, health and productivity: a challenge for the new millennium. Work & Stress 1997, 11:197–214.

2. Van Nimwegen N: Europe at the Crossroads: Demographic Developments in the European Union. Executive Summary, European Observatory on the Social Situation, Demography Monitor 2006—European Observatory and the Social Situation—Demography Network. Brussels: European Commission; 2006.

3. European Commission: Directorate-General for Employment, Social Affairs and Equal Opportunities Unit E.1. In Europe's Demographic Future: Facts and Figures on Challenges and Opportunities. Luxembourg: Office for Official Publications of the European Communities; 2007.

4. Van Nimwegen N, Beets G: Social Situation Observatory. Demography Monitor 2005. Demographic Trends, Socio-Economic Impacts and Policy Implications in the European Union. The Hague: Netherlands Interdisciplinary Demographic Institute; 2006.

5. Humphrey A, Costigan P, Pickering K, Stratford N, Barnes M: Factors Affecting the Labour Market Participation of Older Workers. DWP Research Report 2000. Leeds, West Yorkshire: Corporate Document Services; 2003.

6. Meadows P: Retirement Ages in the UK: A Review of the Literature. Employment Relations Research Series No. 18. London: Department of Trade and Industry; 2003.

7. Lund T, Borg V: Work environment and self-rated health as predictors of remaining in work 5 years later among Danish employees 35–59 years of age. Exp Aging Res 1999, 25:429–434.

8. Emmerson C, Tetlow G: Labour market transitions. In Retirement, Health and Relationships of the Older Population in England: The 2004 English Longitudinal Study of Ageing (Wave 2). Edited by: Banks J, Breeze E, Lessof C, Nazroo J. London: Institute for Fiscal Studies; 2006:41–63.

9. Philipson C, Smith A: Extending Working Life: A Review of the Research Literature. DWP Research Report 299. Leeds, West Yorkshore: Corporate Document Services; 2005.

10. Vickerstaff S, Cox J, Keen L: Employers and the management of retirement. Soc Policy Admin 2003, 37:271–287.

11. Krause N, Dasinger LK, Deegan LJ, Brand RJ, Rudolph L: Psychosocial job factors and return to work after compensated low back injury: a disability phase-specific analysis. Am J Industr Med 2001, 40:374–392.

12. Dasinger LK, Krause N, Deegan LJ, Brand JB, Rudolph L: Physical workplace factors and return to work after compensation low back injury: a disability phase-specific analysis. JOEM 2000, 42:323–333.

13. Higgs P, Mein G, Ferrie J, Hyde M, Nazroo J: Pathways to early retirement: agency and structure in the British Civil Service. Ageing Soc 2003, 23:761–778.

14. Parry J, Taylor RF: Orientation, opportunity and autonomy: why people work after state pension age in three areas of England. Ageing Soc 2007, 27:579–598.

15. Deeg DJH, Westendorp-de Serière M: Autonomy and Well-Being in the Aging Population. I. Report from the Longitudinal Aging Study Amsterdam 1992–1993. Amsterdam: Vrije University Press; 1994.

16. Deeg DJH, Van Tilburg T, Smit JH, de Leeuw ED: Attrition in the Longitudinal Aging Study Amsterdam. The effect of differential inclusion in side studies. J Clin Epidemiol 2002, 55:319-328.

17. Britten N: Qualitative research: qualitative interviews in medical research. BMJ 1995, 11:251–253.

18. Agarwal NC: Retirement of older workers: issues and policies. Hum Res Planning 1998, 21:42–51.

19. Cebulla A, Butt S, Lyon N: Working beyond the state pension age in the United Kingdom: the role of working time flexibility and the effects on the home. Ageing Soc 2007, 27:849–867.

20. De Vaus D, Wells Y, Kenid Y, Kendig H, Quine S: Does gradual retirement have better outcomes than abrupt retirement? Results from an Australian panel study. Ageing Soc 2007, 27:667–682.

21. Armstrong-Stassen M: Encouraging retirees to return to the workforce. Hum Res Planning 2006, 29:38–44.

22. Banks J, Casanova M: Work and Retirement. [http://www.ifs.org.uk/elsa/report_wave1.php] In Health, Wealth and Lifestyles of the Older Population in England: The 2002 English Longitudinal Study of Ageing Edited by: Marmot M, Banks J, Blundell R, Lessof C, Nazroo J. London: Institute for Fiscal Studies;

23. Gruber J, Wise D: Social Security Programs and Retirement Around the World: Micro-Estimation. Chicago: The University of Chicago Press; 2004.

24. Banks J, Emmerson C, Tetlow G: Healthy retirement or unhealthy inactivity: how important are financial incentives in explaining retirement? [https://editorialexpress.com/cgi-bin/conference/download.cgi?db_name=res2007&paper_id=427] 2007.

25. Emmerson C, Tetlow G: Labour market transitions. [http://www.ifs.org.uk/publications.php?publication id=3711] In Retirement, Health and Relation-

ships of the Older Population in England: The 2004 English Study of Ageing (Wave 2) Edited by: Banks J, Breeze E, Lessof C, Nazroo J. London: Institute for Fiscal Studies; 2006.

26. Pope C, Ziebland S, Mays N: Qualitative research in health care. Analysing qualitative data. BMJ 2000, 320(7227):114–146.

The Effects of Human Resource Practices on Firm Growth

Ilias P. Vlachos

ABSTRACT

Although the connection between firm growth and labour is well documented in economics literature, only recently the link between human resources (HR) and firm growth has attracted the interest of researchers. This study aims to assess the extent, if any, to which, specific HR practices may contribute to firm growth. We review a rich literature on the links between firm performance and the following HR practices: (1) job security (2) selective hiring, (3) self-managed teams (4) compensation policy, (5) extensive training, and (6) information sharing. We surveyed HR managers and recorded their perceptions about the links between HR practices and firm growth. Results demonstrated that compensation policy was the strongest predictor of sales growth. Results provide overall support for all HR practices except of job security. Eventually, selecting, training, and rewarding employees as well as giving them the power to decide for the benefit of their firm, contribute significantly to firm growth.

Keywords: human resource practices, firm growth, selective hiring, compensation policy

Introduction

The extent to which, if any, human resource management (HRM) impacts on organizational performance has emerged as the central research question in the personnel/HRM field (see Becker and Gerhart, 1996; Guest, 1997 for reviews). Although initial results indicate that some human resources practices may have a positive effect on organizational performance, most scholars suggest that more conceptual and empirical work is required (Brewster, 2004; Cardon and Stevens, 2004; Givord and Maurin, 2004; Zhu, 2004). For the moment, although Human resources (HR) are considered as the most valuable asset in an organization, they make a difference only for a few organisations (Pfeffer, 1998; Wimbush, 2005).

The link between human resources (HR) and firm growth is well documented in classic economic theory. Overwhelming evidence suggests growth is driven by specialization and division of labour in the processes of generation and attraction/development of technological opportunities. However, at the firm level of analysis, only recently the link between human capital and growth has attracted the interest of researchers.

Firm growth is often seen as an indication of market acceptance and firm success (Fesser and Willard, 1990). Growth is considered as a top strategic priority for most firms yet only few companies achieve growth and ever fewer in maintaining in (Baum and Wally, 2003; Zook and Allen, 2003). Assuming, that firm growth involves more purposeful work and strategic decision making than leaving it to random and chance events, the present study addresses a central research question: How do human resource management practices contribute to firm growth?

The next section reviews the relevant literature on HR practices and firm growth. A discussion of the methodology employed for data collection follows. The last two sections illustrate the data analysis, the discussion of the key results and the provision of possible avenues for future research.

Literature Review

A growing body of empirical research has examined the effect of certain HRM practices on firm performance. Although there is a long list of best HR practices

that can affect either independently or collectively on the organizational performance, results are hard to interpret. In order to determine any effects of HR
practices on firm growth, we choose to examine HR practices initially proposed
by Pfeffer (1998) which according to the literature, can be expected to influence
the firm performance. In his seminal work, Pfeffer (1998) proposed the following seven HRM practices: (1) employment security (2) selective hiring, (3) self-
managed teams and decentralization of decision making (4) comparatively high
compensation contingent on organizational performance, (5) extensive training,
(6) reduced status distinctions and barriers, including dress, language, office arrangements, and wage differences across levels, and (7) extensive sharing of financial and performance information throughout the organization.

The following sections will develop hypotheses concerning the relationship
between HRM practices and firm growth.

Compensation Policy

Performance-based compensation is the dominant HR practice that firms use
to evaluate and reward employees' efforts (Collins and Clark, 2003). Evidently,
performance-based compensation has a positive effect upon employee and organizational performance (see for reviews: Brown et al. 2003; Cardon and Stevens,
2004). However, there is scarce evidence on the effects of compensation policy of
firm growth. Empirical studies on the relationship between performance-related
pay and company performance have generally found a positive relationship, but a
growing body of empirical evidence suggests that it is not just pay level that matters, but pay structure as well (Wimbush, 2005; Singh 2005).

Barringer et al. (2005) conducted a quantitative content analysis of the nar-
rative descriptions of 50 rapid-growth firms and a comparison group of 50 slow-
growth companies. Results demonstrated that employee incentives differentiated
the rapid-growth from the slow-growth firms. Firms that were eager to achieve
rapid-growth provided their employees financial incentives and stock options as
part of their compensation packages. In doing so, firms managed to elicit high
levels of performance from employees, provide employees the feeling that they
have an ownership interest in the firm, attract and retain high-quality employees,
and shift a portion of a firm's business risk to the employees.

Delery and Doty (1996) identified performance-based compensation as the
single strongest predictor of firm performance. Both performance-based compensation and merit-based promotion can be viewed as ingredients in organizational
incentive systems that encourage individual performance and retention (Uen and
Chien, 2004). Collins and Clark (2003) studied 73 high-technology firms and
showed that the relationships between the HR practices and firm performance

(sales growth and stock growth) were mediated through their top managers' social networks.

Cho et al. (2005) suggested that incentive plans is effective in decreasing turn-over rates. Banker et al. (2001) conducted a longitudinal study of the effectiveness of incentive plans in the hotel industry and found that incentive plans were relat-ed to higher revenues, increased profits, and decreased cost. Paul and Ananthara-man (2003) found that compensation and incentives directly affect operational performance.

To be effective, compensation practices and policies must be aligned with organisational objectives. While performance-based compensation can motivate employees, sometimes employees perceive it as a management mechanism to con-trol their behaviour (Lawler and Rhode, 1976). In such a case, employees are less loyal and committed, thus compensation plans have the opposite than desired outcome (Ahmad and Schroeder, 2003; Rodriguez and Ventura, 2003).

Employee turnover can significantly slow revenue growth, particularly in knowledge-intensive industries (Baron and Hannan, 2002). Given that much of the tacit knowledge resides within employees, significant turnover poses a threat to firm performance and its future growth potential. With high turnover rates, firm growth flees away along with leaving managers who often become employers of rival firms or establish themselves rival firms.

Therefore, we propose this hypothesis:

Hypothesis 1: Compensation Policy is positively related to firm growth.

Decentralization & Self-Managed Teams

More and more, employees are required to work in teams, make joint decisions, and undertake common initiatives in order to meet the objectives of their team and organization. Self-managed teams can affect firm growth in two ways: Firstly, a surplus of junior managers in a firm may create and support dynamics of firm growth. The growth stage is perhaps the most dynamic stage of a firm's life cycle. As the business expands, new levels of management are added. Decision-making becomes more decentralized, middle managers gain authority and self-managed teams proliferate as the firm adds more and more projects and customers (Flam-holtz and Randle, 2000; Miller and Friesen, 1984). Secondly, teamwork and de-centralization of decision making promotes employee commitment participation and create a sense of attachment, thus indirectly affecting firm performance (Tata and Prasad, 2004).

Several studies identified self-managed teams and decentralization as impor-tant high-performance HRM practices (Pfeffer, 1998; Wagner, 1994; Yeatts and

Hyten, 1998; Singer and Duvall, 2000). Jayaram et al. (1999) found that decentralised teams have a positive effect on two dimensions of the performance, time and flexibility. Collins and Clark (2003) examined the role of human resource practices in creating organizational competitive advantage and found that top management team social networks (practices such as mentoring, incentives, etc.) mediated the relationship between HR practices and firm performance. Haleblian and Finkelstein (1993) examined the effects of top management team size and chief executive officer (CEO) dominance on firm performance in different environments. Results showed that firms with large teams performed better and firms with dominant CEOs performed worse in a turbulent environment than in a stable one.

Tata and Prasad (2004) found that a company with micro level of centralisation is a receptive environment for self-managed teams. In a study of differential outcomes of team structures for workers, supervisors, and middle managers in a large unionized telecommunications company, Batt (2004) found that participation in self-managed teams is associated with significantly higher levels of employment security, and satisfaction for workers and the opposite for supervisors. Black et al. (2004) examined the impact of organizational change on workers and found evidence that self-managed teams are associated with greater employment reductions.

Therefore, we propose this hypothesis:

Hypothesis 2: Decentralisation is positively related to firm growth.

Information Sharing

Sharing of information may have a dual effect: Firstly, it conveys employees the right meaning that the company trusts them. Secondly, in order to make informed decision, employees should have access to critical information. Communicating performance data on a routine basis throughout the year help employees to improve and develop. Employees presumably want to be good at their jobs, but if they never receive any performance feedback, they may perceive to have a satisfactory performance when in fact they do not (Chow et al., 1999). Furthermore, information sharing fosters organizational transparency which reduces turnover (Ahmad and Schroeder, 2003) and forges synergistic working relationship among employees (Nonaka, 1994).

Information sharing is not a widespread HR practice as someone might have expected it to be. Many companies are vulnerable to share critical information with their employees because in this way employees become more powerful and companies may loose control of them (Pfeffer, 1998). Furthermore, information sharing always involves the danger of leaking important information to competitors (Ronde, 2001). In a study of Japanese consultation committees, Morishima (1991) found a positive association of information sharing with productivity and profitability, and a negative one with labour cost. Constant et al. (1994) pointed out that attitudes about information sharing depend on the form of the information. Burgess (2005) studied employee motivations for knowledge transfer outside their work unit and found that employees who perceived greater organizational rewards for sharing spent more hours sharing knowledge beyond their immediate work group. However, a significant percentage of employees perceived knowledge as a means of achieving upward organizational mobility. Therefore, employees sought information more often than shared it.

Roberts (1995) studied how HR strategy affects profits in 3,000 businesses throughout the world and found that sharing information was related with higher profitability. However, Ichniowski and Shaw (1999) compared US and Japanese steel-making plants and found that employee participation based solely on problem-solving teams or information sharing did not produce large improvements in productivity. In a study of Fortune 1,000 largest manufacturing and service companies on high-performance practices, Lawler et al. (1995) found information sharing to correlate to firm performance but results are inconclusive.

Therefore, we propose this hypothesis:

Hypothesis 3: Sharing of information is positively related to firm growth.

Selective Hiring

This practice can ensure that the right people, with the desirable characteristics and knowledge, are in the right place, so that they fit in the culture and the climate of the organization. Moreover, pinpointing the rights employees would decrease the cost of employees' education and development.

Schuster (1986) argued that selective hiring is a key practice that creates profits. Huselid (1995) examined HR practices of high performance companies and found that attracting and selecting the right employees increase the employee productivity, boost organizational performance, and contribute in reducing turnover.

Cohen and Pfeffer (1986) argued that hiring standards reflect not only organizations' skill requirements but also the preferences of various groups for such standards and their ability to enforce these preferences. Michie and Quinn (2001) proposed that a possible indirect link between selective hiring and organisational performance can be the forging of internal bonds between managers and employees that creates the write culture for productivity growth. Collins and Clark

(2003) argued that the practice of selective hiring results at sales growth. Paul and Anantharaman (2003) pointed out that an effective hiring process ensures the presence of employees with the right qualifications, leading to production of quality products and consequently in increase of economic performance.

Cho et al. (2005) examined pre-employment tests as a key component of selective hiring and found that when employed, these tests can select employees that stay with a company longer. Passing pre-employment tests may give an applicant a stronger sense of belonging to the company, resulting in higher degrees of commitment if employed. Cardon and Stevens (2004) pointed out that for small companies recruiting is often problematic. This can be due to several reasons such as limited financial and material resources and jobs with unclear boundaries responsibilities, which decreases their potential to hire qualified candidates. Therefore, we propose this hypothesis:

Hypothesis 4: Selective hiring is positively related to firm growth.

Training and Development

Training and development may be related to firm performance in many ways. Firstly, training programmes increase the firm specificity of employee skills, which, it turn, increases employee productivity and reduces job dissatisfaction that results in employee turnover (Huselid, 1995). Secondly, training and developing internal personnel reduces the cost and risk of selecting, hiring, and internalising people from external labour markets, which again increases employee productivity and reduces turnover. Training and development like job security requires a certain degree of reciprocity: A company that train and develop systematically its employees advocates them that their market value develops more favourably than in other firms. This increases employees' productivity, commitment, and lowers turnover. Companies may also assist their employees in career planning. In doing so, companies encourage employees to take more responsibility for their own development, including the development of skills viewed as significant in the company (Doyle, 1997).

Barringer et al. (2005) compared rapid-growth and slow-growth firms and found that rapid-growth firms depend heavily on the abilities and efforts of their employees to maintain their growth-oriented strategies. The fast-growth firms used training programs to achieve their objectives and emphasized employee development to a significantly greater extent than their slow-growth counterparts. Therefore, training and employee development practices are more common in rapid-growth firms than slow-growth ones.

Miller (2006) examined the growth strategies in the retail sector and suggested that modern retailers should place more emphasis on the policies and practices that could contribute to staff retention, rather than on the immediacy of recruitment and selection. Zhu (2004) reviewed the changes in the area of human resource development in Japan and observed that some companies and industries have shifted towards a more strategic approach that emphasizes the impact of effective learning at both individual and organizational levels on long-term organizational competitiveness. Husiled (1995) found that the education and development of employees have a significant effect both upon the personnel productivity and the sort-term and long-term indicators of organizational performance.

Ngo et al. (1998) investigated the effects of country origins on HR practices of firms from the United States, Great Britain, Japan and Hong Kong operating in Hong Kong. Study results showed that structural training and development and retention-oriented compensation were related to various measures of firm performance. Paul and Anantharaman (2003), in searching the links between human resource practices and organizational performance, proposed that career development programmes demonstrate a true interest of the organization for the growth of its personnel, which, in turn, stimulates commitment and devotion, which, subsequently, raises personnel productivity and consequently economical output.

Cerio (2003) examined the manufacturing industry in Spain and found that quality management practices related to product design and development, together with human resource practices, are the most significant predictors of operational performance. Michie and Quinn (2001) investigated the relationships between UK firms' use of flexible work practices and corporate performance and suggested that low levels of training are negatively correlated with corporate performance. Therefore, we propose this hypothesis:

Hypothesis 5: The extent of training and development will be positively related to firm growth.

Job Security

Job security creates a climate of confidence among employees which cultivates their commitment on the company's workforce. Job security requires a certain degree of reciprocity: firstly, a company must signal a clear message that jobs are secure; then, employees believing that this is true, feel confident and commit themselves to expend extra effort for the company's benefit; finally, a company that have learnt that job security contributes to its performance, invests again in job security (Pfeffer, 1998). Probst (2002) has developed a conceptual model of the antecedents and consequences of job security. Antecedents include worker characteristics, job characteristics, organizational change and job technology change. Consequences include psychological health, physical health, organizational withdrawal, unionisation activity, organizational commitment and job stress. Jon involvement, cultural values, and procedural justices moderate job security perceptions and attitudes.

Buitendach and Witte (2005) assessed the relationship between job insecurity, job satisfaction and affective organisational commitment of maintenance workers in a parastatal in Gauteng. Study results revealed small but significant relationships between job insecurity and extrinsic job satisfaction and job insecurity and affective organisational commitment. Job satisfaction was also found to mediate the relationship between job insecurity and affective organisational commitment.

However, today's business environments are far from providing job security to their employees. For example, in an analysis of involuntary job loss in France between 1982 and 2002, Givord and Maurin (2004) found evidence that technological changes contribute to keeping the employees for shorter periods of time, thus increasing job insecurity.

When companies do provide job security, then empirical evidence suggests that it has a positive effect on to firm performance. Following Pfeffer (1998), Ahmad and Schroeder (2003) found that among others, job security impacts operational performance indirectly through organizational commitment. Delery and Doty (1996) studied the US banking sector and found some support for a positive relationship between employment security and firm performance. In their study of 101 foreign firms operating in Russia, Fey et al. (2000) found evidence that human resource practices indirectly improve organisational performance. The results showed that not only, there was a direct positive relationship between job security and performance for non-managers, but job security was the most important predictor of HR outcomes for non-managerial employees. Results also suggested a direct positive relationship between managerial promotions based on merit and firm performance.

Michie and Quinn (2001) examined labour market flexibility in over 200 manufacturing UK firms and found that job security is negatively correlated with corporate performance. In contrast, results showed that 'high commitment' organizations are positively correlated with good corporate performance. Kraimera et al. (2005) used psychological contract and social cognition theories to explore the role of full-time employees' perceived job security in explaining their reactions to the use of temporary workers by using a sample of 149 full-time employees who worked with temporaries. Results demonstrated that employees' perceived job security negatively related to their perceptions that temporaries pose a threat to their jobs. On the one hand, for those with high job security, there was a positive relationship between benefit perceptions and performance. On the other hand, for those with low job security, there was a negative relationship between threat perceptions and performance. Therefore, we propose this hypothesis:

Hypothesis 6: The presence of job security is positively related to firm growth.

Figure 1 illustrates the associations between these hypotheses and relevant constructs.

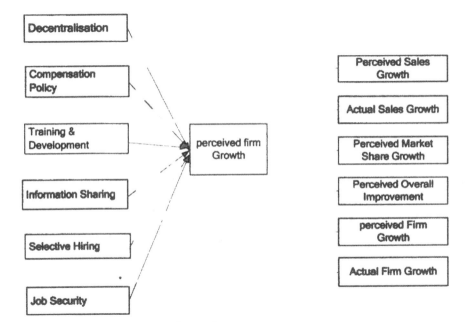

Figure 1: The association between hypotheses and constructs

Method

The Sampling Procedure and Sample

While Figure 1 is a model of the firm performance, we choose to examine it as understood by the individuals who take decisions about firm performance. In doing so, we operationalize and measure individuals' perceptions of the model's variables in their work situations.

In order to develop robust model linking HR practices and firm performance, we drew our sample from food companies operating in Greece for a minimum of five years. We included companies from the food processing and trading sub-sectors, excluding hospitality and retailing. In doing so, we aimed to increase the homogeneity of our population as we as decrease the necessary sample size to achieve robust validity of data analyses.

Testing the research hypotheses in a specific sector adds to the validity of the research design because managerial skills are to a large extent industry-specific. Furthermore, food industry is dealing with subsequent food crises and human resources are considered as a valuable asset to survive and maintain competitive advantage. In-depth interviews were conducted with key decision makers prior to designing a pre-test. The questionnaire was pre-tested with randomly selected firms. Based on the results of the pre-test instrument, the final questionnaire was refined. The respondents were mainly HR managers or, in same instances, the managing directors (MD) of the food firms.

In terms of the empirical research, we posted 372 questionnaires. We got 71 questionnaires, most of them answered by HR Managers (95%). We chose to include both HR and MD responses in the sample size although we recognize that there would be different perceptions about HR practices and organizational performance.

The total response rate was 19.1%. To ensure that the respondents were comparable to non-respondents, analyses of variances were conducted between these groups. We also found no significant differences between HR managers and managing directors. The non-response bias was assessed by comparing early respondents with late respondents (Armstrong and Overton, 1977).

Statistical Analysis

SPSS v.10 on Windows XP was utilized for all analyses. We first had to reduce a large number of variables to a smaller set of components. Principal component analysis is a preferred method for this kind of study. We, then, used hierarchical regression in order to assess the effect of relation, if any, between HR practices and firm growth measures.

Principal component analysis with varimax rotation was conducted to assess the underlying structure for the nineteen HR practices questionnaire. Principal component analysis (PCA) involves a mathematical procedure that transforms a number of (possibly) correlated variables into a (smaller) number of uncorrelated variables called principal components. The first principal component accounts for as much of the variability in the data as possible, and each succeeding component accounts for as much of the remaining variability as possible.

PCA helps with the latter. Having too many features often results in the problem having too many degrees of freedom leading to poor statistical coverage and thus poor generalization. The Varimax rotation is an orthogonal rotation applied to a truncated set of principal components (Harman 1970, Krzanowski 2000). Its application is an attempt to obtain modes that are simple to interpret.

Hierarchical regression models are well suited for this type of analysis. In hierarchical regression, the order of predictor entry, whether individual or in blocks, makes a difference in the results and conclusions. This allows examining the 'effects' of specific independent variables over and above one or more dependant variables.

Surveys using questionnaires often result in small sample size in Greece (Ketikidis et al. 2007; Pasiouras, 2008; Vlachos and Bourlakis, 2006). For example, Ketikidis et al. (2007) used a sample size of 79 observations in six South East European countries including Greece. Pasiouras (2008) used the total population of Greek banks to get 78 observations in order to estimate the technical and scale efficiency of Greek commercial banks.

Measures

Principal component analysis with varimax rotation was conducted to assess the underlying structure for the nineteen HR practices questionnaire. The scales were measured on a Likert format ranging from 1 (strongly disagree) to 5 (strongly agree). Six factors were requested, based on the fact that the items were designed to index the six HR practices. After rotation, decentralisation accounted for 17.53% of the variance, compensation policy for 12.67%, training & development for 12.24%, information sharing for 8.73%, selective hiring for 8.61%, and job security for 6.17%. We used the Anderson-Rubin Method, which ensures orthogonality of the estimated factors, to produce factor scores.

Table 1 contains the items, the scale composite reliability (Cronbach α), and factor loadings for the rotated factors, with loading less than 0.40 omitted to improve clarity.

The first factor, which included items measuring the firm's decentralisation and decision making practices was labelled Decentralisation (seven items, α= 0.906). The second factor, labelled compensation policy, included items measuring the firm's compensation practices and items measuring the firm's policy and HR practices to reduce turnover of employees (four items, α= 0.757). The third factor, labelled training & development, included four items (α=0.647) measuring the firm's emphasis on train and develop its personnel. The fourth factor, labelled information sharing, included two items (α=0.713) measuring the firm's policy to share critical information and performance data with its personnel. The fifth factor, labelled selective hiring, included three items (α=0.556) measuring the firm's policy to recruit personnel that fits its culture and objectives.

The last factor had low internal validity to be included in further analysis. The six factor, labelled job security, included two items (α=0.383) measuring the ability of the firm to create a trustworthy business climate.

Firm Growth

Respondents were asked to indicate their firm's growth as compared to the industry's average in these areas: perceived sales growth, perceived market share growth, perceived overall improvement and perceived firm growth. For perceived items, a 5-point scale ranging from bad (1) to very good (5) was used. Furthermore, we calculated actual sales growth, and actual firm growth based on the last 3 year firm performance. We calculated firm growth using sales and employee figures.

Although we believe the perceived firm growth measures are appropriate, they have some limitations which should be discussed. The first is that they are self-reported responses from HR managers, who may have a stake in seeing positive relationships between their decisions about personnel recruitment, training, development and compensation with achievement of firm's objectives. However, the responses from the sample contain ample variance and means that do not reflect an extremely strong positive bias (see Table 2, variables 2 through 7). If the respondents had greatly inflated their responses, there may have been more consistently positive results than were seen. Secondly, as in all self-reported studies, the possibility of common method variance should be addressed. When both the outcome measure (i.e. firm growth) and the six predictor variables (i.e. compensation policy, decentralisation), are self-reported on the same survey instrument, both measures share common methods variance. There are several techniques that can be used to minimise common method variance (see Podsakoff et al. 2003 for a review of these methods).

We used the Harmon's factor test to examine whether or not common methods variance in the predictor and outcome variables inflates the empirical relationships among the variables. Harmon' test consists of a factor analysis of all relevant variables. If a large degree of common method variance is present, one factor will emerge. Such an analysis was conducted on the firm performance and HR practices variables of this sample. Seven factors emerged, with the first factor (which, in cases of common method variance, would account for most of the variance) only accounting for 18.472% of the variance. Thus, common method variance is unlikely to bias this sample.

Third, management perceptions about concepts like firm growth and organisational performance may actually be more valid indicators than objective data such as profitability, market share and sales, since actual figures are directly related to a vast number of variables, such as trends in the economy, industry factors, and other environmental factors. Therefore, self-reported measures may, in some cases, represent more accurate descriptions than more objective measures (Day, 2003; Podsakoff and Organ, 1986). In the present study, since we are interested in the direction of causation between HR practices and firm effectiveness, the only people with the breadth and depth of knowledge to report adequately about these concepts are the HR managers or managing directors.

Finally, since we were interested in assessing the separate factors of a successful collaboration, we were limited in the number of objective measures that were available within the scope of this study. Because of the previously stated arguments, we concluded that the expert opinions of HR managers or managing directors would be valid and appropriate for this study. The results of data analysis should be acceptable if adequate controls, such as Harmon's one factor test, are reported for the data. While we expect that further research into these firm performance constructs is essential, we believe that they are acceptable for this initial research study.

The Effect of HR Practices on Firm Growth

Table 2 presents the mean, standard deviation, and Pearson's correlation analysis of control variable (sales), firm growth (perceived sales growth, perceived market share growth, perceived overall improvement, perceived firm growth, actual sales growth, and actual firm growth), and HR practices (compensation policy, decentralisation, information sharing, selective hiring, training & development, and job security). The control variable showed low correlation with growth variables as well as each one HR practice.

Compensation Policy had significant association with perceived sales growth ($r=-.328$, $p<.01$) perceived market share growth ($r=.265$, $p<.05$), and perceived overall firm performance ($r=.323$, $p<.01$). Decentralisation had significant association with perceived sales growth ($r=-.284$, $p<.05$) perceived firm growth ($r=.422$, $p<.01$), and perceived overall firm performance ($r=-.271$, $p<.01$). Information sharing had significant association with perceived sales growth ($r=-.282$, $p<.05$), perceived firm growth ($r=.373$, $p<.01$) and perceived overall firm performance ($r=-.345$, $p<.01$). Selective hiring had significant association with perceived sales growth ($r=-.252$, $p<.05$) perceived market share growth ($r=-.510$, $p<.01$), perceived firm growth ($r=-.317$, $p<.05$). Training & Development had significant association with perceived market share ($r=-.274$, $p<.05$) perceived firm growth ($r=.311$, $p<.05$), and perceived overall improvement ($r=.346$, $p<.01$).

Job security, which had low internal validity, showed no significant correlations with any permanence measure. None HR practice showed any significant correlation with actual firm growth variables (sales growth, firm growth).

We then conducted hierarchical multiple regression to determine the best linear combination of HR practices for predicting firm growth. Initially, we entered the control variable (Firm size) in Step 1 of the regression equation. Based on the resource-based view, HR practices will be a competitive advantage if are difficult to emulate. Similarly, large firms may have a resource advantage over smaller firms. Therefore, we included firm size as a control variable, measured by the number of employees. In Step 2, we entered the five HR practices into the regression equations. Finally, in Step 3, we entered the ten interactions of the five factors into the regression equations. Tolerance tests showed no significant collinearity among variables.

We used six measures of firm growth: sales growth (actual, perceived), firm growth (actual perceived), perceived market share growth, and perceived improvement of overall firm performance.

The results are reported in detail in Table 3. Figure illustrates the results of the associations between the research hypotheses and the researched constructs. The combination of HR practices in Step 2 significantly predicted firm growth, in particular perceived firm growth (adjusted R^2=.483; F=11.9, p<.001) with all five variables significantly contributing to the prediction. The beta weights, presented in Table 3, suggest that compensation policy (.2), decentralisation (.41), information sharing (.35), selective hiring (.3), and training & development (.29) were perceived to contribute to firm growth. The change in adjusted R square value was .49, p<.001. This indicates that 49% of the variance of firm growth was explained by the model. According to Cohen (1988), this is a large effect which makes us accept hypotheses 1 to 5.

For all perceived measures of firm growth, HR practices showed a significant effect. On the contrary, HR practices had no significant relation to actual firm growth.

In Step 3, the ten interactions of the five HR practices had a moderate effect only on the perceived firm growth (F= 4.422, p<.001) and the perceived overall firm performance (F= 3.281, p<.001) but with no significant changes in R^2. This indicates that the five HR practices have unique impact on firm growth. Specifically, in Step 2, the changes in adjusted R square value were: perceived sales growth R^2=.336, p<.001; perceived market share growth R^2= .342, p<.001; perceived firm growth R^2=.49, p<.001; and perceived overall firm performance R^2=.399, p<.001.

Table 1: Rotated factor loadings for the six HR practices

	Factor loadings					
	Decentralization	Compensation Policy	Training & Development	Information Sharing	Selective Hiring	Job Security
We encourage decentralized decision making	.864					
We use teams to decide about production problems	.845					
We regularly use teams to perform various task	.725					
All team members contribute to decision making	.724					
We encourage and reward personnel being team players	.638	.551				
We reward personnel to reduce turnover		.784				
We use incentives to boost individual performance		.608				
We select and pay employees based on their contribution		.583				
Employees that care about firm's objectives are rewarded		.539	.458			
Training is a motive for employees to achieve more			.700			
We systematically train and develop our personnel			.635			
We provide training in one key skill	.410		.436			
We train personnel to gain many skills and abilities		.549	.427			
Our employees know well our objectives and strategy				.729		
We inform personnel about their performance				.778		
We use consultant when hiring personnel					.747	
We use pre-recruitment tests					.655	
We select personnel that fits our culture		.449			.476	
We focus on job security				.446		.814
Employees that perform modestly do not get fired						.619
Eigenvalue	8.220	2.279	1.610	1.394	1.279	1.043
Initial percent of variance explained	34.249	9.497	6.709	5.810	5.330	4.347
Rotation sum of squared loadings (total)	4.207	3.040	2.937	2.094	2.067	1.480
Percent of variance explained	17.531	12.667	12.238	8.726	8.612	6.167
Cronbach α (sample N)	0.906	0.757	0.647	0.713	0.556	0.383

Extraction Method: Principal Component analysis. Rotation method: Varimax with Kaiser Normalization.

Table 2: Means, Standard Deviations and Correlation Matrix

	Mean	SD	1	2	3	4	5	6	7
Control variables									
Sales	20,187	74,661	1	,151	,031	,165	,194	-,046	,183
Firm Growth									
Perceived Sales Growth	3.59	0.88		1	-.125	.515**	.585**	.104	.667**
Actual Sales Growth	0.06	0.37			1	-.181	.116	.522**	-.057
Perceived Market Share Growth	3.58	0.96				1	.514**	.016	.398**
Perceived Firm Growth	3.68	0.91					1	.145	.694**
Actual Firm Growth	0.20	0.37						1	.153
Perceived Overall Improvement	3.69	0.87							1
HR practices variables									
Compensation Policy	1	0	.089	.328**	-.061	.265*	.211	.057	.323**
Decentralisation	1	0	.059	.284*	.083	.105	.422**	.230	.271*
Information Sharing	1	0	.126	.282*	-.003	.063	.373**	.172	.345**
Selective Hiring	1	0	.070	.252*	-.178	.510**	.317*	-.007	.233
Training & Development	1	0	.218	.241	.148	.274*	.311*	-.092	.346**
Job Security	1	0	-.100	-.016	-.233	.106	-.103	.131	-.009

** *Correlation is significant at the 0.01 level (2-tailed).*

* *Correlation is significant at the 0.05 level (2-tailed).*

Since the HR practices variables are factor scores, produced by the Anderson-Rubin Method, the scores produced have a mean of 0, a standard deviation of 1, are uncorrelated, the correlations with each other are .00, and thus are not included in this table. Sales: thousands of euros

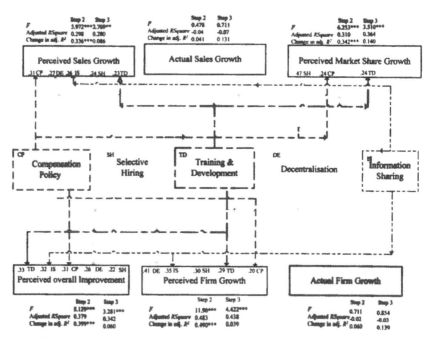

Figure 2: Model results

Table 3: Hierarchal regression results of HR practices on six growth measures

Control variable	Perceived Sales Growth			Actual Sales Growth			Perceived Market Share Growth		
	Step 1 (Control)	Step2 (HR practices)	Step3 (Interaction)	Step 1 (Control)	Step2 (HR practices)	Step3 (Interaction)	Step 1 (Control)	Step2 (HR practices)	Step3 (Interaction)
1. Firm Size	0.15	0.00	0.00	0.03	0.01	0.03	0.16	0.04	0.02
	1.27	0.06	0.05	0.26	0.13	0.22	1.39	0.43	0.20
HR Practices									
1. Compensation Policy		0.31	0.32		-0.05	-0.04		0.24	0.17
		3.14**	2.39*		-0.45	-0.28		2.44*	1.33
2. Decentralisation		0.27	0.26		0.06	0.00		0.09	0.18
		2.72**	2.06*		0.52	0.05		0.95	1.50
3. Information Sharing		0.26	0.18		-0.00	0.04		0.05	0.10
		2.61*	1.49		-0.01	0.30		0.50	0.93
4. Selective Hiring		0.24	0.24		-0.14	-0.21		0.47	0.47
		2.42*	2.04*		-1.18	-1.45		4.76***	4.20***
5. Training & Development		0.23	0.23		0.11	0.08		0.24	0.25
		2.25*	1.97*		0.93	0.55		2.41*	2.24*
Interactions									
1. Compensation Policy * Decentralisation			-0.12			0.24			0.02
			-0.92			1.49			0.22
2. Compensation Policy * Information Sharing			-0.07			-0.15			0.09
			-0.46			-0.82			0.66
3. Compensation Policy * Selective Hiring			0.16			0.02			-0.39
			1.21			0.14			-2.98**
4. Compensation Policy * Training & Development			-0.03			0.10			0.04
			-0.26			0.63			0.37
5. Decentralisation * Information Sharing			0.05			0.09			-0.08
			0.43			0.61			-0.72
6. Decentralisation * Selective Hiring			0.08			0.06			-0.19
			0.58			0.35			-1.46
7. Decentralisation * Training & Development			0.17			-0.17			0.00
			1.34			-1.07			0.00
8. Information Sharing * Selective Hiring			0.10			0.05			-0.16
			0.67			0.28			-1.16
9. Information Sharing * Training & Development			0.00			-0.14			0.17
			0.05			-0.87			1.42
10. Selective Hiring * Training & Development			-0.18			0.15			0.05
			-1.53			1.01			0.43
F	1.618	5.972***	2.709***	0.068	0.478	0.711	1.941	6.253***	3.510***
Adjusted R-square	0.008	0.298	0.280	-0.01	-0.04	-0.07	0.013	0.310	0.364
Change in adjusted R-square	0.022	0.336***	0.086	0.000	0.041	0.131	0.027	0.342***	0.140

Standardized regression coefficients are reported. Within cells, first row figure is beta coefficients and second row the t-test values, significant at: *p <0.10 **p <0.01 ***p <0.001

Table 3: (Continued)

Control variable	Perceived Firm Growth			Actual Firm Growth			Perceived firm performance Improvement		
	Step 1 (Control)	Step2 (HR practices)	Step3 (Interaction)	Step 1 (Control)	Step2 (HR practices)	Step3 (Interaction)	Step 1 (Control)	Step2 (HR practices)	Step3 (Interaction)
Firm Size	0.19	0.01	0.07	-0.04	-0.06	0.00	0.18	0.01	0.00
	1.63	0.22	0.69	-0.37	-0.52	0.04	1.54	0.11	0.02
R Practices									
Compensation Policy		0.20	0.15		0.05	-0.10		0.31	0.37
		2.37*	1.28		0.47	-0.65		3.28**	2.91**
Decentralisation		0.41	0.40		0.16	0.18		0.26	0.13
		4.77***	3.47**		1.39	1.16		2.77**	1.06
Information Sharing		0.35	0.27		0.15	0.27		0.32	0.30
		4.07***	2.54*		1.28	1.85*		3.39**	2.60*
Selective Hiring		0.30	0.28		0.00	-0.12		0.22	0.18
		3.58***	2.66*		0.00	-0.84		2.38*	1.62
Training & Development		0.29	0.30		-0.06	-0.11		0.33	0.35
		3.38**	2.81**		-0.51	-0.78		3.41**	3.09**
Interactions									
Compensation Policy* Decentralisation			-0.09			0.19			-0.17
			-0.84			1.24			-1.40
Compensation Policy* Information Sharing			-0.01			-0.11			0.06
			-0.09			-0.63			0.42
Compensation Policy* Selective Hiring			-0.10			0.00			0.06
			-0.86			0.02			0.48
Compensation Policy* Training & Development			-0.01			-0.25			-0.02
			-0.14			-1.58			-0.15
Decentralisation* Information Sharing			-0.12			0.21			0.13
			-1.06			1.36			1.11
Decentralisation* Selective Hiring			0.06			0.09			0.13
			0.47			0.56			0.99
Decentralisation* Training & Development			-0.05			-0.09			-0.10
			-0.43			-0.60			-0.86
Information Sharing* Selective Hiring			0.05			-0.07			0.16
			0.38			-0.43			1.13
Information Sharing* Training & Development			-0.05			-0.14			-0.02
			-0.43			-0.90			-0.23
Selective Hiring* Training & Development			-0.06			0.08			0.00
			-0.56			0.59			0.00
F	2.689	11.90***	4.422***	0.144	0.711	0.854	2.381	8.129***	3.281***
Adjusted R-square	0.023	0.483	0.438	-0.01	-0.02	-0.03	0.019	0.379	0.342
Change in adjusted R-square	0.037	0.490***	0.039	0.002	0.060	0.139	0.033	0.399***	0.060

Standardized regression coefficients are reported. Within cells, first row figure is beta coefficients and second row the t-test values, significant at: $p <0.10$ ** $p <0.01$ *** $p <0.001$

Discussion

The primary purpose of this study was to evaluate the impact of HR practices on firm growth. In summary, a review of existing literature finds that there are HR practices positively linked to organizational performance (Pfeffer, 1998; Becker and Gerhart, 1996; Guest, 1997; Cardon and Stevens, 2004; Givord and Maurin, 2004; Zhu, 2004). Based on a comprehensive literature review, we hypothesised that the following HR practices are related to firm growth: (1) Compensation policy, (2) Decentralization & self-managed teams, (3) Information Sharing (4) Selective Hiring, (5) Training and Development and (6) Job Security.

However, a review of literature pertaining to organizational performance shows that firm growth, an indication of market acceptance and firm success as well as a top priority of most companies (Baum and Wally, 2003; Zook and Allen, 2003; Fesser and Willard, 1990), has been studied mostly as a latent variable of organisational performance (Pfeffer, 1998; Cardon and Stevens, 2004; Givord and Maurin, 2004).

Consequently, this paper argues that the selection of specific HR practices becomes a strategic decision. Therefore, HR managers should be able to report on the concrete results of specific HR practices on specific firm growth measures. Briefly, a survey of HR managers demonstrated that HR practices are linked to firm growth. The findings of the study lead to a number of interesting implications for HRM theorists and practitioners. The first (and rather obvious) implication can be derived from the evidence found that all HR practices are related to firm growth, a finding consistent with a variety of extant theories and studies,. Hence, firm growth as a strategic priority depends on human capital: selecting, developing, and rewarding the best people as well as revealing to them critical company information in order to make informed decisions which they are authorised to take.

More profound implications can be derived from the findings regarding the links between specific HR practices and firm growth measures. All five HR practices contributed to perceived sales growth, overall firm performance improvement, and firm growth. Selective hiring, compensation policy, and training & development were the predictor of perceived market share growth. In particular, selective hiring was strongly correlated to perceived market share growth (r2=.47, p<.01). On the contrary, decentralisation and information sharing did not contributed significantly to market share growth.

Compensation policy was related to all perceived firm growth measures, being the strongest predictor of sales growth and the weakest of firm growth. Linking sales with compensation benefits can be an explanation of the high correlation between compensation policy and sales growth. Decentralisation and team working was significant factor of firm growth. This finding may provide some justification of the claim that as the business expands, decision-making becomes more decentralized and self-managed teams proliferate as the firm adds more and more projects and customers (Flamholtz and Randle, 2000; Miller and Friesen, 1984).

Training and development was related to all firm growth measures but it showed higher correlation to overall firm performance improvement. Beta weight was 0.33 (r2 3.41, p<0.001). This finding may have a profound implication: Given that firms were well established, they may have already run many in-company training programmes and noticed and reported concrete evidence of the benefits of training and development.

Information sharing comes with pros and cons. Information sharing has the inherent vulnerability that informed employees will become more powerful and companies may loose control of them (Pfeffer, 1998). Even worse, information sharing involves the danger of leaking important information to competitors (Ronde, 2001). On the other hand, information sharing tells employees that the company trusts them and thus gives them sensitive information to make informed decisions which will shape the future of the company. The findings demonstrate that information sharing does positively relate to firm growth. Information sharing was significantly correlated to sales growth, firm growth, and overall firm performance improvement. Respondents did not perceive that job security was an important HR practice. This finding can be attributed to the fact that most respondents were HR managers who might be reluctant to report an insecure job environment in their company's workplace.

The findings as a whole suggest that a positive relationship exists between the extent to which companies implement HR practices and firm growth achievements. This overall result corroborates previous empirical studies on the links between HRM and firm performance. These findings provide tentative support of the contention that HR practices can create a competitive advantage.

Future research could clarify the causal relationship between HR practices and firm performance. Another research stream is examining HR practices in sets in order to assess their collective effect. The conceptual basis of further research can be extended. An interesting avenue for future research is the market-based competitive advantage approach, which declares that the market determines who is competitive or not (Reed et al., 2000). The market-based approach can provide another theoretical basis than resource-based view of competitive advantage, in order to examine the effect of HR practices on firm performance.

A series of limitations bounds the findings, conclusions, and implications of this study. The most obvious limitations of this study stem from the sample used and the measures employed. We examined a small set of HR practices that seem to have an effect on firm growth in Greek food industry. Given that managerial skills are to a large extent industry-specific, generalizability of research findings beyond the food industry remains an open question. Furthermore, given the dynamic nature of firm growth, this study measured one instance of this dynamic phenomenon. The effects of HR practices can take years to materialize into organizational performance. For example, selective hiring and training can produce results after years. Often, high performance work practices have better results in bundles than implemented in isolation. This study focused on established firms with more than 5 years of operation. However, the stage of a firm's lifecycle, either growth, mature, decline or revival stage (Ciavarella, 2003) can be an important factor in applying specific HR practices. Another limitation of the findings is the use of self-report questionnaires to collect data on all measures. This limits our ability to draw conclusions about the causal nature of the relationships between HR practices and firm growth. In a future study there would be of great value to see how different HR and MD responses are.

These limitations suggest that the interpretation of research findings need to be cautious they also indicate a number of potentially fruitfully avenues for future research. Except from testing the research hypotheses in other settings and environments, the combined effect of HR practices, and which practice works better with another one is yet another open question. A large quantitative survey could also control for mediating and/or moderating variables between human resource management and firm performance.

References

Ahmad S., and Schroeder R.G., 2003. The impact of human resource management practices on operational performance: recognizing country and industry differences, Journal of Operations Management, 21: 19–43.

Armstrong, J.C. and Overton, T.C. 1977. Estimating Non-response Bias in Mail Surveys, Journal of Marketing Research, 14: 396–402.

Banker, R.D., Lee, S.Y., Potter, G., Srinivasan, D., 2001. An empirical analysis of continuing improvements following the implementation of a performance based compensation plan, Journal of Accounting and Economics, 30 (1): 315–350.

Baron, J. N., & Hannan, M. T. 2002. Organizational blueprints for success in high-tech start-ups: Lessons from the Stanford project on emerging companies. California Management Review, 44(3): 8–36.

Barringer, B. R., Jones, F. F., and Neubaum, D. O., 2005. A quantitative content analysis of the characteristics of rapid-growth firms and their founders, Journal of Business Venturing, 20: 663–687.

Batt, R., 2004. Who Benefits from Teams? Comparing Workers, Supervisors, and Managers, Industrial Relations, 42(1): 183–212.

Baum, J. R., and Wally S., 2003. Strategic decision speed and firm performance, Strategic Management Journal, 24 (11): 1107—1129.

Becker, B., and Gerhart, B., 1996. The impact of Human Resource Management on organisational performance: Progress and prospects, Academy of Management, 39 (4): 779–801.

Black, S.A., Lynch, L.M., and Krivelyova, A., 2004 How Workers Fare When Employers Innovate, Industrial Relations, 43(1): 44–66. Brewster, C., 2004. European perspectives on human resource management, Human Resource Management Review 14: 365–382.

Buitendach, J. H. Witte, H. De, 2005. Job insecurity, extrinsic and intrinsic job satisfaction and affective organisational commitment of maintenance workers in a parastatal, South African Journal Business Management, 36(2).

Burgess, D., 2005. what motivates employees to transfer knowledge outside their work unit?, Journal of Business Communication, 42(4): 324–348.

Cardon, M. S., Stevens, C. E., 2004. Managing human resources in small organizations: What do we know?, Human Resource Management Review, 14: 295–323.

Cerio, J. Merino-Diaz De, 2003. Quality management practices and operational performance: empirical evidence for Spanish industry, International Journal of Production Research, 41, No. 12, 2763– 2786.

Cho, S., Woods, R. H., Jang, S., Erdem, M., 2005. Measuring the impact of human resource management practices on hospitality firms' Performances, International Journal of Hospitality Management.

Chow, C. W., Harrison, G. L., McKinnon, J. L., and Wu, A., 1999. Cultural Influences on Informal Information Sharing in Chinese and Anglo-American Organizations: An Exploratory Study, Accounting, Organizations and Society, 24: 561–582.

Ciavarella, M. A. 2003. The adoption of high-involvement practices and processes in emergent and developing firms: a descriptive and prescriptive approach, Human Resource Management, 42(4): 337–356.

Cohen, J., 1988. Statistical power and analysis for the behavioral sciences 2nd ed.. Hillsdale, NJ: Lawrence Erlbaum Associates.

Cohen, Y., and Pfeffer, J., 1986. Organizational Hiring Standards, Administrative Science Quarterly, 31(1): 1–24.

Collins C. J., and Clark K. D., 2003. Strategic human resource practices, top management commitment, team social networks and firm performance: the role of human resource practices in creating organizational competitive advantage, Academy of Management Journal, 46(6): 740–751.

Constant, D., Kiesler, S., and Sproull, L. 1994. What's Mine Is Ours, or Is It? A Study of Attitudes about Information Sharing, Information Systems Research 5(4): 400–421.

Delery, J. E, Doty, D. H., 1996. Modes of theorizing in strategic human resource management: tests of universalistic, contingency and configurational performance predictions, Academy of Management Journal, 39(4): 802–835.

Doyle, M., 1997. Management development, in Beardwell, I. and Holden, L. eds Human Resource Management: A Contemporary Perspective,. London: Pitman.

Fesser, H.R., Willard, G.E., 1990. Founding strategy and performance: a comparison of high and low growth high tech forms, Strategic Management Journal, 11(2): 87–98.

Fey, C. E., Bjorkman, I., Pavlovskaya, A., 2000. The impact of human resource management practices on firm performance in Russia, International Journal of Human Resource Management, 11(1): 118.

Flamholtz, E. G., & Randle, Y. 2000. Growing pains: Transitioning from an entrepreneurship to a professionally managed firm. San Francisco: Jossey-Bass.

Givord, P., and Maurin, E., 2004. Changes in job security and their causes: An empirical analysis for France, 1982–2002, European Economic Review, 48: 595—615.

Guest, D., 1997. Human resource management and performance: a review and research agenda, International Journal of Human Resource Management, 8, 263–276.

Haleblian, J., and Finkelstein, S., 1993. Top Management Team Size, CEO Dominance, and Firm Performance: The Moderating Roles of Environmental Turbulence and Discretion, Academy of Management Journal, 36: 844–863.

Harman, H.H., 1970. Modern Factor Analysis 2nd revised ed., Chicago, IL: University of Chicago Press.

Huselid, M. A., 1995. The impact of human resource management practices on turnover, productivity and corporate financial performance, Academy of Management Journal, 38(3): 635–672.

Ichniowski, C., and Shaw, K., 1999. The effect of human resource management systems on economic performance: an international comparison of US and Japanese plants, Management Science, 75 (5): 704–721.

Jayaram, J., Droge, C., Vickery, S. K., 1999. The impact of human resource management practices on manufacturing performance, Journal of Operations Management, 18 (1): 1–20.

Ketikidis, P.H. Koh, S.C.L. Dimitriadis, N. Gunasekar, A. and Kehajova, M., 2008. The use of information systems for logistics and supply chain management in South East Europe: Current status and future direction, , Omega, 36 (4): 592–599.

Kraimer, M.L., Wayne, S.J., Liden, R.C., Sparrowe, R.T., 2005. The role of job security in understanding the relationship between employees' perceptions of temporary workers and employees' performance, Journal of Applied Psychology, 90 (2): 389–98.

Krzanowski, W.J., 2000. Principles of Multivariate Analysis: A User's Perspective, revised ed., Oxford: Oxford University Press.

Lawler, E. E., and Rhode, J. G., 1976. Information and Control in Organizations, Goodyear Publishing Company, Pacific Palisades, CA.

Lawler, E. E., Mohrman, S. A. and Ledford, G. E. Jr., 1995. Creating High Performance Organizations, San Francisco: Jossey-Bass

Michie, J., and Sheehan-Quinn M., 2001. Labour Market Flexibility, Human Resource Management and Corporate Performance, British Journal of Management, 12 (4): 287–306.

Miller, D., & Friesen, P. H. 1984. Organizations: A quantum view. Englewood Cliffs, NJ: Prentice Hall.

Miller, D., 2006. Strategic human resource management in department stores: An historical perspective, Journal of Retailing and Consumer Services, forthcoming.

Morishima, M., 1991. Information sharing and firm performance in Japan, Industrial Relations, 30 (1): 37–61.

Ngo, H., Turban, D., Lau, C., and Lui, S., 1998. Human resource practices and firm performance of multinational corporations: influences of country origin, International Journal of Human Resource Management, 9 (4): 632–652

Nicholis, C. E., Lane, H. W., and Brechu, M. B., 1999. Taking self-managed teams to Mexico, Academy of Management Executive, 13 (3): 15–25.

Nonaka, K. 1994. The Knowledge creating company, Harvard Business Review, 69: 96–104.

Pasiouras, F., 2008. Estimating the technical and scale efficiency of Greek commercial banks: The impact of credit risk, off-balance sheet activities, and international operations, Research in International Business and Finance, 22 (3): 301–318.

Paul, A. K., Anantharaman, R. N., 2003. Impact of people management practices on organizational performance: analysis of a causal model, International Journal of Human Resource Management, 14 (7): 1246–1266.

Pfeffer, J., 1998. Seven practices of successful organizations, California Management Review, 40 (2): 96–124.

Probst, T. M., 2002. The impact of job insecurity on employee work attitudes, job adaptation, and organizational withdrawal behaviours. In J. M. Brett & F. Drasgow Eds. The psychology of work: Theoretically based empirical research. Mahwah, NJ: Lawrence Erlbaum Associates.

Roberts, K., 1995. The Proof of HR is in the Profits, People Management, February, 42–43.

Rodriguez, J. M., and Ventura J., 2003. Human resource management systems and organizational performance: an analysis of the Spanish manufacturing industry, International Journal of Human Resource Management, 14 (7): 1206–1226.

Rønde, T., 2001. Trade Secrets and Information Sharing, Journal of Economics & Management Strategy, 10 (3): 391–417.

Schuster, F. 1986. The Schuster Report. New York: John Wiley and Sons.

Singer, J., and Duvall, S. 2000. High-Performance Partnering By Self-Managed Teams In Manufacturing, Engineering Management Journal, 12 (4): 9–15.

Singh, K., 2005. The effect of human resource practices on firm performance in India, Human Resource Development International, 6 (1): 101–116.

Tata, J., and Prasad, S., 2004. Team self-management, organisational structure, and judgments of team effectiveness, Journal of management issues, 16 (2): 248–265.

Tosi, H. L., Misangyi, V. F., Fanelli, A., Waldman, D. A., and Yammarino, F. J., 2004. CEO charisma, compensation, and firm performance, The Leadership Quarterly, 15: 405–420.

Vlachos, I. P. and Bourlakis, M., 2006. Supply Chain Collaboration between retailers and manufacturers: Do they trust each other? Supply Chain Forum: An International Journal, 7(1): 7081.

Wagner, J. A. 1994. 'Participation's Effect on Performance and Satisfaction: A Reconsideration of Research Evidence,' Academy of Management Review, 19: 312–31.

Wimbush, J. C., 2005. Spotlight on human resource management, Business Horizons, 48: 463–467.

Yeatts, D. E., and Hyten, C., 1998. High-performing self-managed work teams, a comparison of theory and practice, Thousand Oaks, CA: Sage

Zhu, Y., 2004. Responding to the challenges of globalization: human resource development in Japan, Journal of World Business, 39: 337–348.

Zook, C., and Allen, J., 2003. Growth outside the core, Harvard Business Review, December.

Common Factors between Swedish and Chinese Entrepreneurial Leadership Styles

Ingmar Bremer

ABSTRACT

This paper includes a comparative study of the entrepreneurial leadership of both Sweden and China, taking into consideration such factors as their political and economic history, leadership styles, and regulatory changes. It will conclude with an analysis of the factors that both entrepreneur leadership styles have in common, as well as substantial differences between fundamental approaches to business development.

Introduction

In recent years, researchers have contributed different causes as responsible for the success of a country's economic system, and as a result, differing models for economic growth suggest multiple possible paths for success. Two countries of notable global success, attributable to each of its entrepreneurial leadership skills, are Sweden and China. The world is changing fast, and China is now an important part of the global economy. However, cooperation in Europe is growing closer and broader. Sweden is a small nation with a history of major success on the global market, success that has been attributable to the Swedish business sector's strong position and skilled company leaders. This paper will offer a comparative study of the entrepreneurial leadership of both Sweden and China, taking into consideration such factors as their political and economic history, leadership styles, and regulatory changes. It will conclude with an analysis of the factors that both entrepreneur leadership styles have in common.

The fact that entrepreneurship is a catalyst for economic growth and development is well known. Small businesses in the United States, for example, account for 58% of the private work force, 51% of GNP and about 75% of net new jobs (Asel, 2003). Entrepreneurship is even more important to the growth of developing economies where small businesses frequently account for 80% or more of employment and virtually all job growth (Asel, 2003). Differing economic, cultural and political circumstances abroad also suggest the need for a better understanding of entrepreneurship with a local context (Asel, 2003). Fortunately, the ability to study entrepreneurship abroad is expanding rapidly as a result of the emergence of global private equity markets and microfinance. International entrepreneurship spans cultural boundaries and involves a variety of stakeholders, including the entrepreneur, investors and policy makers (Asel, 2003).

Entrepreneurs operate at the margins of the economy exploiting opportunities overlooked by incumbents. They innovate to develop promising, but untested markets and flexibly managing scarce resources in an uncertain, often unforgiving environment (Asel, 2003). International entrepreneurship thus offers a rich tapestry to explore many of the issues that are at the heart of business strategy and economic development (Asel, 2003). Companies play a key role with regard to achieving long-term sustainable development based on economic growth, environmental considerations and social commitment. Finally, an economically thriving society with low inflation creates an important base for business growth.

Entrepreneurial Leadership Entrepreneurial leadership is leadership that is based on the attitude that the leader is self-employed. Leaders of this type take initiative and act as if they are playing a critical role in the organization and energize their people, demonstrate entrepreneurial creativity, search continuously for new opportunities and pursue them, take risk, venture into new areas and provide strategic direction and inspiration to their people (Kotelnikov, 2005). These leaders also take responsibility for the failures of their team, learn from these failures and use them as a step to ultimate success and strategic achievement. Entrepreneurial leadership involves instilling the confidence to think, behave and act with entre-preneurship in the interests of fully realizing the intended purpose of the organi-zation to the beneficial growth of all stakeholders involved (Kotelnikov, 2005). In the new era of rapid changes and knowledge-based enterprises, managerial work becomes increasingly a leadership task. Leadership is the primary force behind successful change, as leaders empower employees to act on the vision (Kotelnikov, 2005). They execute through inspiration and develop implementation capacity networks through a complex web of aligned relationships (Kotelnikov, 2005).

Venture values are different from established corporate shared values. Research indicates that entrepreneurial independence demands space for action and trust, while independence in a corporation implies responsibility and control imposed from above (Kotelnikov, 2005). Entrepreneurship is important because any coun-ty's economy demands agility, experimentation, adaptation, and rapid response in order to be first to market. Corporate experimentation comprises analysis, review, somber consideration of facts, and willingness sacrifice speed for thoroughness (Kotelnikov, 2005). Entrepreneurial paranoia, or the impending belief that com-petitors are catching up, is overshadowed by an essential need to build corporate consensus and minimize perceived risk (Kotelnikov, 2005). Entrepreneurial lead-ership skills are important because leading innovation is a delicate and challeng-ing process.

As a result, a true leader must encourage expansive thinking in order to gener-ate new ideas, but also filter through these ideas to decide which to commercial-ize. "Loose tight" leadership alternates the creation of space for idea generation and free exploration with a deliberate tightening that selects and tests specific ideas for further investment and development (Kotelnikov, 2005). Looseness usu-ally dominates the early stages of the innovation process; in the later stages, tight-ening becomes more important to scrutinize the concepts and bring the selected ones to the market (Kotelnikov, 2005). Those who remain loose too long generate plenty of ideas but have difficulty commercializing them. Those who lock into the tight mode choke off all but most obvious ideas, thus confining innovation to incremental line extensions of existing products that add little value (Kotelnikov, 2005).

An examination of the literature regarding entrepreneurial leadership reveals that creativity is a continuous activity for the entrepreneur, a method of always seeing new ways of doing things with little concern for how difficult they might be or whether the resources are available. But the creativity in the entrepreneur is combine with the ability to innovate, to take the idea and make it work in prac-tice (Kotelnikov, 2005). This seeing something through to the end and not being satisfied until all is accomplished is a central motivation for the entrepreneur. Indeed once the project is accomplished the entrepreneur seeks another mountain to climb because for him or her creativity and innovation are habitual, something that he or she just has to keep on doing (Kotelnikov, 2005).

An "entrepreneur" has been defined as a person who habitually creates and innovates to build something of recognized value around perceived opportunities (Kotelnikov, 2005). The best entrepreneurs have the ability to devise new combinations dependent on their ability to discern relationships between seemingly disparate items. In other words, creativity is the juxtaposition of ideas which were previously thought to be unrelated, and it is the entrepreneurs ability to combine ideas in a unique way or to make useful associations among ideas. Entrepreneurial leadership includes creating an atmosphere where you and others are comfortable expressing new ideas, an atmosphere where ideas are not immediately evaluated and attacked (Kotelnikov, 2005).

The term "entrepreneur" is originally a French word—entreprendre—that means to undertake (Mamede & Davidsson, 2003). According to Casson (1987), it seems to have been introduced into economics by Richard Cantillon in 1755. It was through J.B. Shay in the early 1980s that the expression became recognized, referring to a person who shifted economic resources out an area of lower and into an area of higher productivity and greater yield (Mamede & Davidsson, 2003). The term "entrepreneurship" was coined in the early 1900s, to refer to the actions conducted by the entrepreneur. Wennekers, Thurik and Buis (1997), defined entreprenuership, for research purposes, as the ability and willingness of individuals, both on their own and within organizations: to perceive and create new economic opportunities (new products, new production methods, new organized schemes and new product market combinations); to introduce new ideas in the market, in the face of uncertainty and other obstacles, by making decisions on location, form and the use of resources and institutions; and compete with others for a share of the market.

Entrepreneurial Research and Development and Economic Growth

Although economic growth and development have similar meanings and are sometimes treated interchangeably, there are some distinctions that should be considered. While economic growth mainly refers to the capacity of a nation to become wealthier through the production of more goods and services, economic development ultimately implies that citizens of that nation be better off (Mamede & Davidsson, 2003). Saemundson and Kirchhoff (2002) define economic growth and development as an expression frequently used to refer to improvement in social well being within nations. In economic terms, development has traditionally denoted the capacity of a country, whose initial economic situation has been relatively static for a long time, to generate and maintain growth rates on the order of 5% to 7% or more of its gross national product (Todaro and Smith, 2003). According to Todaro and Smith (2003), before the 1970s, development was normally seen as an economic phenomenon in which rapid increase in the gross national product would trickle down to the population in the form of jobs or other economic opportunities or at least generate the proper conditions for the distribution of the economical and social benefits of growth.

Though different perceptions regarding the concept may exist, the traditional economic vision of development was reconsidered during the 1970s (Mamede & Davidsson, 2003). The experience of developing nations during the 1950s and 1960s, in which the realization of economic growth targets did not mean improvement in the levels of living of their population, indicated that the existing definition of the term was not adequate (Mamede & Davidsson, 2003). As a result, economic development was redefined in terms of reduction or elimination of poverty, inequality, and unemployment within the perspective of a growing economy (Mamede & Davidsson, 2003).

Research indicates that entreprenuership can be both the cause and effect of economic development in the sense of wealth distribution. Countries in which wealth is concentrated in the hands of a small fraction of the population face greater difficulties in coordinating the major components of progress (Mamede & Davidsson, 2003). These three components are labor, capital, resources and innovation. According to Mamede and Davidsson (2003), considering that the three driving forces of entrepreneurial success—founders, opportunity recognition, and resource requirements—are more likely to occur in a combined way, there are better chances to prosper in regions in which wealth is more equitably distributed. These researchers have also observed that members of such societies are in a more favorable condition to get involved in entrepreneurial endeavors.

National and international research and development and innovation policies are being improved around the world, in order to increase economic growth and achieve higher living standards (Erskine, 2003). Understanding of the drivers of technological progress and the key factors that underlie successful research and development and innovation is intensifying (Erskine, 2003). A review of a large number of studies that assess the factors that have helped drive successful research and development and innovation in countries that are research and development and innovation leaders confirms a few general conclusions. First, it is very difficult to determine exactly what underlies a successful national research and development effort, and it is easy to conclude that everything depends on everything else, but it is clear that innovation systems and processes must be considered, not just specific technical issues with the promotion of research and development (Erskine,

2003). Culture, and in particular an entrepreneurial spirit and a willingness to risk and experience failure, is vital to innovation (Erskine, 2003).

Research indicates that it is still unknown how to change a nation's culture, but all the available evidence confirms that incentives that reward particular behavior do tend to have results and that education in processes not well understood. Private expenditure on research and development in any country will be insufficient to maximize the nation's productivity potential, unless it is subsidized, either through taxes or grants or some other mechanism (Erskine, 2003). International studies suggest that the social return for such subsidization is high. Research and development expenditures are likely to have a greater commercial impact if aggregate these funds are allocated with commercialization potential as a key criterion (Erskine, 2003). This is best fulfilled through competitive and market-driven or industry-driven mechanisms for allocating research and development funds (Erskine, 2003). Research indicates that education, tax and immigration policies that ensure availability of skilled and motivated labor are a feature of almost all the leading countries. A review of the literature reveals that the pace and intensity of global innovation is accelerating and that all the international evidence is that leadership from the top can make a critical difference.

Difficulties faced by poor countries, wherein low average income is a limiting factor of savings and investments, tend to reinforce each other in what is known as the vicious cycle of poverty, in which low savings and investment is followed by low pace of capital formation, that results in low levels of productivity, which does not all lead to improvements in the levels of average incomes (Mamede & Davidsson, 2003). The consequences of such cycles, usually worsened by significant inequalities in the distribution of wealth, negatively impact the level of entrepreneurial activity of a nation or region (Mamede & Davidsson, 2003). Baumol (1993) argues that even if entrepreneurs are not in complete control of their economic destiny, they influence its direction as few others are able to do. Baumol (2003) also sees the entrepreneur as responsible for a significant amount of historic growth of modern society. Baumol (2003) sees the entrepreneurial talent and motivational mechanisms of entrepreneurial activity as one of the main explanations for the successful growth of some economies in contrast with others.

Studies have been conducted to assess what the international best practices are, in order to identify the key factors in each of the countries that are critical for that success. It is now well accepted that innovation and research and development are positively associated with productivity growth. Research and development provides an important contribution to output and total factor productivity growth (Erskine, 2003). The empirical evidence typically shows that a 1% increase in the stock of research and development leads to a rise in output of 0.05-0.15% (Erskine, 2003). There is also evidence that research and development may play a different role in small and large economies (Griffith et al., 1998). In smaller economies, it primarily serves to facilitate technology transfer from abroad. The belief that less advanced countries would catch up with the technological world leaders as technological knowledge is diffused or transferred through the world has been severely shaken over the past decade by a widening in the productivity gap between countries (Erskine, 2003).

The opportunities for wealth creation in and the increasing economic importance of 'knowledge-based' industries has heightened the need to understand the processes underlying technological progress (Erskine, 2003). Firms, industries and countries are now engaged in very direct competition to produce technological progress, to create wealth, jobs and human and social well-being. Innovation and research and development have become vital activities in an increasingly knowledge-based world (Erskine, 2003). No country leads in every sphere of innovation, but some dominate in particular industries. Research indicates that considering research and development, the USA is the global leader; the UK also ranks highly, as a recent success in biotechnology leadership and because of its relevance to the development of Australia's education system and legal framework (Erskine, 2003). Other countries of interest would most likely include Singapore, South Korea and Taiwan, and even perhaps China, where research and development effort is intensifying most rapidly and the policy framework is developing the fastest (Erskine, 2003).

The question of whether east Asia can compete in global markets has recently been evaluated in a 2002 World Bank report. According to the report, the factors that determine whether or not countries such as China can compete include the building of research and development capital; the business environment, including ease of entry by firms, level of competition, and protection of intellectual property; and the effectiveness of the education system in producing an adequate supply of skilled and technical workers; the links among businesses, universities, and public and private research institutes that stimulate innovation and its commercialization (Yusuf & Evenett, 2002).

Also included among the factors are the interaction among firms and agglomeration economies in industrial clusters; the extent of technology generation and absorption by firms through their own research and development, licensing, assistance from lynchpin buyers in a production network, new equipment purchases, and support from equipment or component suppliers; the degree of access to an international pool of professionals and to centers of excellence in East Asia and the West; and the development status of production networking, supply chain management, and logistics (Erskine, 2003).

According to Stern et. al.., (2000), innovative capacity depends on the overall technological sophistication of an economy and its labor force, but also on an array of investments and policy choices by both government and the private sector. Innovative capacity is related to but distinct from non-commercial scientific and technical advances, which do not necessarily involve the economic application of new technology (Stern et. al., 2000). Differences in national innovative capacity reflect variation in both economic geography and innovation policy.

Other researchers have examined finance and its influence on economic growth and technical progress, concluding that the fundamental financing problem for firms undertaking research and development is uncertainty over the outcome of the research and development. The firm and any financier suffer from a significant information asymmetry about the prospects for future income flows, and typically a financier will be unwilling to accept research and development as collateral to a debt (Hall, 2002). Equity finance is thus an imperative for research and development conducting firms. According to Hall (2002), this is an obvious limitation in economies with poor markets for venture capital. Finance and access to finance have become more important determinants of research and development effort as international capital has become more mobile across borders and as "research and development costs per invention" have increased (Hall, 2002).

Evidence on the "funding gap" for research and development has been surveyed, with a focus on financial market reasons for under investment in research and development that persist even in the absence of externality-induced under investment (Hall, 2002). The conclusions are: 1) small and new innovative firms experience high costs of capital that are only partly mitigated by the presence of venture capital; 2) evidence for high costs of R&D capital for large firms is mixed, although these firms do prefer internal funds for financing these investments; 3) there are limits to venture capital as a solution to the funding gap, especially in countries where public equity markets are not highly developed; and 4) further study of governmental seed capital and subsidy programs using quasi-experimental methods is warranted (Hall, 2002).

Leadership Studies and Analysis

Since its introduction over twenty years ago, charismatic leadership has been strongly emphasized in the US management literature (Bass, 1985; House,1977; Shamir, House & Arthur, 1993). The benefits of charismatic or transformational leadership are thought to include broadening and elevating the interests of followers, generating awareness and acceptance among the followers of the purposes and mission of the group, and motivating followers to go beyond their self-interests for the good of the group and the organization (Bass, 1985). Charismatic or transformational leaders articulate a realistic vision of the future that can be shared, stimulate subordinates intellectually, and pay attention to the differences among the subordinates. Tichy and Devanna (1990) highlight the transforming effect these leaders can have on organizations as well as on individuals. By defining the need for change, creating new visions, and mobilizing commitment to these visions, leaders can ultimately transform organizations (Hartog et. al.., 1999).

According to Bass (1985) the transformation of followers can be achieved by raising the awareness of the importance and value of desired outcomes, getting followers to transcend their own self-interests and altering or expanding followers' needs. Bass (1985) defined the transactional leader as one who: recognizes what followers want to get from their work and tries to see that followers get what they desire if their performance warrants it; exchanges rewards for appropriate levels of effort; and responds to followers' self-interests as long as they are getting the job done. Numerous research studies have been conducted in this area, and, collectively, the empirical findings demonstrate that leaders described as charismatic, transformational, or visionary have positive effects on their organizations and followers, with effect sizes ranging from .35 to .50 for organizational performance effects, and from .40 to .80 for effects on follower satisfaction, commitment, and organizational identification (Fiol et al., 1999).

Studies have been carried out in many different countries, and research in this area also shows that transformational leadership is closer to perceptions of ideal leadership than transactional leadership. As Lord and Maher (1991) note, being perceived as a leader is a prerequisite for being able to go beyond a formal role in influencing others. They hold that leadership perceptions can be based on two alternative processes. First, leadership can be inferred from outcomes of salient events, and attribution is crucial in these inference-based processes (Lord & Maher, 1991). For example, a successful business 'turnaround' is often quickly attributed to the high quality 'leadership' of top executives or the CEO (Hartog et. al.., 1999). Leadership can also be recognized based on the fit between an observed person's characteristics with the perceivers' implicit ideas of what 'leaders' are (Hartog et. al.., 1999).

Cultural groups may vary in their conceptions of the most important characteristics of effective leadership. As such, different leadership prototypes would be expected to occur naturally in societies that have differing cultural profiles (Bass, 1990a; Hofstede 1993). Historical research indicates that in some cultures, one might need to take strong decisive action in order to be seen as a leader, whereas in other cultures consultation may be a better approach. Additionally, the evaluation and meaning of many leader behaviors and characteristics may also strongly vary in different cultures. In a culture that endorses an authoritarian style, leader sensitivity might be interpreted as weak, whereas in cultures endorsing a more nurturing style, the same sensitivity is likely to prove essential for effective leadership (Hartog et. al.., 1999).

Research indicates that leadership exists in all societies and is essential to the functioning of organizations within societies (Wren, 1995). Because individuals have their own ideas about the nature of leaders and leadership, they develop idiosyncratic theories of leadership. As such, an individual's implicit leadership theory refers to beliefs held about how leaders behave in general and what is expected of them. This type of attribution process provides a basis for social power and influence (Lord & Maher,1991). In recent years, decision-making models in business organizations have emerged as a significant factor in the determination of the organization's success or failure. Organizations require that individuals carry out job assignments dependably, make creative suggestions, and carry out self-training (Katz, 1958). However, the organization does not obtain all these behaviors simply through hiring the employee.

Research has noted the distinction between membership and decision making behaviors required by organizations and the quite different sources of these behaviors. In one such study, the motivation to acquire and keep organizational membership from productivity was distinguished (March & Simon, 1958). Membership motivation results from a favorable inducements-contributions balance. Employees must perceive a continuing favorable balance if they are to remain members. The motivation to perform represents a much more complex psychological contract between the individual and the organization involving perceived alternatives, perceived consequences of these alternatives, and individual goals (March & Simon, 1958). Organizations have no choice but to provide membership motivation if they wish to remain organizations.

Process or theories explain the operation of motivation, or the factors that influence an individual to choose one action rather than another. Process theories are subdivided into cognitive and non-cognitive approaches. Cognitive theories see behavior as involving some mental process. Non-cognitive theories see behavior as caused by environmental contingencies. The major cognitive theories are equity theory, goal-setting theory, and expectancy theory. All of them focus on perceptions of the outcomes that flow from behavior.

Equity theory suggests that motivated behavior is a form of exchange in which individuals employ an internal balance sheet in determining what to do. It predicts that people will choose the alternative they perceive as fair. The components of equity theory are inputs, outcomes, comparisons, and results. Inputs are the attributes the individual brings to the situation and the activities required. Outcomes are what the individual receives from the situation. The comparisons are between the ratio of outcomes to inputs and some standard. Results are the behaviors and attitudes that flow from the comparison, but other standards of comparison, including oneself in a previous situation, seem equally probable (Adams, 1965).

Goals setting theories argue that employees set goals and that organizations can influence work behavior by influencing these goals. The major concepts in the theory are intentions, performance standards, goal acceptance, and the effort expended. These concepts are assumed to be the motivation. Participation in goal setting should increase commitment and acceptance. Individual goal setting should be more effective than group goals because it is the impact of goals on intentions that is important. In goal-setting theory the crucial factor is the goal. Tests of the theory show that using goals leads to higher performance than situations without goals, and that difficult goals lead to better performance than easy ones (Mitchell, 1979). Although participation in goal setting may increase satisfaction, it does not always lead to higher performance.

Expectancy theory supports the contention that people choose the behavior they believe will maximize their payoff. It states that people look at various actions and choose the one they believe is most likely to lead to the rewards they want the most. The elements in the theory are expectancies that certain outcomes will occur and the anticipated satisfaction of those outcomes. Although the formal elements are expectancies and valences, in most formulations expectations are divided into two types: expectancy, or the expectation that effort will lead to performance, and instrumentality, or the expectation that performance will lead to reward.

Expectancy theory has been tested extensively. The usual approach is to obtain expectancies, instrumentalities, and valences by questionnaire or interview and to relate these responses to self-reported or measured choices, such as occupational choice, job satisfaction, effort, or performance (Mitchell, 1980). It has been found that expectancy theory can do an excellent job of predicting occupational choice and job satisfaction and a moderately good job of predicting effort on the job. Expectancy theory implies that the anticipation of rewards is important as well as the perceived contingency between the behaviors desired by the organization and the desired rewards. The theory also implies that since different people desire different rewards, organizations should try to match rewards with what employees want.

Although these implications suggest that following the requirements of expectancy theory will lead to performance motivation in organizations, organizations should be aware of possible difficulties. Employees may not believe that good performance does in fact lead to more desired rewards, and convincing them may require more changes than the organization is prepared to make. Poor selection and training of employees, for example, even with maximum effort, results in poor performance. Finally, it should be noted that the components of decision-making models are beliefs that require a good deal of information and a rather complex cognitive process in determining action. Some employee groups do want the rewards the organization has to offer, do want to believe that greater effort results in improved performance, and do want to believe that better performance leads to greater rewards.

The way in which the social environment is interpreted is strongly influenced by the cultural background of the perceiver. This implies that the attributes that are seen as characteristic or prototypical for leaders may also strongly vary in different cultures (Hartog, et. al.., 1999). Hunt, Boal and Sorenson (1990) propose that societal culture has an important impact on the development of superordinate category prototypes and implicit leadership theories. They hold that values and ideologies act as a determinant of culture specific superordinate prototypes, dependent on their strength.

The research in this area mentions three elements attributable to the leadership styles of different cultures; a stress on market processes, a stress on the individual, and a focus on managers rather than workers. As a result there is a growing awareness of need for a better understanding of the way in which leadership is enacted in various cultures and a need for an empirically grounded theory to explain differential leader behavior and effectiveness across cultures (House, 1995). Culture profiles derived from Hofstede's theoretical dimensions of cultures, yield many hypotheses regarding cross-cultural differences in leadership. Hofstede's dimensions of culture are: uncertainty avoidance, power distance, masculinity-femininity, individualism-collectivism, and future orientation. High uncertainty avoidance cultures, with the resulting emphasis on rules, procedures and traditions may place demands on leaders not expected in low uncertainty avoidance cultures (Hartog et. al.., 1999).

According to Hofstede, innovative behaviors may therefore be expected in low uncertainty avoidance cultures. Cultures that are more masculine are probably more tolerant of strong, directive leaders than feminine cultures, where a preference for more consultative, considerate leaders appears likely (Hartog et. al.., 1999). Research indicates that preferences for a low power distance in societies could result in other desired leader attributes than a preference for high power distance (Hartog et. al.., 1999). Other research indicates that managers in high power distance countries report more use of rules and procedures than do managers from low power distance countries. The most cited study, by Gerstner and Day (1994) focused on cross-cultural comparisons of leadership prototypes. In this study, respondents completed a questionnaire asking them to assign prototypically ratings to 59 leadership attributes. Comparing the ratings from a sample of American students (n=35) to small samples (n= between 10 and 22) of foreign students from 7 countries, they found that the traits considered to be most, moderately or least characteristic of business leaders varied by respondents country or culture of origin. However, this study has several limitations; small sample sizes, student samples, only foreign students currently in the US to represent other cultures in the sample, and employing a not cross-culturally validated English-language trait-rating instrument (Hartog et. al.., 1999). Despite these limitations, presenting conservative biases, reliable differences in leadership perceptions of members of various countries were found.

A new study, focusing on the entrepreneurial leadership characteristics of Sweden and China, would no doubt be useful, because sampling is a problematic issue in cross-cultural studies. As has been noted in cross cultural research, using national borders as cultural boundaries may not be appropriate in countries that have large subcultures (Hartog, et. al.., 1999). In large, multi-cultural countries such as China it is not even clear which sample would be most representative. As a result, the samples from all countries need to be relatively homogeneous within countries. An ideal sample would consist of representatives from the financial industry, food industry, and telecommunication industry. These industries are fairly universal and thus, such organizations could be identified in participating countries. Additionally, these industries differ in terms of the rate of change typically experienced.

The proposed study would consist of interviews with Swedish and Chinese entrepreneurs being asked the following questions. The model consists of 5 roles with two to three competencies each with questions. A random sample of the questions to be asked are as follows:

1. Designing (Developing executable business models)

    a. Recognizing opportunities for value creation

        - I anticipate the future course of events

        - I understand needs of other people, social groups and organizations

        - I have an ability to see the forest through the trees

        - I see possibilities of combining different products, services, or technology to create new value

        - I successfully identify alternative uses for different products, services, or technologies

        - I differentiate between executable and non-executable opportunities

    b. Turning ideas into specific action plans

        - I understand the economics of the business

        - I understand what is needed to make a business successful

        - I have a long-term view

        - I recognize risks and plan how to mitigate them

- I convert business vision into specific plans which can be realized
- I break big projects into smaller pieces of manageable size

c. Developing a clear and convincing vision for the venture

- I set and communicate a clear direction for the venture
- I consider the whole situation rather than details only
- I convey my ideas in a clear and understandable way
- I can talk about complex things in simple terms
- I come up with powerful metaphors and images
- I ensure that employees and other stakeholders understand personal benefits of achieving the vision

2. Assembling (assembling stakeholders and resources into a **performing organization**)

a. Creating performing organizations and teams

- I set clear and challenging performance and behavior standards and goals
- I identify required competencies and find people who possess them
- I integrate people with different backgrounds into a cohesive working system
- I introduce systems and procedures to facilitate performance
- I develop incentives to attract and motivate people
- I identify resource requirements of the business and effectively meet them through various channels

b. Possessing High Emotional intelligence

- I analyze my feelings before acting on them
- I make sure that my behavior is appropriate to the situation
- When someone is talking to me, I give my full attention
- I can read other people's feelings quite well
- I make sure people feel at ease with me
- I get people to open up by being easily approachable

c. Extracting value from social networks

- I have a large and diverse network of contacts
- I am able to make transactions with others on favorable terms
- I can ask for favors

- I am effective in formulating specific requests to other people
- I fully leverage my contacts
- I easily develop new contacts in different areas to help out the business

d. Developing others

- I personally mentor some people in my organization
- I regularly review how my people develop
- I allocate adequate financial and organizational resources to the development of people
- I adjust organizational structure to provide better developmental opportunities for my people
- I advise people to leave my company when I see that they have reached the ceiling in their development
- I reward and promote people with leadership potential

Additional questions would consist of questions addressing topics such as leading by example, enthusiasm for the venture, role models, rules, and interacting with people at different levels of organization and outside of it. Additional questions would revolve around goals, determination, focus, distractions, risks and external events. Other possibilities include social interaction, constructive disagreement, improvements, and performance strengths and weaknesses.

Next, criteria would be established for items to be considered universally endorsed as contributors to outstanding leadership. Possible criteria would be that 95% of country scores had to exceed a mean of 5 on a 7 point scale for that attribute, and the grand mean score for all countries had to exceed 6 for the attribute. In addition to examining the universally endorsed attributes, the results would also show which attributes were found to be viewed universally as ineffective and which were found to be culturally contingent. Universally endorsed leader attributes, as well as attributes that are universally seen as impediments to outstanding leadership and culturally-contingent attributes would be presented. It is predicted that the results support the hypothesis that specific aspects of charismatic or transformational leadership are strongly and universally endorsed across cultures. Sweden and China will be compared utilizing such a proposed study in the section following an examination of the economic, political and entrepreneurial leadership in both countries.

Entrepreneurial Leadership in Sweden

Research indicates that there is strong commitment and determination among entrepreneurs throughout Sweden to work for growth and increased prosperity.

When companies produce goods and services, they also generate jobs and tax revenue, and are responsible for research and for training employees. To new Swedes, employment in companies and self-employment are important ways into Swedish society (Advantage Sweden, 2005). Productivity is high, the labor force is well-trained, research and development is world class and its global business network is extensive (Advantage Sweden, 2005). In an international perspective, Sweden has a low investment level, and this undermines its future competitiveness. Over one million Swedes of working age are on sick leave, have taken early retirement, are unemployed or are living on social allowance (Advantage Sweden, 2005). There is imbalance in the age structure in Sweden; after 2010, the number of people aged over 80 will increase faster than the number gainfully employed. (Advantage Sweden, 2005).

In Sweden, the dependency burden is increasing as the proportion of entrepreneurs in Sweden has never been as low as it currently is (Advantage Sweden, 2005). Research indicates that Sweden faces several big challenges, including international cooperation. According to Advantage Sweden (2005), trade and personal relations bind together people from different cultures, and build peace and tolerance. Business affirms a freer and more open world, where democracy and market economies lay the foundations for better living conditions. Thus, international cooperation is a necessity to counteract environmental problems, poverty and terrorism (Advantage Sweden, 2005). Closer and broader European cooperation is important to enable Swedish business to be competitive at global level (Advantage Sweden, 2005). European Union enlargement creates new possibilities, but also sets new challenges such as competitiveness, growth and jobs (Advantage Sweden, 2005).

Sweden appears to have a distinct advantage over the potential growth of China's economy. Many Swedish companies, both big and small, are world leaders. As a result, Sweden has a strong foundation on which to build, as well as access to important raw materials, a well-trained labor force, and a good level of research. There is strong environmental commitment, and at the local level, there is generally good consensus between unions and employers, and between business people and politicians (Advantage Sweden, 2005). Wage formation, state finances and inflation have stabilized in recent years. Research indicates that to create even better conditions for favorable development, both companies and the public sector must continuously become better and more effective in their operations and must raise skills and quality (Advantage Sweden, 2005). That will make Sweden even more attractive to investors and to overseas visitors.

International competition has never been as intense as now. For example, in 1997, one million vacuum cleaners were manufactured in China, and in 2005, 25 million (Advantage Sweden, 2005). However, more and more overseas companies and owners choose to invest in Sweden, so the conditions for trade are improved through the removal of trade barriers and harmonization of regulations. Additionally, legislation in the European Union is implemented in an effective way in Sweden, through the removal of duplicate regulation and harmonization of legislation so that competition between companies is free and fair. This is important because an advantage is created through a stable and competitive legislative framework, implemented consistently and smoothly (Advantage Sweden, 2005). Regulations that are difficult to overview, an increasing number of public bodies and unpredictable implementation put unnecessary constraints on companies (Advantage Sweden, 2005). This hampers company performance, and thereby companies' competitiveness.

Since Sweden is a sparsely populated country located far from the major markets on the continent, for Sweden to have an edge, there is a need for a well-constructed and well-functioning infrastructure, as well as a competitive transport network (Advantage Sweden, 2005). If Sweden's growth is to continue, there is also a need for secure, long-term access to energy at competitive prices (Advantage Sweden, 2005). The energy supply must meet the highest reliability and environmental requirements. According to Advantage Sweden (2005), the use of information technology creates many new opportunities, and is an important base for enterprise in the future, and for continued growth in productivity and competitiveness. An effective capital supply for the start-up and expansion of companies is also important.

In order for companies to start and expand, there is a need for both a technological and a mental infrastructure that makes it attractive and straight forward to be an entrepreneur. In Sweden, attitudes towards business people have become increasingly favorable (Advantage Sweden, 2005). Every year, Swedish companies complete 73 million forms for submission to 75 different authorities (Advantage Sweden, 2005). In Sweden, it is difficult to start up companies due to the high tax rate on labor, which acts as a deterrent to both existing and new service-sector companies, at the same time as the informal sector is expanding. Good quality in basic education and good opportunities for adults to learn new work skills are important to a strong and competitive business sector (Advantage Sweden, 2005). Quality must permeate the entire school system, not only vocational training. Collaboration must improve between the business sector and both basic and tertiary education (Advantage Sweden, 2005). Increased international cooperation in education gives new perspectives, creates understanding of other cultures and strengthens Sweden.

Entreprenuership evolves through faith in people's will and ability to take responsibility, to have dreams, to want to develop, and to dare to seek new challenges. This is how an efficient public sector is created, but this requires that work and entrepreneurship are economically worthwhile. Furthermore, there must also be fundamental security for both employees and company leaders, as 34 per cent of students do not complete their upper secondary education within the three years (Advantage Sweden, 2005). To encourage increased entrepreneurship, the Confederation of Swedish Enterprise in the coming years will work to ensure that it is economically worthwhile to work, to save and to invest in companies so that the legal framework is changed so that entrepreneurs are given better conditions for expansion in the private service sector (Advantage Sweden, 2005). Another goal is for entrepreneurship and enterprise to become a self- evident part of all education so that quality is raised in the entire education system and that collaboration improves between school and business. Also, workforce immigration should be permitted and that the integration of immigrants is carried out in an active and resolute way. The end result will be that people shall have reasonable prospects of saving for the start-up capital to realize their ideas.

To strengthen Sweden's competitiveness, investment in development and innovation is needed. Therefore, conditions for research and development must be given high priority (Advantage Sweden, 2005). A clearer link is demanded between state research investments and the needs of the business sector, making it easier for research results to reach the market in the form of new products and new services, and can create more growth companies (Advantage Sweden, 2005). The legislation governing public companies, intellectual property rights and venture and capital markets must be developed to encourage and facilitate enterprise with innovative business development and the production of good sand services in Sweden (Advantage Sweden, 2005). For a company to develop, it must make a profit. Companies without profit requirements are not under the same pressure to increase efficiency and offer customers quality and new solutions. Thus, competition stimulates new ideas, new methods and efficient production (Advantage Sweden, 2005). Competition also favors consumers, through lower prices and better quality (Advantage Sweden, 2005).

In Sweden there is considerable knowledge within the public sector, which through private enterprise can reach overseas markets, generating new jobs in Sweden. Today, there are a number of obstacles in the way of this process. It is crucial that these obstacles be removed and that public procurement should always take place openly, simply and through sound competition (Advantage Sweden, 2005). For example, company registration and start-up must be a simple, brief procedure. It must be made easier to build up equity in a company for financing development (Advantage Sweden, 2005). The tax and levy burden must not be allowed to impede Sweden in international competition (Advantage Sweden, 2005). The informal sector creates unfair competition and creates difficulties for responsible companies.

It is becoming increasingly attractive to own, start up, run and develop profitable companies in Sweden. More entrepreneurs are needed, and the necessary dynamics of enterprise mean the start-up of companies and the liquidation of companies. Risk-taking must give the possibility of profits, at the same time as bankruptcy should not necessarily mean that one loses the chance to try again (Advantage Sweden, 2005). In a comparison between 28 countries of how many new companies were started, Sweden ranked 21st (Advantage Sweden, 2005). The research also indicates that Sweden needs more people to work and pay tax on their income. It appears that too many people of working age do not work, but have taken early retirement, are on sick leave, are unemployed or are in labor market schemes (Advantage Sweden, 2005).

Young people, elderly people and immigrants often have difficulty in finding employment in Sweden. Outmoded labor market regulations and rules governing taxation and allowances reduce mobility on the labor market (Advantage Sweden, 2005). Complicated rules and tax regulations lead to undeclared work. High payroll costs, major risk factors for companies, such as costs in connection with sickness and comprehensive legislation, have created high recruitment thresholds (Advantage Sweden, 2005). Few employees change employer, even if they are not content. The labor market of tomorrow demands increased mobility, regulations on working hours that lead to more hours of work input and solutions that are suited to both the company and the employees (Advantage Sweden, 2005). Wage formation must be based on the conditions of individuals and companies. Unemployment insurance and social insurance are important factors in stimulating labor market mobility (Advantage Sweden, 2005). Thus, systems must be coordinated, must stimulate work and must provide benefits during certain periods (Advantage Sweden, 2005).

In Sweden, through collective agreements that give stability and support for both development and reorientation, labor market players can increase companies' competitiveness and capacity to create new jobs (Advantage Sweden, 2005). The current legislation on labor disputes does not provide the necessary balance between the players, since even minor union actions can swiftly bring disproportionately far-reaching consequences to both companies and the community (Advantage Sweden, 2005). A more internationalized labor market creates possibilities and challenges. Security on the labor market is not primarily a question of keeping a job, its about being able to find a new job if the old one disappears (Advantage Sweden, 2005). Statistics reveal that the average Swede works for 8 per cent of his or her lifetime (Advantage Sweden, 2005).

The economic background of Sweden reveals that Sweden has faired fairly badly in terms of economic growth for almost three decades, but has faired very well in terms of employment, and in terms of low unemployment, until about

1990. At that time Sweden had the highest employment rate in the world, 81 percent of the population between 18-64 years were gainfully employed (Henrekson, 2005). Since then, there has been a dramatic change in terms of employment. At the peak of the employment boom in 1989-90 there were about 4.5 million jobs in Sweden (Henrekson, 2005). That figure dropped by about 600,000 jobs in just a couple of years time, and in late 1993 the economy began to bounce back, and 150-200,000 jobs were gained, but now those jobs have been lost again (Henrekson, 2005).

This research indicates that the recovery of the Swedish economy after the severe crisis of 1991-93 has been one of jobless growth. So far there has not been any permanent change in the job level, at the private sector and in the public sector.

Since entrepreneurship is a key to job growth in the private sector, the jobs have to be created in existing firms or new firms. Thus, the challenge is to be build institutions and rules of the game in the Swedish economy that render strong employment expansion possible (Henrekson, 2005). Such incentives include employing more people in existing businesses or starting new businesses for good, viable ideas. A disaggregation of the employment record in Sweden shows that employment growth looking over the entire post-war period has been bleak for the private sector (Henrekson, 2005). There are fewer jobs in the private sector now than there was 47 years ago, despite the fact that there are almost 2 million more Swedes now than there were in 1950.

In the Swedish economy, large corporations play a very dominant role. There are a number of studies showing that Sweden is perhaps the single industrial economy with the highest dominance of large firms in the whole OECD area (Henrekson, 2005). There has been a low share of self-employment, and corporate ownership has been very concentrated, with a reliance on large corporations. Research indicates that corporate taxation is very important from an entrepreneurial perspective. Historically, Sweden has historically had corporate taxation which has been very beneficial to institutional owners and to debt financing (Henrekson, 2005). It has been an extreme characteristic of the Swedish tax system benefiting institutional ownership to the detriment of private, individual ownership, and the tax system has encouraged a high debt-equity ratio (Henrekson, 2005).

The only types of firms that can benefit from this type of tax system consist of institutional ownership; as a result the Swedish engineering industry, Swedish raw material based large companies and construction companies have benefited from these tax rules. In contrast, small and new firms, must be individually owned. Also firms which are labor intensive or knowledge intensive have very little collateral, so they have to work with a high-equity ratio (Henrekson, 2005). Likewise, new firms based on a new innovation, where it takes a long time for the finished product to reach the market, and where the risk level is high require a low debt-equity ratio (Henrekson, 2005).

Sweden now has a 40-60 percent tax rate schedule, rather than the 30-50 schedule that was instituted in the 1991 tax reform. A recent report shows that Sweden has the highest tax burden of all countries on low incomes, about 62 percent of labor income for a typical low income earner is taxed away (Henrekson, 2005). On the consumer's side, demand may be very low because those who are going to buy the service will have to pay out of their own after-tax income. A very high total tax burden also makes it very difficult to save in Sweden, and high taxes also render it very difficult to accumulate wealth. As a result, an individual is unlikely to have any capital to support a business venture, leading to less venture capital and fewer firm start-ups.

Labor security legislation has also affected entreprenuership in Sweden. There is evidence suggesting that the employment security provisions fall more heavily on smaller firms and some other classes of firms (Henrekson, 2005). Sweden has a much more centralized wage formation structure and a narrower wage dispersion, meaning that in the Swedish setting, small firms have to pay a higher wage in the initial stage of their life cycle than otherwise. As a result, this increases their wage costs and makes it more difficult for them to get started and obtain the impetus to finally become a large firm. Especially noteworthy is the dramatic increase in employment in health and medical care and social services. These services are labor-intensive, and in many instances are very suitable for production by a small firm (Henrekson, 2005).

The entrepreneurial process is such a pervasive feature of a market economy that the most efficient way to encourage firm births is to enhance the environment for all business activity. Thus, Sweden should work to create a stable and internationally competitive economic framework for all types of firms (Henrekson, 2005). This framework should offer sufficient incentive for change and for investment in real capital, education, and knowledge capital, and it should be neutral in terms of an enterprise's orientation, size, and organizational principles (Henrekson, 2005). The research indicates that if Sweden succeeds in this endeavor, Sweden can become as powerful a job machine as the United States.

Holmberg and Akerblom (2003) studied Swedish leadership styles, and their analysis reveals that institutional contexts seem to generate different implicit models of leadership, but within the same national framework. Excellent leadership is evidently executed and enacted as aspects of socially constructed institutions and socially grounded culturally values (Holmberg & Akerblom, 2003). According to a common understanding of the culture concept, collective conceptions of leadership are therefore expressions of the culture at large in which both leaders and followers are embedded (Holmberg & Akerblom, 2003). Therefore, a Swedish leadership style would consequently be an expression of the Swedish culture.

Researchers have noted that Swedish leadership is vague and imprecise, and the typical Swedish order is 'See what you can do about it (Holmberg & Akerblom, 2003)!' Researchers have attributed this to a far-reaching delegation of authority; managers who say 'See what you can do about it!' demonstrate trust for their co-workers. It is also a matter of the execution of control by a common understanding of the problem, rather than direct orders (Holmberg & Akerblom, 2003). This must be regarded as a strength with the egalitarian Swedish society (Edström &Jönsson, 1998). Due to the cultural similarity among the Scandinavian countries in an international perspective, Swedish leadership is furthermore described within the broader notion of Scandinavian management.

In ethnographic descriptions of Sweden, it is often asserted that Swedes have a strict border between public and private life, whereas in many other parts of the world, the two are inseparable (Daun, 1989). Independence and solitude are important and positive concepts for Swedes in general (Daun, 1989), something which is enacted in the private sphere. Hampden-Turner & Trompenaars (1993) assert that Swedes more than any other culture begin with the individual, his or her integrity, uniqueness, freedom, needs, and values, yet insist that the fulfillment and destiny of the individual lies in developing and sustaining others by the gift of his or her own work and energy.

Holmberg & Åkerblom (1998) found Sweden to be both an extremely collective and extremely individualist society. Their findings can be contrasted with the result of Hofstede (1980), in which Sweden was labeled an individualistic culture. One explanation to this difference is that Hofstede did not distinguish between the small family group, or clan, and the much wider group constituting the society as a whole. This distinction is obviously important in the Swedish case, where the two life worlds (public and private) preferably are kept separate in time and space (Holmberg & Akerblom, 2003). In Hofstedes (1980) seminal work Sweden was ranked among the least uncertainty avoiding cultures in contradiction to the contemporary study by Holmberg & Åkerblom (1998), who found Sweden to be a highly uncertainty avoiding culture with a strong future orientation.

The development of the consensus culture is connected to the fact that the Swedish population is unusually homogeneous, compared to other countries (Holmberg & Akerblom, 2003). For example, Swedes share the same history, same language, same religion; and differences between different groups within the nation are comparatively small (Holmberg & Akerblom, 2003). Everyone's opinions, ideas and experiences are respected and listened to, since all are potential contributors to the accomplishment of the task in place or to the solution of the problem being dealt with (Holmberg & Akerblom, 2003). Mutual understanding, collective consideration and compromised solutions are favored (Holmberg & Akerblom, 2003).

Entrepreneurial Leadership in China

Rapid economic development over 20 years has led some commentators to claim China could deliver sustained global growth, however, it has started to falter, and risks becoming a destabilizing factor in the world. China, for two decades the world's fastest growing economy, has become a major force in the global economy. But as the ostensibly 'communist' regime in Beijing struggles to put the brakes on an economy which is experiencing an extreme form of overheating, euphoria among the capitalist class internationally has given way to nervousness (Coates, 2004). As Steven Roach, chief economist at investment bank Morgan Stanley, warns, "the world may be unprepared for the impact of a Chinese slowdown (Coates, 2004)."

Last year, according to official statistics, China's gross domestic product (GDP) grew by 9.1 percent (Coates, 2004). For years, independent economists have viewed official Chinese statistics with skepticism, believing them to be exaggerated. Today, many believe the figures understate reality which predicts that the economy may have grown by 11 or 12 percent in 2003 (Coates, 2004). One reason for the discrepancy is that city and provincial governments are playing down local growth data in order to avoid penalties from Beijing aimed at reining in overheated sectors such as property, steel and cars (Coates, 2004). Investment in new steel capacity rose by 87 percent last year and total output is set to double again in two to three years (Coates, 2004). The director of a stainless steel mill on the Yangtze river, owned jointly by South Korea's Posco and China's largest private steel company, Shangang, recently told the UK Financial Times that in a few years his complex alone will be making as much steel as the whole country of France (Coates, 2004).

In China, the steel sector is an example of the uncontrolled expansion of capacity taking place throughout the economy, much of which is 'blind' or 'duplicative' according to the government (Coates, 2004). This is creating huge imbalances such as chronic shortages of electricity, water and raw materials. Blackouts, often forcing factories to halt production, are commonplace even in the most developed cities (Coates, 2004). Despite huge investment in recent years, road, rail and port capacity is overloaded. These shortages are being exploited by capitalists and corrupt officials for huge speculative gains (Coates, 2004). For example, shipping costs for freight in northeast Asia rose by 400% last year on the basis of surging Chinese orders, with scrap metal, coal and iron ore for the steel industry accounting for half this sea-borne traffic (Coates, 2004). While mining and energy transnationals made bumper profits from the Chinese boom, other branches of the world economy have been squeezed by higher prices for raw materials (Coates, 2004).

The question of whether China can continue to grow at its current rate for the next two decades has been speculated by financial advisors. Media comment on China in this area has struck a more cautious tone as a result of signs including an explosion of credit, rampant over capacity (nine tenths of manufacturing goods are in over supply), and the return of inflation (2.8% in the first quarter of 2004) (Coates, 2004). President Hu Jintao, and his prime minister, Wen Jiabao, have assured financial markets that 'resolute' measures are being taken to rein in excessive investment and engineer a 'soft landing' for the economy but, so far, with no discernible impact (Coates, 2004). "China is in a situation of severe over-investment," notes Credit Suisse First Boston's Hong Kong office (Coates, 2004). Investment is chasing diminishing returns, and according to The Economist, China currently needs $4 of investment to generate each additional dollar of annual output, compared with $2-3 in the 1980s and 1990s (Coates, 2004).

China's money supply grew by 20 percent last year, and bank credit (new loans) by 56 percent (Coates, 2004). Additionally, the sharp rise of the US dollar in 1995, to which most Asian currencies were linked, priced some exports out of world markets. China, although it exports 25 percent of national output, is less dependent on the world market (Coates, 2004). The super-Keynesian measures of the government, implemented in response to the Asian crisis to boost demand by slashing interest rates six times since 1997, and by financing huge infrastructure projects, have increased the specific weight of the home market (Coates, 2004).

China is now the world leader in many branches of manufacturing, including cellular phones, colour TVs and computer monitors. Since the start of its global export offensive 20 years ago, manufacturing industry in China has shifted from low-tech sectors like textiles, toys and simple manufactures to computers and electronics which now account for 60 percent of exports (Coates, 2004). Reflecting the increased role of high-tech production, China accounted for 14 percent of global semiconductor consumption in 2003 (Coates, 2004). Additionally, 16 million manufacturing jobs have actually disappeared since 1995, as Chinese industry has upgraded its technology. Shanghai Baosteel Group, for example, the world's sixth largest steel producer, cut its workforce to 100,000 from 176,000 five years ago (Coates, 2004). As industry in the southern and eastern provinces has become more capital intensive, low-tech production has shifted to the poorer (and cheaper) inland provinces (Coates, 2004). This right now is where there is greatest resistance to government attempts to curb new investment (Coates, 2004).

China still lags behind the advanced capitalist countries in the application of new technology, but the gap is closing. A million engineering graduates leave Chinese universities every year and there is an ongoing transfer of technology from the huge network of foreign partnerships and joint ventures (Coates, 2004). A survey by the Japanese newspaper, Nihon Keizai Shimbun, based on interviews with 350 Japanese corporations, concluded that, "in the field of technical development China would catch up with Germany and Japan within ten years (Coates, 2004)." China's integration into the capitalist world economy means that many facets of US and European industry are now dependent on components or finished products from Chinese factories. "In a crisis," warned Ted Dean, managing director of consultancy firm, BDA, "Chinese labor could become as destabilizing a force for the world economy as oil prices (Coates, 2004)."

These indisputable facts are often cited by capitalist commentators to present a picture of unstoppable economic progress: a 20-year Chinese boom (Coates, 2004). Take this example into consideration: with 282 million mobile phone subscribers, China is the world's biggest market. But growth rates are already slowing, with fewer new subscribers in the first months of 2004 (Coates, 2004). Overproduction consisting of too many phones combined with too few buyers has caused prices to plummet, which in turn squeezes profit margins. Research indicates that the re-emergence of inflation or rising prices, in China is mainly due to the rising cost of capital goods, some farm products and services such as education. A more serious problem, however, is the longer-term potential for deflation, or falling prices, arising from such extreme levels of overcapacity (Coates, 2004). Deflation not only squeezes profits, it magnifies the problem of debt, making repayments costlier in relative terms (Coates, 2004). This is a potential time-bomb for the Chinese economy which has financed its investment boom with unprecedented levels of credit (Coates, 2004).

For years, Chinese labor has been a source of super-profits for global corporations and local capitalists. Manufacturing wages averaged just 61 US cents (€0.52, £0.34) an hour last year, compared with $16 in the US and $2 in Mexico (Coates, 2004). One hundred thousand Chinese workers die every year from industrial accidents or work-related illnesses (Coates, 2004). Low wage levels impose severe limits on the growth of a mass consumer market, as Chinese workers can only afford to buy back a fraction of what they produce. While average per capita incomes have risen rapidly in the last 20 years, the gap between rich and poor is now the biggest in the world (Coates, 2004). This has been a largely urban boom, with average incomes in the cities six times those of rural ones. Shanghai, with 16 million inhabitants, has the same per capita GDP as Portugal (Coates, 2004). But the poorest region, Guizhou, has a per capita GDP lower than Bangladesh (Coates, 2004). Although incomes for China's 800 million rural population are now rising due to a rise in prices for farm goods, the Financial Times pointed out that, "a consumer society has largely failed to materialize among two thirds of China's population (Coates, 2004)."

The pressure of migration from the countryside, predicted to be up to 400 million set to move to the cities by 2020, will most likely hold down wage levels. There are numerous plans for expansion in east Asia, such as a new $15 billion natural gas pipeline from Xinjiang province to Shanghai to bring cleaner fuel to the coastal areas, though uneconomical from a market standpoint (Coates, 2004). Additionally, eighty-six new subway lines are under construction. These policies, rather than aiming to improve living conditions for the masses, aim to create a more effective framework for the exploitation of Chinese labor. In the absence of democratic control of these projects by workers' organizations, waste, corruption and abuses such as environmental degradation and the forcible relocation of local communities are legion (Coates, 2004).

According to prime minister Wen, the Chinese economy has reached a critical juncture (Coates, 2004). For example, in April of 2004, the central bank raised the minimum level of deposits that banks must keep in reserve from 7 percent to 7.5 percent (Coates, 2004). Smaller banks were ordered to halt all lending temporarily, a measure backed up by police measures including a crackdown on 'illegal' sales of farmland, and beefed-up environmental and other controls at new factories and construction sites. Furthermore, housing construction in China is overwhelmingly pitched towards the luxury market and over capacity in the form of vacant properties is widespread. Research indicates that property prices rose by 25 percent last year and are approaching US levels in cities like Shanghai and Beijing. This points to the danger of a crash in land prices which, in turn, could trigger a banking collapse (Coates, 2004). Higher interest rates would be the most effective way to regain some control over credit levels and investment, but the results may be too dramatic (Coates, 2004).

More than anything, the Chinese regime fears political instability, and a movement of the working class (Coates, 2004). Labor protests in China are numerous, among unemployed workers, laid-off from the state sector. These movements have so far been isolated, local outbursts, which have been defused by a combination of concessions and repression from the authorities (Coates, 2004). Given the now pivotal role it plays in the global economy, it is clear that any re-run of the Asian crisis in China, would have major international implications (Coates, 2004). China's role as the number one market for capital goods (minerals, fuel, building materials and machinery) made it the main locomotive of global growth in 2004. World GDP grew by 3.2% in 2003, with China contributing a third of this growth, or 1.1%, while US capitalism accounted for just 0.7% (Coates,

2004). In 2003, China accounted for 70% of Japan's total export growth, and 40% of South Korea's.

Last year, China became the world's third largest importer after the US and Germany. For the first time since 1993, it is heading for a trade deficit in upcoming years, with imports exceeding exports on an annual basis. The surge in Chinese demand in 2003 drove world prices for industrial raw materials up by 73% (Coates, 2004). China is the world's biggest steel producer, accounting for one fifth of global output in 2003 with 220 million tons, or as much as the US and Japan combined (Coates, 2004). In 2003, China also became the world's third largest market for motor vehicles with sales growing 60% (Coates, 2004). By 2007, production is predicted to reach 15 million vehicles, against sales of 7 million. Unfortunately, these prices have already begun to fall, as steel prices rose 35% in the twelve months to February 2004, car prices fell 5.1%. Fierce competition between car-makers makes it impossible to pass on rising costs to consumers, so profit margins are falling (Coates, 2004).

Today, China, with one quarter of the world's population is seen as a great opportunity for many corporations. For the expatriate businessperson and their family, China can be one of the most exciting and arduous international assignments, however, researchers warn that before considering any international assignment in China, a family needs to take stock of its motivations, expectations, strengths and weaknesses (Goodman, 2005). Contemporary China is a combination of Confucianism, Communism and a free market spirit of entrepreneurship. To be successful in China the expatriate must understand how the mixture of these forces impacts day-to-day living (Goodman, 2005). In China, there is no business without guanxi or relationship. Relationships take a considerable time to develop and are based on many continuous signs of good faith (Goodman, 2005). Though difficult to establish, once a relationship exists it tends to be long lasting and is full of many mutual obligations and favors; these mutual obligations are remembered and are balanced out over time (Goodman, 2005). The actual "value" ascribed to each favor may differ due to cultural factors.

Traditional Chinese values are based on human feelings rather than political or religious principles; respect for the feelings of others helps to hold society together. Considerable time and effort are spent on "face working" particularly one's own face as well as that of others (Goodman, 2005). Causing someone to "lose face" is humiliating and will not be forgotten (Goodman, 2005). Thus, so important is the preservation of face that it is sometimes preferable to agree to a decision even if there is no intent to carry out the decision. Additionally, China is in a state of rapid change. This has resulted in a situation where the rules and regulations of government and business and the authority to enforce the rules are constantly changing. In China, health issues are an important concern, as air pollution is very bad due to the burning of coal. Furthermore, the Chinese work ethics and educational systems are based on socialism.

The Chinese private equity industry has become the largest private equity industry in Asia in recent years despite the tremendous regulatory hurdles and institutional uncertainties that venture capital firms face. In 2001, China, together with Hong Kong, captured 30% of Asia's private equity investment to overtake Japan for the first time (Batjargal, 2004). By the middle of 2002, the total venture capital fund pool in mainland China reached $7.15 billion. Although the first domestic venture capital organization was set up in 1986, development of the private equity industry intensified only after March 1998, when the Chinese government adopted a number of policy schemes to promote venture investments (Batjargal, 2004). In the first two quarters of 2002, venture capital firms raised $156 million in funds, a steep decline from$1.86 billion in 2001 (Batjargal, 2004).

In the first two quarters of 2002, 36 foreign firms invested $87 million while Chinese firms invested$70 million (Batjargal, 2004). Until 1998, venture capital firms were regarded as financial institutions that provided privileged loans to small firms. The main legal form of venture capital firms, limited liability partnership, is not recognized in mainland China's laws. As a result, all venture capital firms are registered and operate as limited liability companies, adding confusion as well as serious risks to the processes by which venture capital firms raise, invest, and manage funds (Batjargal, 2004). The assets of the venture capital firm are not separated legally from those of the fund, thus increasing agency risks in venture investments, such as misuse of funds.

Research on personal networks of entrepreneurs revealed that entrepreneurs obtain information and advice from network members (Birley 1985) and access bank loans through contacts (Uzzi 1999). The idea of social capital in the Chinese context captures the indigenous social phenomenon called guanxi, or the Chinese version of social networks and networking (King 1991). Researchers defined guanxi as a web of extended family relationships (Kipnis 1997), a cluster of patron-client exchange relationships for instrumental purposes (Walder 1986). Research indicates that Guanxi capital promotes inter-personal trust, facilitates job mobility, and enhances firm performance (Batjargal, 2004). A study of private equity in China emphasizes the important role guanxi plays in venture capital practices, as a substantial portion of the cash that goes into private equity funds originates from government sources. As a result, guanxi relationships with government officials are often regarded as a defining factor for securing government investments in venture capital funds.

Investors are likely to invest in only those projects that are expected to produce acceptable net present values. Informal socialization such as social eating, an important component of guanxixue, or the art of net-working. This enables investors to know the values and beliefs of entrepreneurs better, and facilitate interpersonal and cognitive trust in entrepreneurs' abilities and intentions (Batjargal, 2004). Cultural features of the Chinese, such as a strong sense of role obligation, favoritism, and inclinations to categorize people into in-group and out-group circles also facilitate better communication between investors and entrepreneurs who know each other.

The Chinese context adds culture-specific variables that also affect investment selections through referrals. In the culture of shame, a favor giver (the one who recommends some-one to a third party) is regarded as a face giver, and a favor receiver (the one who gets access to the third party through the recommendation) is regarded as a face receiver (Batjargal, 2004). Successful transactions between face giver (referee), face receiver (fund seeker), and investor will enhance the face—mianzi (social standing, symbolic resources, and reputation)—of all parties (Batjargal, 2004). Referrals may improve odds of obtaining venture capital for entrepreneurs because of opportunity filtering, matching, and trust benefits that mitigate social risks indecisions. In the Chinese context, venture capitalists are likely to invest more in common stock rather than other senior securities such as convertible preferred stock, nonconvertible preferred stock, debt coupled with common stock, or common stock purchase warrants (Batjargal, 2004).

The Chinese prefer to keep details of guanxi deals confidential and resolve potential issues and problems through tacit understandings and actions. A recent survey found that about 60% of Chinese entrepreneurs preferred social solutions for dispute settlement (Krug and Hendrischke 2002). Precise calculations of dividends, conversion, liquidation, and antidilution terms may hurt the commitment of the entrepreneurial team and are likely to be perceived as unenforceable by investors and entrepreneurs (Batjargal, 2004). The stronger the tie between the entrepreneur and the venture capitalist, the fewer the number of contractual covenants that protect venture capitalists' interests. Peculiarities of Chinese negotiation behavior are likely to lead to increases in venture values. A sense of balance, modesty, and mutuality is likely to smooth out negotiation processes where acceptable compromises are crafted (Batjargal, 2004). A cultural inclination of the Chinese to favor those whom they know also contributes to the risk-mitigating role of personal relationships in venture financing in the Chinese context.

The human quality of emotional affection is also a factor in the Chinese culture and rendering of human obligations. A Confucian exchange tactic of giving more in expectation of getting more is at work (Malik 1997). By increasing firm values, investors manufacture and accumulate social receivables, and these advance monetary favors provide leverage over entrepreneurs. Finally, in China, social relationships embedded in local cultures and traditions do affect entrepreneurial process and venture investment decisions. Changes in network structures, compositions, and relations over time, is an important issue, given the social and economic transformations that are taking place in China. An implication for entrepreneurship research is to examine the impact of the way in which venture capital was raised on firm performance.

Comparison of Swedish and Chinese Entrepreneurs

Researchers have argued that new firm creation, innovation and competition are the three major aspects through which entreprenuership can contribute to economic development in the sense of wealth distribution. Every year, Swedish companies complete 73 million forms for submission to 75 different authorities (Advantage Sweden, 2005). Indicated above, in Sweden, it is difficult to start up companies due to the high tax rate on labor, which acts as a deterrent to both existing and new service-sector companies, at the same time as the informal sector is expanding. In applying these facts, it would appear that entreprenuership in Sweden is not as strong as it could be due to the difficulties facing new firm creation, innovation and competition. In China, there has been an economic boom as more and more and more new firms are created. Due to the fact that a million engineering graduates leave Chinese universities every year, there is an ongoing transfer of technology from the huge network of foreign partnerships and joint ventures (Coates, 2004). These new graduates begin the creation of new firms, however, innovation and competition in China appear to be very high. China may not be able to continuously put out new firms and new innovations, as competition is very fierce, and already it is predicted that the Chinese economy will fail.

New firm creation is an ability and a willingness of individuals to perceive and create new economic opportunities (Mamede & Davidsson, 2003). The innovative process has been defined as occurring within new firms which generally does not arise out of the old ones, but start producing alongside them (Mamede & Davidsson, 2003). This is relative to Swedish firms, because many old firms exist, small and large in Sweden. Entering the markets with their innovations entrepreneurs challenge the dominating firms, and their willingness is motivated by the desire of creating wealth for themselves, and to succeed they strive in for the product or solution they believe in (Mamede & Davidsson, 2003). If successful in creating demand for their innovation they expand their business to new markets and in doing so they also influence economic structures in other regions (Mamede & Davidsson, 2003). In Sweden, many older firms exist which are already strong and have the capability to innovate new ideas. As a result, in Sweden, new wealth is not only created by this process, but also distributed along with the previous one.

In China, however, there has been a giant boom of new firms and innovations, which do not have a traditional foundation to stand on, such as in Sweden. In China, there exists the possibility, since competition is so fierce, that the activities of the new firms may negatively affect the existing ones causing them to ultimately decline. This is because the new entrepreneurs acquire the market shares that previously belonged to the older companies, thus acquiring some of their wealth. As time goes by the older companies are not able to retain their workforce and have to dismiss their employees. Some of them declare bankruptcy, and a as consequence creditors, employees and shareholders lose part of their wealth (Mamede & Davidsson, 2003). At the same time, the new expanding firms employ new workers, pay increase dividends to their shareholders, and intensify their purchases from suppliers (Mamede & Davidsson, 2003). Thus, China bears the example of its wealth as being in the process of constantly changing hands, along with the creation of new firms.

Innovation is the process of introducing new ideas in the market in the face of uncertainty and other obstacles (Wennekers, Thurik & Buis, 1997). Another important link between entreprenuership and wealth distribution is innovation. The new products and new processes that result of innovative activity are seen by many economists as the main source of dynamism in capital development (Mamede & Davidsson, 2003). Research indicates that the introduction of new innovations can generate changes and cycles in the economy, causing wealth to become increasingly concentrated in the hands of a few large firms, thus destabilizing society. In China, there is always something new coming out in the market. China has a great number of steel products, and technological advances create many new products. Through a strong belief in their ideas and dedicated effort, they manage to allocate resources in a better way, develop a greater appeal to buyers and succeed in creating demand for their new products and solutions (Mamede & Davidsson, 2003).

Competition has been defined simply as to compete with others for a share of that market (Wennekers, Thurik & Buis, 1997). Competition is one of the most important forces in the market, and often a determining factor for the future of many enterprises (Mamede & Davidsson, 2003). The success of these firms is in a large extent associated with the way they assess their business environment in order to meet the needs of the market. In China, the needs of the market were increasing due to the population boom, however in recent years, the output is exceeding the amount of purchases in the country. The competition in China is steadily increasing, at a faster pace that the competition in Sweden. As a result, in China, the disposition to compete and face the risks and uncertainties involved in the competitive process is an important element of what it truly means to be an entrepreneur.

Furthermore, not all types of competition are beneficial to the mechanism of wealth generation and distribution. While it is perceived as a positive effect for many nations as it increases the levels of trade and the total production, to others it is harmful (Mamede & Davidsson, 2003). Examples of this fact are the developing economies in east Asia. Some countries have experienced significant growth throughout the nineties and have managed to increase their standards of living. However, other countries, by opening their markets to international competition, have been inundated with imports, unable to sell their exports. This is occurring presently in china, as production is beginning to fall behind purchases. This causes lower levels of growth and worse standards of living.

The competition that creates and distributes wealth is one that results from innovation and new firm creation (Mamede & Davidsson, 2003). In Sweden, this is favorable, as entrepreneurs are willing to pay the price assuming the risks of their choices. In Sweden, it appears that the chance of risk is less than that in China. As people gain confidence, improve the financial situation, and have access to information, they also develop political will and are less likely to accept corrupt governments and inadequate living conditions (Mamede & Davidsson, 2003). Consequently, they seek better education for themselves and their children, along with the improvements in the household and community (Mamede & Davidsson, 2003). It is clear from the research that entrepreneurs in Sweden already realize this, and are initiating changes to improve the educational system, whose graduates secure the future of their country.

As they create their new firms, innovate and strive for the ideas they believe in, entrepreneurs in Sweden not only succeed in harvesting good profits, the deserved outcomes of their efforts, but also in contributing to the prosperity of organizations and nations (Mamede & Davidsson, 2003). As a result, it appears that Sweden has secured their position as prime movers of progress, and as the engine of both economical and social change (Mamede & Davidsson, 2003). Much emphasis has been given to an existing association between entrepreneurial leadership and economic growth. Many studies have been developed, or are being carried out, in order to analyze the links between entreprenuership and economic growth. Evidence shows that this relationship is complex and that more data are necessary in order to determine the causal mechanisms of this association (Reynolds, et. al.., 2001).

The Global Entreprenuership Monitor (GEM) is a unique, unprecedented effort to describe and analyze entrepreneurial processes within a wide range of nations. By doing so, GEM focuses on one of the most important forces driving and carrying economic change, one that has until now remained elusive for researchers due to a lack of reliable, internationally comparable data (Reynolds et. al., 2002). The major objectives of the GEM report include measures for the differences in the level of entrepreneurial activity between countries, to probe for a systematic relationship between entreprenuership and national economic growth, to uncover factors that lead to higher levels of entreprenuership, and to suggest policies that may enhance the national level of entrepreneurial activity. In the 2002 GEM assessment, representative samples of 1,000 to 5,000 randomly selected adults in each country were selected to provide a harmonized measure of the prevalence of entrepreneurial activity (Reynolds et. al., 2002).

The GEM report also includes up to 50 face to face interviews with experts in their country, chosen to represent the entrepreneurial framework features. These same experts were additionally asked to complete a standardized questionnaire in order to obtain a precise measure of their judgments about their country as a suitable context for entrepreneurial activity (Reynolds et. al., 2002). Finally, standardized national data was collected from international data sources such as the World Bank and United Nations. The 2002 GEM report indicated that the level of entrepreneurial activity was lowest in Central Europe, and highest in the developing Asian countries, such as China. The GEM report also indicated that age and gender have a very stable relationship to entrepreneurial activity, as men are twice as likely to engage in entrepreneurial conduct than are women. Additionally, those ages 25 to 44 are most likely to be involved with all types of entrepreneurial activity. In countries women are more likely to be involved where there is equality in career opportunities, whereas in developing countries low participation of women may reflect the lack of jobs and an inadequate education (Reynolds et. al., 2002).

Of the 2.4 billion persons comprising the labor force represented in the 37 countries of the 2002 GEM report, 286 million are either actively involved in starting a business or are the owner-manager of a business less than 42 months old (Reynolds et. al., 2002). In China, the total population was estimated at 1,284,000,000 for 2002. The total labor force in 2002 was 814,470,000. By comparison, in 2002, there was a total population of 8,876,000 in 2002 in Sweden, with a total labor force of 5,433,000 in 2002. The GEM report indicates that entrepreneurial activity is uniformly low in the east Asian groups, as well as within most of the members of the European Union. In contrast, the Anglo nations have a relatively higher level of activity, and the developing Asian countries have the highest total entrepreneurial activity rates. Paradoxically, many of the most and least entrepreneurial countries are located in Asia where they often share the same cultural background (Reynolds et. al., 2002).

The 2002 GEM report also indicates the changes in the percentile of the growth of gross domestic products over a three year period. Sweden's percentile of growth in gross domestic products for 1999 was 4.51%, in 2000, 3.61%, and in 2001, 1.21%. The change from the previous year for Sweden was .90% from 1999 to 2000, and 2.40% from 2000 to 2001. Sweden's total entrepreneurial activity for 2001 was 6.68%, and for 2002, 4.00%. China's statistics were not located on the 2002 GEM report.

The GEM report also indicated a constantly negative relationship between the quality of the infrastructure and the level of necessity entreprenuership, as well as the lack of relationship between framework conditions (Reynolds et. al., 2002). Necessity entreprenuership was most prevalent in developing nations such as Thailand, India and China, where financial support, education, training, and infrastructure are clearly absent (Reynolds et. al., 2002). Entreprenuership-enhancing programs and policies implemented in a number of developed countries, principally in the European Union, have only resulted in modest levels of necessity entreprenuership (Reynolds et. al., 2002). This research indicates that there is substantial uniformity across the GEM countries with regard to the concepts, language, and judgments utilized. Additionally, it supports the notion that this uniformity is especially prominent among the more developed nations and may have evolved very similar infrastructures in support of entrepreneurial activity.

Most new firms receive their initial financial support from informal investments made by family, friends, and associates. An extremely small proportion of the most promising firms receive funding from venture capital firms, which are a specialized form of formal investment. Informal flows were estimated in the 2002 GEM report by means of asking all those in the adult population surveys if they had made an investment in a new firm, not their own, the past three years. The 2002 GEM report indicates the amount of venture capital invested as a percent of gross domestic product for each of the countries on the report. Nations that enjoyed year-to-year increases included Sweden, with a 101 percent increase. A large portion of all businesses are owned and managed by families or groups of relatives. Sweden was one of the 10 countries in which family owned businesses were started with family sponsored entreprenuership. In Sweden, the low estimate of family sponsored entrepreneurships was 26%, with the high estimate being 52%. Again, China was not included in these statistics.

Conclusion

Finally, researchers' Ralston, Gustafson, Cheung and Terpstra (1993) analyzed and interpreted the results of a study based on the convergence and divergence of managerial values in the United States, Hong Kong and the People's Republic of China. Although this study did not include Sweden, the results of the study are consistent with a review of the literature used for this paper. The study, which utilized four Western-developed measures, found that both culture and the business environment interact together to create a unique set of managerial values in a country. The goal of the study was twofold: to help understand convergence or divergence of managerial values, and to investigate similarities and differences of managerial values in the study countries.

The study examined the contrasting themes of convergence and divergence. The convergence approach proposes that managers in industrialized nations would embrace the attitudes and behaviors common to managers in other industrialized nations despite the numerous cultural differences. The divergence view proposes that individuals would retain diverse, culturally based values despite any economic and social similarities between their nations. The countries were chosen based on criteria defined in a previous study. The United States represented a capitalist business environment at the height of technological development. On the other extreme, the People's Republic of China represented a socialist legal and political system with communist origins. Serving as a link between these two extremes, was Hong Kong, with a well-developed financial system at the forefront of world commerce.

It was hypothesized that convergence would be found if the Hong Kong managers adopted Western values, and divergence would be found if they maintained Eastern values. It was hypothesized that the U.S. and the People's Republic of China would be polarized on the variables in the study. The results of the data supported the theory that there were significant differences between managers in the U.S. and People's Republic of China. The data provided little support for the convergence hypothesis, and some support for the divergence hypothesis. The majority of the findings for measures developed with both Eastern and Western constructs supported the cross-vergence view.

The data of the study summarizes the prevailing view found in the examination of the entrepreneurial leadership styles of Sweden and China. As a result, it appears that values must be viewed individually and not together as an entity. It has been determined that some values may change while others do not, some may change more rapidly, and that other values may evolve from a combination of influences. The results of the Ralston et. al.. (1993) study were similar to those of a previous study, which taken together, theorize the possibility of a concurrent convergence, divergence and cross-vergence which depend on the values measured and the countries studied. It was also concluded that different national cultures would contribute to the unique behaviors of managers in the different industrialized nations.

A review of the literature on the entrepreneurial leadership styles in Sweden and China leave open a few important aspects that would assist in the interpretation and performance of future studies. One important possibility raised is that it would be necessary to recognize that values may differ between groups within a nation. The implications for future research that this raises is that different values in the same nation may need to be looked at from different angles not previously thought of. For example, comparable elements such as the differences between male and female managers in the same nation, or the differences in managerial styles between the present managers and the next generation of managers could be examined. Other cultural differences could be taken into consideration, such as social class or environmental influences of the countries studied. The political scene of the country, liberal or conservative are also additional factors that can be taken into consideration.

Finally, the results of the examination of the entrepreneurial leadership styles in Sweden and China have offered support for previous research and other studies. It is highly likely that the differences in entrepreneurial leadership in these countries have contributed to their respective successes and failures. Future research using different value sets is likely to be the final deciding factor in interpreting this important research question, the results of which have many implications in forecasting, globalization, and the international economy.

Bibliography

Adams, J.S. (1965). Inequity in Social Exchange. Advances in Experimental Social Psychology. pp. 267–299.

Adler, P. & S. Kwon. (2002). Social capital: Prospects for a new concept. Acad. Management Rev. 27(1) 17–60.

Advantage Sweden. (2005). A Programme for the Future of Companies and Jobs. Retrieved June 2, 2005 from http://sn.svensktnaringsliv.se/sn/publi.nsf/Publikationerview/F22E8690AC0776EAC1256FEF002E2C41/$File/PUB200504-015.pdf.

Asel, P. (2003). International Entreprenuership Course Description. Retrieved June 6, 2005 from http://icp.gmu.edu/course/syllabi/03fa/ITRN769–001.pdf.

Batjargal & Liu. (2004). The Role of Social Capital. Organization Science 15(2), pp. 159–172.

Baumol, W. (1993). Entreprenuership, Management, and the Structure of Payoffs. Cambridge: Massachusetts Institute of Technology.

Baumol, W. (1993). Formal Entrepreneurial Theory in Economic: Existence and Bounds. Journal of Business Venturing, 8, 197–210.

Bass, B.M. (1985). Leadership and Performance Beyond Expectations. New York: Free Press.

Bass, B.M. (1996). A new paradigm of leadership: An inquiry into transformational leadership. Alexandria: U.S. Army Research Institute for the Behavioral and Social Sciences.

Bass, B.M. & Avolio, B.J. (1989). Potential biases in leadership measures: how prototypes, leniency and general satisfaction relate to ratings and rankings of transformational and transactional leadership constructs. Educational and Psychological Measurement, 49, 509–527.

Bian, Y. (1997). Bringing strong ties back in: Indirect ties, networkbridges, and job searches in China. Amer. Sociological Rev. 62, 366–385.

Bruton, G. & D. Ahlstrom. (2003). An institutional view of China's venture capital industry. J. Bus. Venturing 18(2) 233–259.

Coates, L. (2004). Is China Headed for a Crash? Retrieved June 6, 2005 from http://appli1.oecd.org/olis/2001doc.nsf/linkto/eco-wkp(2001)39/$FILE/JT00118568.pdf.

Coleman, J. (1988). Social capital in the creation of human capital. Amer. J. Sociology 94 S95–S120.

Dorfman, R. (1991). Economic Development from Beginning to Rostow. Journal of Economic Literature, 29, 573–591.

Dorfman, P.W., Howell, J.P., Hibino, S., Lee, J.K., Tate, U. & Bautista, A. (1997). Leadership in Western and Asian Countries: Commonalties and Differences in Effective Leadership Processes across Cultures. Leadership Quarterly, 8(3), 233–274.

Drucker, P. (1985). Innovation and Entreprenuership. New York: Harper & Row.

Erskine, A. (2003). Critical Factors in Successful R &D: An International Comparison. Retrieved June 7, 2005 from http://www.ausicom.com/uploads/03_0401_ersk.doc.

Foti, R.J. & Luch, C.H. (1992). The influence of individual differences on the perception and categorization of leaders. Leadership Quarterly, 3, 55–66.

Gerstner, C.R. & Day, D.V. (1994). Cross-cultural comparison of leadership prototypes. Leadership Quarterly, 5, 121–134.

Hall, B. (2002). The Financing or Research and Development. Retrieved June 5, 2005 from http://www.nber.org/papers/w8773.

Hartog, D., House, R., Hanges, P. Dorfman, P., Ruiz-Quintanilla, A. (1999). Emics and Etics of Culturally Endorsed Implicit Leadership Theories: Are Attributes of Charismatic/Transformational Leadership Universally Endorsed? Retrieved June 3, 2005 from http://jonescenter.wharton.upenn.edu/papers/1999/wp99-02.pdf.

Henrekson, M. (2005). Entrepreneurial and Business Conditions in Sweden: Implications for Employment. Retrieved June 11, 2005 from http://www.usemb.se/Publications/jobcreation/henreks.htm.

Hofstede, G (1980). Culture's consequences: International differences in work-related values. Beverly Hills,CA: Sage Publications Inc.

Hofstede G. (1993). Cultural constraints in management theories. Academy of Management Executive, 7(1), 81–94.

House, R. J., Wright, N. S. & Aditya, R. N. (1997). Cross-Cultural Research on Organizational Leadership. A Critical Analysis and a Proposed Theory. In P. C. Earley & M. Erez (eds.), New Perspectives in International Industrial/Organizational Psychology. San Francisco: The New Lexington Press.

Holmberg, I. & Akerblom, S. (2003). The Production of Outstanding Leadership—An Analysis of Leadership Images Expressed in Swedish Media. Retrieved June 7, 2005 from http://www.hhs.se/NR/rdonlyres/9F54A323-4BD3-4BE9-B4F4-2C72CF1DC3A7/0/production_of_leadership.pdf.

Hunt, J.G. (1991). Leadership: A new synthesis. Newbury park, CA: Sage.

Hwang, K. (1987). Face and favor: The Chinese power game. Amer. J. Sociology 92(4) 944–974.

Kaplan, S., P. Stromberg. (2001). Venture capitalists as principals: Contracting, screening and monitoring. Amer. Econom. Rev. PapersProc. 91(2) 426–430.

Katz, D. (1958). The Motivational Basis of Organizational Behavior. Behavioral Science, 9, pp. 131–146.

Kirchoff, B. (1994). Entreprenuership and Dynamic Capitalism: The Economics of Business Firm Formation and Growth. Westport: Praeger Publishers.

Kotelnikov, V. (2005). Ten3 BUSINESS e-COACH—New Wonder of the World. Retrieved June 1, 2005 from http://www.1000ventures.com/business_guide/crosscuttings/leadership_entrepreneurial.html—56k –

Lipton, M. & Ravallion, M. (1995). Poverty and Policy. Amsterdam: North Holland.

Lord, R. & Maher, K. (1991). Leadership and Information Processing: Linking Perceptions and Performance. Boston: Unwin-Everyman.

Malik, R. (1997). Chinese Entrepreneurs in the Economic Development of China. Praeger, London, U.K.

Mamede, R. & Davidsson, P. (2003). Entreprenuership and Economic Development—How can entrepreneurial development lead to wealth distribution? Retrieved June 27, 2005 from http://aplicaciones.icesi.edu.co/ciela/anteriores/Paper/pmed

March, J.G. & Simon, H.A. (1958). Organizations. John Wiley: New York.

Meindl, J. R. (1990). On Leadership: An alternative to the conventional wisdom. Research in Organizational Behavior, 12, pp. 159–203.

Mitchell, T.R. (1979). Organizational Behavior. Annual Review of Psychology, 30, pp. 243–281.

Ralston, D.A., Gustafson, D.J., Cheung, F.M. & Terpstra, R.H. (1993). Differences in Managerial Values: A Study of U.S., Hong Kong and PRC Managers. Journal of International Business Studies, 24, 249–276.

Reynolds, P., Bygrave, W., Autio, E., Cox, L., Hay, M. (2002). Global Entrepreneurship Monitor, 2002 Executive Report. Retrieved June 8, 2005 from http://www.tuta.hut.fi/units/Isib/research/gem/GEM_REPORT_2002_

Saemundsson, R. & Kirchoff, B. (2002). Economic Development, Technological Innovation and Entreprenuership. Goteborg: Chalmers University of Technology.

Shamir, B. (1993) Toward the integration of transformational, charismatic and visionary theories. In: M.M. Chemers & R. Ayman (Eds.), Leadership theory and research: perspectives and directions, 81–107.

Shamir, B., Arthur, M.B. & House, R.J. (1994). The rhetoric of charismatic leadership: a theoretical extension, a case study and implications for research. Leadership Quarterly,5(1), 25–42.

Slaughter, M. (1996). Entreprenuership: Economic Impact and Public Policy Implications: an overview of the field. Kansas City: Kauffman Center.

Stern, S., Porter, M., Furman, J. (2000). The Determinants of National Innovative Capacity. Retrieved June 4, 2005 from http://www.nber.org/papers/w7876.

Timmons, J. (1994). Opportunity Recognition: The Search for Higher Potential Ventures. New York: Wiley and Sons.

Todaro, M. & Smith, S. (2003). Economic Development. Harl Education Limited.

Tracy, B. (2003). Get Smart! Management Success Newsletter. November 2003.

World Bank. (2001). Attacking Poverty. World Development Report. New York: Oxford University Press.

World Bank. (1993). The East Asian Miracle: economic growth and public policy. World Bank Policy Report. New York: Oxford University Press.

Yu, T. (1997). Entreprenuership and Economic Development in Hong Kong. London: Routledge.

Yusuf, S. & Evenett, S. (2002). Can East Asia Compete? Innovation for Global Markets. World Bank Report, September 2002.

Paris on the Mekong: Using the Aid Effectiveness Agenda to Support Human Resources for Health in the Lao People's Democratic Republic

Rebecca Dodd, Peter S. Hill, Dean Shuey and
Adélio Fernandes Antunes

ABSTRACT

Background

This study examines the potential of aid effectiveness to positively influence human resources for health in developing countries, based on research carried out in the Lao People's Democratic Republic (Lao PDR). Efforts to make aid more effective—as articulated in the 2005 Paris Declaration and recently re-iterated in the 2008 Accra Agenda for Action—are becoming an increasingly prominent part of the development agenda. A common criticism, though, is that these discussions have limited impact at sector level. Human resources for health are characterized by a rich and complex network of interactions and influences—both across government and the donor community. This complexity provides a good prism through which to assess the potential of the aid effectiveness agenda to support health development and, conversely, possibilities to extend the impact of aid-effectiveness approaches to sector level.

Methods

The research adopted a case study approach using mixed research methods. It draws on a quantitative analysis of human resources for health in the Lao People's Democratic Republic, supplementing this with a documentary and policy analysis. Qualitative methods, including key informant interviews and observation, were also used.

Results

The research revealed a number pathways through which aid effectiveness is promoting an integrated, holistic response to a range of human resources for health challenges, and has identified further opportunities for stronger linkages. The pathways include: (1) efforts to improve governance and accountability, which are often central to the aid effectiveness agenda, and can be used as an entry point for reforming workforce planning and regulation; (2) financial management reforms, typically linked to provision of budget support, that open the way for greater transparency and better management of health monies and, ultimately, higher salaries and revenues for health facilities; (3) commitments to harmonization that can be used to improve coherence of donor support in areas such as salary supplementation, training and health information management.

Conclusion

If these opportunities are to be fully exploited, a number of constraints will need to be overcome: limited awareness of the aid effectiveness agenda beyond a core group in government; a perception that this is a donor-led agenda; and different views among partners as to the optimal pace of aid management reforms. In conclusion, we recommend strategic engagement of health stakeholders in the aid effectiveness agenda as one means of strengthening the health workforce.

Background

Human resources for health (HRH) are characterized by a rich and complex network of interactions and influences—both across government and the donor community. Workforce planning and recruitment are influenced by public administration systems; salary rates and conditions for health workers intersect with those of the broader civil service; and pre-service vocational training, in-service training and continuing professional development engage stakeholders not only in education, but also in trade and foreign policy. At a higher level, whole-of-government agendas such as poverty reduction, decentralization and privatization also influence the profile, regulation and deployment of the health workforce. This complexity provides a good prism through which to assess the potential of the aid effectiveness agenda to support HRH development. This in turn gives us an insight into the dynamics of the development process and opportunities for aid management reform.

The Paris Declaration on Aid Effectiveness [1] has been endorsed by more than 100 developing and developed countries as well as by key multilateral agencies, the international finance institutions and civil society organizations. It sets out principles to guide donor support built around the three pillars of the aid effectiveness agenda: harmonization and simplification of donor policies and procedures; alignment behind national priorities and use of country systems; and a focus on results as measured in improved development outcomes. Support for the Paris Declaration was recently reiterated at the Third High-Level Forum on Aid Effectiveness, a meeting of development partners and developing countries held in September 2008, though stakeholders also noted a range of challenges to its implementation. Among these were the need to broaden the range of actors in government involved in aid effectiveness processes and to intensify efforts to apply aid effectiveness approaches at sector level [2].

This study examines the potential of aid effectiveness to positively influence HRH in developing countries, based on research carried out in the Lao People's Democratic Republic (hereafter the Lao PDR). The capital of Lao PDR is Vientiane. On the banks of the Mekong River, with its broad boulevards and distinct French colonial heritage, it gives its name to a localized version of the Paris Declaration: the Vientiane Declaration, signed in September 2006 by 23 partner countries and organizations providing aid to the Lao PDR.

According to the Organisation for Economic Co-operation and Development (OECD), donors committed USD 36.7 million to health in the Lao PDR in 2005, and USD 20.8 million in 2006 (Table 1). These figures are in line with those published by the Government of the Lao PDR, which recorded disbursements of USD 36.6 million to health in financial year 2005–2006 [3]. OECD lists 173 separate health or population "activities" (in OECD terminology) for Lao covering the period 2001–2006, with a median value of USD 0.23 million. In general, an "activity" signifies allocation of funds to a specific project or programme. However, donors sometimes choose to report at a more detailed level, in which case a "reported activity" may represent a component of a project. But there are also cases where activities are aggregated, so a single "reported activity" can be the sum of several activities.

Table 1. Health aid commitments to the Lao PDR (USD, millions)

	2001	2002	2003	2004	2005	2006	Total
Australia	13.67	0.19	0.08	1.53	0.59	0.19	16.25
Belgium	0.84	0.77	0.77	0.43	1.18	1.43	5.42
Canada		4.31		0.50		0.04	4.85
France	0.35	0.59	1.25	1.49	1.46	1.90	7.04
Germany		1.27			0.50	0.57	2.34
Ireland						0.11	0.11
Italy				0.04			0.04
Japan		2.66	5.31	9.82	5.42	10.10	33.31
Luxembourg	0.48		9.17	4.19	3.58	2.20	19.63
New Zealand				0.01		0.48	0.49
Norway		0.10		0.06	0.05		0.21
Sweden	1.92				0.00	1.08	3.00
United Kingdom				0.56			0.56
United States		2.03	2.11	0.68	0.00		4.82
EC	2.23		0.97				3.20
GFATM			19.67		7.48		27.15
IDA					15.00	1.13	16.13
UNAIDS	0.23	0.24	0.17		0.28		0.93
UNFPA	2.48	2.28	1.47				6.22
UNICEF	1.20	0.94	0.79	0.97	1.10	1.52	6.52
Total	23.40	15.39	41.76	20.26	36.65	20.77	158.23

Source: Creditor Reporter System, OECD/DAC

The largest entry for this period was a USD 15.9 million grant from the Global Fund to Fight Aids, Tuberculosis and Malaria (GFATM) for infectious disease control, but the majority were for much smaller amounts, with 134 of the 173 activities having a value of less than USD 1 million dollars. This suggests a high degree of fragmentation in donor support, and quite high transaction costs for government in managing many separate activities. Activities are classified broadly—for example, as "basic health care" or "reproductive health care," thus it is not possible to disaggregate specific amounts spent on human resources for health.

This level of donor support is low in comparison to many other low-income countries [4], but it is still three times higher than government spending. Per capita health expenditure was estimated at USD 22 per capita in 2006, of which 75% comes from households [5]; of public expenditure, between 70% and 75% is financed by donors, the remainder by government [6]. Further, the landscape of health donors is complicated: Japan, Luxembourg and the GFATM are the major contributors, but there are 12 other bilateral donors active in health as well as the European Commission, World Bank, Asian Development Bank and various United Nations agencies. This points both to the importance and influence of external support in the sector and to the synergies offered by the aid effectiveness agenda in making optimal use of limited resources.

Methods

This research adopted a case study approach using mixed research methods. It drew on a quantitative analysis of HRH in the Lao PDR undertaken by the World Health Organization (WHO) and the Ministry of Health (MOH) [7], supplementing this with a documentary and policy analysis, examination of the academic literature, government and donor agency policy, reports and publications, unpublished research and reviews. Qualitative methods, including key informant interviews and observation, focused on the potential linkages between HRH and the aid effectiveness agenda.

A total of 23 key-informant interviews were conducted. Stratified selection was used to ensure a balance of informants across ministries of health and finance, the Public Administration and Civil Service Authority (PACSA) and development partners. All major partners active in health and human resources development were interviewed: the Asian Development Bank, European Commission, France, Japan, Luxembourg, the Joint United Nations Programme on HIV/AIDS (UNAIDS), the United Nations Development Programme (UNDP), the United Nations Population Fund (UNFPA), the United Nations Children's Programme (UNICEF), WHO and the World Bank, as well as major non-governmental organizations (NGOs). Information on the GFATM activities was collected from its web site, and via those partners active in the Country Coordinating Mechanism, which oversees GFATM activities.

The question guide used during the interviews was developed prior to the field component, and reviewed by colleagues working on HRH in WHO Geneva. Two interviewers (RD and PSH) attended each interview, alternating roles as lead interviewer and note-taker.

Notes from interviews were transcribed within 12 hours and their accuracy and comprehensiveness corroborated by both interviewers. Findings were triangulated across different interviewees, and a preliminary presentation of the key findings made to the WHO country office to test the initial analysis. An internal peer review process within WHO was also carried out.

An Overview of HRH Challenges in the Lao PDR

The workforce analysis undertaken by WHO and the MOH [7] highlights a range of HRH challenges in the Lao PDR. These include inadequate training, low salaries and inadequate non-monetary incentives, all of which have led to a geographical maldistribution of health workers and poor productivity. Skilled professionals are concentrated in the capital and economically better-off regions and there are corresponding gaps at the periphery. This situation is typical of many low-income countries and is not specific to the Lao PDR [8,9].

Table 2 and Fig. 1 show that while the ratio of health workers to population has grown steadily over the last three decades, the most senior category of the profession (mainly physicians) has grown most. Medical-to-nursing ratios fell from 1:9.9 in 1976 to 1:3.7 in 1995, with 2005 figures showing only 1.8 nurses per medical staff (physicians and medical assistants) [7]. Physicians-to-nursing/medical assistants rations also fell over time from 1:54.8 in 1976 to 1:5.4 in 1995, reaching 4.5 nurses/medical-assistants per medical graduate in 2005 [7]. This structure has been purposefully established over time, as a government decision that saw high-level medical education as the preferred solution to inadequate health coverage [10].

Table 2. Evolution of health worker density per 100 000 inhabitants from 1976 to 2005

Professional level	Years of training	1976	1980	1985	1990	1995	2000	2005
Postgraduate/High-level*	<4	0.03	0.05	0.15	0.28	0.34	0.36	0.40
Mid-level*	2 to 3	0.13	0.26	0.65	0.66	0.67	0.69	0.75
Low-level *	<2	1.58	1.56	1.84	1.42	1.18	1.08	1.02
Total		1.74	1.88	2.64	2.36	2.19	2.13	2.17

*Classification reflects that used by Ministry of Health in the Lao PDR
Source: Extracted from, Fernandes Antunes A, Khampasong T, Shuey D, Xayseda S, Vangkonvilay P, Manivong L, Ministry of Health of Lao People's Democratic Republic MOH: Human Resources for Health: Analysis of the situation in Lao PDR. Ministry of Health, Lao People's Democratic Republic: Vientiane; 2007.

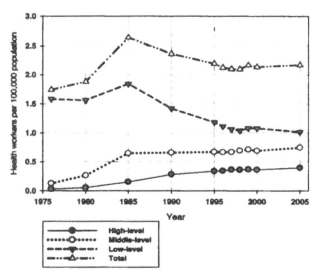

Source: Extracted from, Fernandes Antunes A, Khampasong T, Shuey D, Xaysida S, Vangkonvilay P, Manivong L, Ministry of Health of Lao People's Democratic Republic: Human Resources for Health: Analysis of the situation in Lao PDR. Ministry of Health, Lao People's Democratic Republic: Vientiane; 2007.

Figure 1. Evolution of density for the three main types of health worker (low-, mid- and high-level staff) from 1976 until 2005.

Recent data on intake numbers for medical training and appointment quotas for different cadres at provincial level continue to reflect historical patterns. In 2005, there were 4163 students enrolled in medical training, of whom 28% were "high-level" (and 14% physicians), 63% were "mid-level" (and 41% nurses), and just 8% were "low-level" or primary-care workers. In terms of allocation, in 2005 physicians accounted for 48 of 441 (11%) of health staff allocated across the Lao PDR. There is also a strong bias in favour of the centre in the allocation of new staff, with 39% of new recruits being sent to Vientiane in 2005, including 28 of the 48 newly-qualified doctors. By contrast, most of the senior posts in rural and poor regions remain unfilled, forcing local authorities to rely on low-level staff.

Overall, health workers are disproportionately concentrated in the capital: Vientiane has 3.63 health workers per 1000 inhabitants (Fig. 2). Of the remaining 17 provinces, 15 have a health worker density of less than 2.5 health workers per 1000, and in the more remote, southern provinces density drops to 1.4 per 1000. This distortion is even more pronounced when it comes to high-level and mid-level health service providers (physicians, medical assistants and nurses), with 1.84 such health workers per 1000 in the capital and all other provinces recording rates of less than one health worker per 1000 people [7].

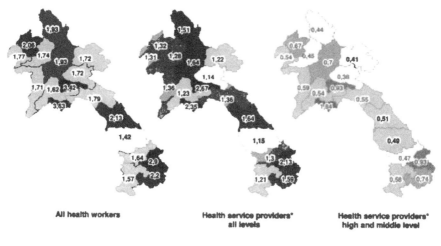

All health workers   **Health service providers***   **Health service providers***
                                        all levels   **high and middle level**

*includes only physicians/doctors, medical assistants and nurses

Source: Extracted from, Fernandes Antunes A, Khampasong T, Bhuey D. Xayaida S, Vangkonvilay P, Manivong L, Ministry of Health of Lao People's Democratic Republic MOH: Human Resources for Health: Analysis of the situation in Lao PDR. Ministry of Health, Lao People's Democratic Republic: Vientiane; 2007.

Figure 2. Maps showing the ratios of the different health worker categories per 1000 inhabitants per province.

Low salaries (discussed further below) are one important reason that health workers have a strong preference for urban areas, where they have opportunities to earn supplementary income from private practice. In the Lao PDR as elsewhere, educational and career-development opportunities, better schools and health care for families attract and retain staff in cities.

Midwifery skills are a conspicuous gap in the health workforce [11]. While nursing graduates are expected to have competence in both nursing and midwifery, graduates typically have very limited clinical obstetric experience, as very few births take place in public facilities. Only 103 midwives and 63 auxiliary midwives currently work in clinical obstetric roles [11]. With maternal mortality in the Lao PDR estimated at 405 per thousand live births [12] and only 19% of deliveries assisted by skilled birth personnel, establishing a cadre of health workers with midwifery skills is a recognized priority for government and donors alike. The low skills of nursing graduates also points to the broader issue of inadequate standards in training, which affects all cadres of the workforce.

Results and Discussion

In this section we explore the intersections between HRH and aid effectiveness in the Lao PDR in relation to four specific issues: workforce planning; training; salaries and supplements; and financial management. In each case we present current challenges, map existing examples of how aid effectiveness is being used to address those challenges and discuss opportunities for further action. We argue that one of the most promising aspects of the aid effectiveness agenda is its broad scope and complex network of cross-governmental links, which provides a mechanism for mediating across the web of stakeholders and interest groups that characterize HRH. A number of concerns are also presented.

Workforce Planning

As discussed above, the current workforce profile in the Lao PDR presents challenges in relation to the distribution of health staff and the balance between health cadres—with distortions towards the centre and a relative undersupply of primary care workers: "Many hospitals do not have enough nurses, which creates problems for basic patient care" (said a senior MOH staff member).

The quota system that allocates staff to provinces locks-in the historical dominance of doctors over nurses. Each year provinces and programmes submit a request for new posts, based on exits (deaths, transfers, retirements) and estimated needs. These requests are compiled by the Ministry of Health and then forwarded to the PACSA for consideration. Informants suggest that because requests from the provinces are so disproportionate to supply and because PACSA does not have the necessary technical perspective to discriminate between competing staffing needs in an environment of resource constraints, historical patterns tend to be maintained. According to a staff member of a multilateral agency: "PACSA does not have an overview of staffing allocation or technical awareness... but it is open to more rational case presentations."

Two aid effectiveness initiatives are affecting this challenge. First, within the health sector, structures for dialogue have been established that allow a shared analysis of inefficiencies in the quota system. Based on two important reports on the health workforce—by WHO and the MOH in June 2007 and by UNFPA in 2008—the Sector Working Group on health is forging a common understanding on this issue between donors and with government. The Sector Working Group is chaired by the MOH and co-chaired by WHO and Japan. It meets twice a year at ministerial and ambassadorial level to discuss overall policy directions in the sector, and four times a year at the operational level (deputy-directors of MOH departments and health advisers from the development partners) to focus on operational coordination. Three subgroups have also been established: on financing, human resources and maternal and child health.

Second, looking across sectors, efforts to strengthen capacity for planning are being implemented under the auspices of the Vientiane Declaration Action Plan.

Capacity development frameworks have been developed for key sectors (transport, education and health) and in relation to cross-cutting issues (aid effectiveness and emergency preparedness). These will build managerial skills—e.g. for planning and budgeting—within the central government and in selected line ministries. Of specific relevance to health workforce planning is the development of a database on human resources management by PACSA, with United Nations support. This database was in turn adapted by the Ministry of Health, and used to register all health workers in five provinces, providing information on workforce capacities and gaps to be used in planning.

This combination of sectoral and cross-sectoral aid effectiveness initiatives establishes the necessary structures and capacities to strengthen planning and governance functions in the ministry of health and in central government, and opens the door to reform the quota system. This in turn paves the way for a more rational, integrated and needs-based approach to workforce planning in health.

Training

Challenges in relation to training of the health workforce include the lack of intersection between pre-service vocational and in-service training, poor coordination between partners providing support for training, and the need to increase the level of clinical experience offered to medical students.

One of the central findings of the research, triangulated across a range of respondents, is that donor support for both pre-service and in-service training has been non-harmonized and supply-led, with government reluctant to take a lead role in coordination. For example, the lack of coordination between partners supporting specialist training is such that they cannot agree what language should be used to deliver classes. Offers of support often come directly from developed-country hospitals direct to the MOH, and remain ad hoc rather than integrated into a comprehensive system of postgraduate training. Coordination of in-service and short training between vertical programmes is [also] an issue. We would like these to be integrated, but don't know how," said a senior MOH staff member.

Poor coordination in support for training has been exacerbated by a stop-start approach to training of new cadres: training for medical assistants was supported, then discontinued and may yet start again; training for midwives has followed the same pattern [11]. Primary Health Care workers were created as a low-level cadre, but are now being upgraded to medical assistants [7]. Donors were often involved in the decision to make changes in cadres, although government took the final decision.

With its emphasis on harmonization, the aid effectiveness agenda has catalysed a number of initiatives to address the coordination challenge. First, a strategic plan on HRH development is in the making, which will provide a framework behind which donors can in future align their support. Second, some partners are already aligning their support for primary health care training with the MOH's Healthy Villages scheme. Third, France is leading an effort to coordinate offers of support to medical specialist training. Key to the success of these initiatives will be the close and continued involvement of government.

On curriculum revision, the Sector Working Group subgroup on HRH provides a mechanism to address the relative neglect of training for nursing, midwifery and allied professions and to provide a greater emphasis on clinical experience. "In practice, training is theoretical, not competence-based," commented one bilateral partner. The lack of good practical training sites is a key issue in this regard. The research revealed a common concern among development partners supporting the sector on these points and a shared view that the HRH subgroup was the best forum for formulating a response. Upgrading the capacity of health workers appears as the third strategic programme area in the health chapter of the Lao PDR's Sixth Socio Economic Development Plan [15], providing a further impetus for donors to take a more coherent approach to this issue.

Simultaneously, the ASEAN Free Trade Agreement (AFTA) is driving a review of health training curricula. Health partners and government could use this review as an entry point to pursue reforms, including improving clinical competences. Under AFTA, free movement of nurses is allowable once national training curricula meet certain quality criteria. A process to determine equivalence among doctors is under negotiation, which is also driving reform of their curriculum. This reframes health professional training in terms of regional development and provides a political impetus, beyond the MOH, to raise curriculum standards. But there are also concerns. MOH interviewees are worried that the public system will suffer a brain drain of health professionals if foreign-managed facilities are established, as AFTA allows.

This points to the need for coherence across different aspects of development policy: an area where the aid effectiveness agenda has the potential to deliver, but has yet to do so. Though the drivers of AFTA are primarily economic, the agreement has clear implications for health worker development, not only in the Lao PDR but also across South-East Asia. Development partners interested in setting comparable quality standards across the region will need to ensure coherence between their support for economic development (including trade liberalization) and support for health. By taking a holistic view of the development agenda, aid effectiveness discussions provide a forum where this synergy could be achieved.

Salaries and Supplements

There is universal agreement among development partners in the Lao PDR that the salaries of health workers are unacceptably low, reported by MOH to be just USD 50 per month in remote areas. Low salaries translate into low productivity, with patient contacts in the Lao PDR standing at roughly 7% of international averages [16].

Even so, opportunities for increasing base pay levels are limited. Some 80% of the domestically-financed health budget is already spent on salaries [7], which means that available fiscal space for further increases is very limited. Moreover, increasing salaries for health workers independently from other civil service staff was regarded by informants as inappropriate: "We need a national solution—not one just for MOH," suggests one donor partner. The Ministry of Finance's view is that low salaries are not the most pressing problem facing the sector: "Is the problem really salaries, or the system as a whole? I'm not convinced that raising salaries will improve health. The whole system needs reform." Given these views and the fact that a 20% increase in civil service pay was awarded in October 2007, further government-funded increases in health worker pay are unlikely in the near future.

This begs the question: Could salary increases be funded by donors? Most donor support for health is classified as capital expenditure in the national budget (see Table 3), but in practice much of this is spent on things that would normally be classified as recurrent costs, such as salary supplements. However, the potential to fund base salary increases through donor support appears to be limited. The authors encountered a resistance to this idea within the Ministry of Finance: "Paying salaries is the business of government," said one senior staff member.

Further, donors argue that government needs to first demonstrate its commitment to increasing salaries. As overall government spending on health appears to be decreasing—dropping from 6.4% to 3.2% of the total budget between 2004–2005 and 2005–2006 [17], the chances of this are not high. Projected revenues from a planned hydroelectric scheme are one promising source of funds for salary increases [18]—the Nam Theun 2 dam should generate USD 20 billion over its lifetime. While there is a commitment to spending a good share of this revenue on the social sectors, the exact amounts and modalities are not yet clear.

Table 3. Total public and public health expenditure, 2002–2005 (as % of GDP)

	2002	2003	2004	2005
Total expenditure (including debt)	19.6	19.5	15.7	19.9
Health expenditure as % of total public	0.98	1.13	0.68	1.14
• Domestic expenditure	0.49	0.34	0.28	0.31
• Foreign financed	0.49	0.79	0.4	0.83
Structure of expenditure				
• Capital expenditure, in total	0.65	0.9	0.43	0.87
• Domestically financed	0.16	0.1	0.04	0.04
• Foreign financed	0.49	0.79	0.4	0.83
• Recurrent expenditure, total	0.33	0.23	0.25	0.27
• Salaries/Wages	0.21	0.16	0.19	0.17
• Operations and Maintenance	0.11	0.07	0.06	0.1

Through its focus on human development, poverty reduction and the MDGs the Vientiane Declaration provides donors with the mandate needed to advocate pay increases in the social sector. The opening statement of the Vientiane Declaration is as follows:

> *We, the Government of the Lao People's Democratic Republic and the Partners in Development, seek to take appropriate monitorable actions to make aid more effective and assist the country in achieving the Millennium Development Goals (MDGs) by 2015 and the long-term development goal of exiting the status of least-developed country by 2020.*

The mechanisms of aid effectiveness—coordination groups, etc—provide the means through which this advocacy can be carried out.

A convincing analysis of how new monies could be used to fund pay increases in the health sector is now needed; the MOH and WHO have already done some work in this area [7]. Sector and inter-sector coordination mechanisms could be used to develop common positions, mobilize support and overcome the political obstacles outlined above. A coherent position within donor agencies—between their poverty reduction and health teams—is essential.

In an environment where base salary levels and productivity are low, the indirect incentives and allowances provided by donors to health staff implementing their projects become very important. These include travel and meeting allowances, access to transport and computers, and so on. Interviewees report that there is no standardization of incentives between partners or with the MOH, with some partners paying supplements that are much higher than others. Further, the payment of travel allowances is creating perverse incentives in terms of service delivery. Lack of transparency on this issue made it difficult for the research team to gather firm evidence, but anecdotal reports suggest that problems are significant: "Nurses working in HIV wards earn USD 100 a month more than general nurses, working in the adjacent ward." "Staff prefer to do outreach rather than facility-based immunization in order to get the overnight per diem," reports United Nations staff. In some cases, supplementation practices ran counter to donor policy, but were pursued nonetheless.

The Sector Working Group is trying to tackle this issue, but progress is slow. An attempt to standardize rates across the United Nations and some partners fell apart when others failed to join. There are also differing views within the Group on how proactive donors should be in pushing this issue with government. "Every sector needs to find its own way—not necessarily follow other countries," said one bilateral partner, adding that, according to the principle of ownership, partners should be more patient in waiting for government to take the lead in coordination. Others disagree, feeling that a more open and candid dialogue is needed within the Group: "Difficult issues simply aren't discussed," said one multilateral partner.

Still others feel that, given the incentives associated with current ways of doing business, government is unlikely to initiate change: "The direct project allowances of top managers in the MOH and their income from indirect revenues such as per diems creates a strong incentive to maintain the status quo" said a United Nations informant.

This tension—of differing expectations and approaches within the donor community—is an emerging theme in reports monitoring the implementation of the Paris Declaration, and is thus not unique to the Lao PDR [19].

Financial Management

Budget support is the process by which donors deliver their financial assistance directly into the government budget and it is mixed with domestic revenues [20]. It is seen by some as one of the more effective forms of aid because it avoids many of the costs and inefficiencies associated with multiple projects, it is easier to align with recipient priorities and it opens the way to a broader, strategic dialogue on economy-wide issues [21]. The counter argument is that if accountability and governance are poor—as they often are in developing countries—resources may well be misspent.

Whatever its pros and cons, budget support has become increasingly associated with effective aid [22]. In the Lao PDR as in many other countries, budget support is linked to efforts to improve the public financial management systems through which money is channelled. This, in turn, can have a positive impact on the health sector and HRH, as discussed below.

Currently, budget support in the Lao PDR is delivered through the World Bank's Poverty Reduction Support Operation (PRSO), which is financed by the World Bank, the European Commission and Japan. In 2008, the PRSO was worth USD 20 million, equivalent to just under 10% of the overall government budget. The European Commission also links additional support of EUR 1 million per annum, 2009–2011, to progress towards certain conditions related to the PRSO, including finalization of a health sector financing strategy. While details of this strategy are not yet defined, it is expected to improve planning, management and monitoring of health resources through links to a Medium Term Expenditure Framework that would provide a common planning and monitoring framework for government and donor resources.

A second example of how aid effectiveness reforms positively influence financial planning in health is a proposed new budget law, supported by World Bank as part of public financial management reform, which would ensure that central government received a share of the revenues collected at provincial level. The bulk of domestic revenues is currently raised and spent at provincial level [23]. This means that each province's capacity to provide health services is contingent on its own revenue-raising potential, and that the centre has very little leverage to regulate. This, combined with the financial and administrative autonomy of facilities, has created a situation in which fees charged by health providers differ from province to province and there is no standardized approach to regulation of private practitioners. The public financial management reforms associated with budget support have the potential to strengthen the centre, and in so doing to improve opportunities for regulation.

Despite these synergies, the authors encountered limited knowledge and commitment to aid effectiveness beyond "upstream" ministries such as planning and finance. The agenda has yet to engage line ministries such as health, lower levels of government, or nongovernmental partners. Further, there is a widely-held view that the Vientiane Declaration is a donor product that does not yet have the full support of government. "The Vientiane Declaration has been pushed primarily by donors," said one United Nations staff member. (Literature on Sector Wide Approaches notes that partners, not government, are often at the forefront of coordination efforts [13,14].)

Respondents offered a range of likely reasons for this. First, the potential of aid effectiveness to deliver improvements in development outcomes is not always immediately apparent. "The current debate is too broad and superficial," said one bilateral partner. Second, the transaction costs associated with coordination are often high—as demonstrated by difficulties encountered by the Sector Working Group in standardizing incentives and allowances. "The benefits for the MOH are unclear," said a United Nations staff member. Third, there are substantial incentives associated with current ways of delivering aid that are difficult to overcome.

Conclusion

In this article we have focused on what aid effectiveness can do for HRH, demonstrating how this policy instrument is promoting an integrated, holistic response to a range of complex challenges. Some of these challenges are themselves the result of ineffective donor behaviour. Others are rooted in the multisectoral nature of HRH issues. In both cases, the aid effectiveness agenda offers solutions. Examples from the Lao PDR that may provide lessons for other countries include the following.

- Efforts to improve governance and accountability, which are often central to the aid effectiveness agenda, can be used as an entry point for reforming workforce planning and regulation.
- Financial management reforms, typically linked to provision of budget support, open the way for greater transparency and better management of health monies, which in turn have the potential to deliver more resources to the health sector.
- Aid effectiveness' emphasis on harmonization can be used to improve coherence of donor support in areas such as salary supplementation and training.
- The expressed desire for alignment with government policy provides an incentive for the government to develop policies—include HRH plans—that donors can support.

But the pathways of influence are neither simple nor direct. This review has highlighted the difficulties that emerge when aid effectiveness approaches are applied to a specific component of the health system—human resources for health. Two issues emerge, which are also reflected in the global literature. The first is that while aid effectiveness has a conceptual and rhetorical appeal, when operational details are added the consensus may break down, particularly if the status quo is challenged or in-country working methods disrupted. The challenge that the Lao PDR has faced in standardizing salary supplements exemplifies that "the devil is in the details."

The second issue is that aid effectiveness principles are most likely to be operationalized when linked to a substantive reform agenda. The links between budget support and public financial management reform provides a tangible illustration. This is also a lesson that emerges from the literature: SWAps are often a driving force behind health sector reform. In the Lao PDR, human resources development could provide such a framework. The research identified multiple points of intervention in the critical pathways for HRH development where the potential contribution of the aid effectiveness agenda is significant.

Lending confidence to this analysis is the early evidence provided that, in some areas, positive synergies are already emerging and aid effectiveness is already contributing to the resolution of more complex, cross-cutting HRH issues that are difficult to solve from a health sector perspective alone. To optimize the yield from this potential, health sector decision-makers will need to actively engage their counterparts working on aid effectiveness and overcome identified challenges. Conversely, these counterparts will need to be open to collaboration at sector level. In our view, this is an effort worth making, with the potential to deliver benefits to both sides.

Competing Interests

The authors declare that they have no competing interests.

Authors' Contributions

RD conceived the project, developed the research design, undertook the key informant interviews, prepared the analysis and drafted the manuscript; PSH assisted with the research design, undertook the key informant interviews, collaborated in the analysis and offered critical comments in the drafting and review of the manuscript; AFA and DS undertook the quantitative human resources analysis that informed the study and offered critical comments in the drafting and review of the manuscript. All authors have read and approved the final manuscript.

Acknowledgements

This research was commissioned by WHO as an input to the Third High-Level Forum on Aid Effectiveness, held in Accra in September 2008.

References

1.   OECD: Paris Declaration on Aid Effectiveness. OECD: Paris; 2005.

2. OECD: Aid Effectiveness: A progress report on implementation of the Paris Declaration. In Third High-Level Forum on Aid Effectiveness 2–4 September 2008. OECD: Accra; 2008.

3. Government of the Lao PDR: Foreign Aid Report 2005–2006. Committee for Planning and Investment, Government of the Lao PDR: Vientiane; 2007:5.

4. OECD/DAC: Effective Aid—Better Health: Report prepared for the Accra High-Level Forum on Aid Effectiveness. OECD/DAC: Paris; 2008.

5. Government of the Lao PDR: [http://www.who.int/nha/country/lao.pdf] Lao People's Democratic Republic—National Expenditure on Health. 2008.

6. WHO: Western Pacific Country Health Information Profiles. World Health Organization, Western Pacific Region: Manila; 2007.

7. Fernandes Antunes A, Khampasong T, Shuey D, Xaysida S, Vangkonvilay P, Manivong L, Ministry of Health of Lao People's Democratic Republic: Human Resources for Health: Analysis of the situation in Lao PDR. Ministry of Health, Lao People's Democratic Republic: Vientiane; 2007.

8. Sergent CF, Johnson TM: Medical Anthropology: Contemporary Theory and Method. Praeger: Westport; 1996.

9. WHO: Working Together for Health: World Health Report 2006. World Health Organization: Geneva; 2006.

10. Phomtavong S, Akkhavong K, Xaisida S: Strengthening the quality of human resources for health oriented toward the district and village levels in Lao PDR. In Asia Sub-Regional Action Learning Network on HRH. Edited by: Boupha B. WHO: Bangkok; 2005.

11. MOH/UNFPA: Assessment of Skilled Birth Attendance in Lao PDR. Ministry of Health and United Nations Population Fund: Vientiane; 2008.

12. National Statistics Centre, 2005 Census [http://www.nsc.gov.la/Population-Census2005.htm]

13. Walt G, Pavignani E, Gilson L, Buse K: Managing external resources in the health sector: are there lessons for SWAps (sector-wide approaches)? Health Policy Plan 1999, 14(3):273–84.

14. Walt G, Pavignani E, Gilson L, Buse K: Health sector development: from aid coordination to resource management. Health Policy Plan 1999, 14(3):207–18.

15. Government of the Lao PDR: Sixth National Socio-Economic Development Plan (2006–2010). Committee for Planning and Investment, Lao People's Democratic Republic: Vientiane; 2006.

16. Dereché C, Bigdeli M, Manivong K, Sanasisane S, Shuey D: Measuring public hospital costs and activities in Lao PDR. Juth Pakai 2005, 1:34–43.

17. World Bank: Lao PDR Economic Monitor, April 2008. World Bank: Vientiane; 2008.

18. World Bank: Quick Facts on NT2. [http:/ / siteresources.worldbank.org/ IN-TLAOPRD/ Resources/ 293582-1092106399982/ 492430-1092106479653/ quick-fact.pdf]

19. OECD: The 2008 Survey on Monitoring the Paris Declaration. OECD: Paris; 2008.

20. OECD: Harmonising Donor Practices for Effective Aid Delivery, in DAC Guidelines and Reference Series. OECD: Paris; 2003.

21. Killick T, Lawson A: Budget Support to Ghana: A risk worth taking? Briefing Paper 24. Overseas Development Institute: London; 2007.

22. Lister S: Evaluation of General Budget Support: Synthesis Report. IDD and Associates: Birmingham; 2006.

23. Stuart-Fox M: Politics and Reform in the Lao People's Democratic Republic, Working Paper No. 126. Asia Research Centre: Perth; 2005.

Strategic Human Resources Management: Aligning with the Mission

U. S. Office of Personnel Management

Executive Summary

Human resources alignment means integrating decisions about people with decisions about the results an organization is trying to obtain. By integrating human resources management (HRM) into the agency planning process, emphasizing human resources (HR) activities that support broad agency mission goals, and building a strong relationship between HR and management, agencies are able to ensure that the management of human resources contributes to mission accomplishment and that managers are held accountable for their HRM decisions. This is especially important in light of the Government Performance and Results Act's (GPRA) push to align all agency activities, including HRM, toward achieving defined agency strategic goals and measuring progress toward those goals.

In fiscal year 1999, the U.S. Office of Personnel Management (OPM) embarked on a special study to determine how much progress Federal agencies have made toward aligning HRM with agency strategic goals in support of HRM accountability and agency mission accomplishment. Our key findings and conclusions are summarized as follows:

- *Many more agencies than expected include HR representatives in the agency planning process and integrate human resources management goals, objectives, and strategies into agency strategic plans. However, most agencies are still struggling in this area. Therefore, agency executives and HR leaders need to work together to fully integrate HRM into the planning process so that it will become a fundamental, contributing factor to agency planning and success.*

- *Although some agency HR offices have begun focusing on organizational activities that assist agency decision-making, most are still emphasizing internal HR office efficiency efforts. While internal issues are important to the success of any HR program, HR offices also need to examine the "big picture" and find ways to impact the success of the agency as a whole.*

- *Most agencies are in some way measuring the efficiency and/or effectiveness of the HR function. These measures, however, are generally output-oriented, focus on internal HR processes and activities, and are used to make improvements to HR-specific policies and procedures. As HR refocuses its activities to broader organizational issues, HRM measures also need to be expanded to gauge the impact HRM has on agency goals and mission. Then, the measurement data can be used to inform agency-level decisions.*

- *The relationship between HR and management is becoming more collaborative. HR executives are beginning to earn a seat at the management table. HR offices are becoming more consultative and involved in day-to-day line management activities. Nevertheless, there is still a long way to go if HR is to become a strategic partner at all levels. To do so, HR needs to build its own internal competencies to deal with organizational issues, educate itself on agency and program missions, and find ways to offer creative and innovative solutions to organizationwide issues.*

Although many National Performance Review (now known as the National Partnership for Reinventing Government) initiatives, such as downsizing, reorganizing, streamlining, and delegating HR authorities, were meant to improve HR's ability to focus on organizational issues, they have not taken hold as quickly or thoroughly as hoped. Therefore, HR is still doing most of the process work, and its ability to focus on alignment has been limited. However, as HR's role in agency planning, activities, and decision-making advances—

and it is advancing—so too will the alignment of human resources management with agency mission accomplishment.

Introduction

What is Alignment?

Strategic human resources management...strategic alignment...alignment with mission accomplishment. These are just a few of the terms being used to describe the new, evolving role of Federal human resources management (HRM). What do these terms really mean? If you were to ask agency personnelists, managers, or employees, you would probably get a wide range of answers. So, it's important to establish from the beginning what we are really talking about.

Human resources management alignment means to integrate decisions about people with decisions about the results an organization is trying to obtain. Our research indicates that agencies that successfully align human resources management with agency mission accomplishment do so by integrating HRM into the agency planning process, emphasizing HR activities that support mission goals, and building strong HR/management relationships.

In addition to being a vital contributor to Hierarchy of Accountabilityagency mission accomplishment, HRM alignment is the ultimate level of HRM accountability, as demonstrated in the Hierarchy of Accountability. While HRM accountability must begin with basic legal compliance, it ultimately encompasses all four levels of the pyramid, including demonstrating how HRM supports achievement of the agency strategic goals.

Why Align?

Why the sudden emphasis on aligning HRM activities with agency mission accomplishment? Basically, it comes down to demonstrating the value of human resources management to the agency. In the past, one of HR's primary roles has been to ensure compliance with laws, rules, and regulations. Although this is still, and will always be, a necessary function, many recent developments have led to a strong emphasis on results.

The National Performance Review (NPR) took on the task of reinventing government to make itwork better, cost less, and get results. NPR mandated many initiatives that changed the focus of HR from just compliance toward results, including downsizing the HR function, delegating HR authorities to line managers, calling for HR to demonstrate its business value, and enhancing customer service.

Through these initiatives, management of human resources would become more responsive to mission-related needs because it would take place at the line level, and the HR staff would be able to expend more of its energy on broader organizational issues.

The Government Performance and Results Act (GPRA) of 1993 has also played a large part in focusing agencies on results. The purpose of GPRA is to improve Federal program effectiveness, accountability, service delivery, decision-making, and internal management, thereby improving confidence in the Federal Government. This is achieved by demonstrating organizational results through strategic planning and performance measures. Although the primary focus of GPRA is on programmatic functions, agencies are also required to describe how administrative resources, such as HR, are being used to achieve strategic goals. Further, the General Accounting Office (GAO) and the Office of Management and Budget (OMB) have evaluated many of these efforts, and are calling for agencies to improve their discussions of HRM alignment in strategic and annual plans. Therefore, the human resources function is increasingly being aligned to the agency strategic plan, which requires HR to show how it is supporting mission accomplishment.

Alignment has already occurred in other key administrative functions. When Congress devel-oped a statutory framework to introduce performance-based management into the Federal Government, it initiated financial, information technology, and procurement reforms through such mandates as the Chief Financial Officer Act and Information Technology Management Reform Act. Human resources management is the administrative missing link to this comprehensive package.

The private sector has recognized that it is not just financial and technological capital that provide companies with the competitive edge, but people, or human capital. Without attracting and retaining the right people, in the right jobs, with the right skills and training, an organization cannot succeed. Therefore, people have been recognized as companies' most important asset. As the Federal Government moves toward a performance-based management approach, we, too, need to realize the importance of our human resources. A huge percentage of agencies' budgets is spent on human resources—salaries, benefits, training, work life programs, etc. Nowhere else do you make that substantial an investment and not measure the return.

Not only do human resources provide the competitive edge, but several recent studies have confirmed that the quality and innovation of HR practices impact business results. These studies were able to draw a correlation between increased quality of HR practices and increased business success. Among other benefits, HR alignment with mission accomplishment increases HR's ability to anticipate its customers' needs, increases the agency's ability to implement strategic business goals, and provides decision-makers with critical resource allocation information.

Finally, HR alignment is a vital process to advance agency accountability. By defining, maintaining, and assessing HRM goals and measures, communicating them throughout the agency, and using the information to make management decisions, agencies are able to ensure that the management of human resources contributes to mission accomplishment and that managers are held accountable for their HRM decisions in support of mission accomplishment.

The Study

Once we defined what alignment means and why it is important, we wanted to find out where agencies currently stand in terms of aligning their human resources management with agency mission accomplishment. Therefore, the Office of Personnel Management (OPM) embarked on a special study designed to explore the following objectives:

- Assess how well human resources management is linked to agency mission accomplishment;

- Explore the role played by the HR staff in agency strategic planning;

- Determine how the HR service providers work with line managers to carry out agency strategic goals; and

- Identify best practices aligning HRM with the agency strategic plan and goals.

In order to obtain information pertaining to these objectives, we did the following:

- Reviewed 31 agency strategic and 28 annual performance plans;

- Conducted an extensive literature and Internet search;

- Gathered information from agency HR professionals, supervisors, and employees at 17 agencies of various size through the fiscal year 1998 and 1999 OPM Oversight reviews and

- Interviewed nine additional leading agency HR Directors.

Strategic Planning

Agencywide Planning

To some agencies, strategic planning is a way of life. To others, it's an exercise. To almost all, it's a requirement. As part of GPRA, agencies, unless specifically exempted, follow a continuous, three step strategic planning process:

Strategic planning allows agencies to map out where they are, where they want to go, and how they plan to get there. Some agencies adopted the idea of strategic planning even before GPRA was enacted, whereas others are just beginning to understand its potential benefits. The results of the fiscal year 1999 Merit System Principles Questionnaire (MSPQ), an OPM Governmentwide survey of supervisors and employees, show that agencies are beginning to embrace not only the concept, but also the practice, of strategic planning.

The strategic planning process varies from agency to agency. On one end of the spectrum are the agencies which have very collaborative processes involving senior management, line supervisors and employees, and stakeholders throughout the entire process. On the other end are the agencies which develop plans at the top management level with little input from the line or stakeholders or that plan functionally, having each program office submit its own goals and strategies with little to no collaboration among offices. The typical strategic planning process is a mixture of these:

The management of agency human resources is an integral part of how an agency is going to achieve its mission goals. Without people, there is no one to do the work. Therefore, integrating HRM into the agency strategic plan is the first step in aligning it with the mission.

Even though GAO and OMB are pushing for improvement of HRM alignment discussions in strategic and annual plans, GPRA's primary focus is still on agency programs, rather than corporate functions. Therefore, we assumed at the beginning of this study that not many agency strategic plans would have addressed HRM's role in mission accomplishment. We were pleasantly surprised. Out of the 31 strategic plans reviewed, 87 percent had addressed HRM in some way. Below is a breakdown of how integration between HRM and the agency plan is achieved, a count of how many strategic plans have integrated HRM in a particular way, and some examples of actual agency approaches.

The table can be somewhat misleading, however. Although some agencies are clearly ahead of the pack, integration of HRM in agency plans is still evolving. When looking at the actual placement of strategic plan HRM discussions, they are generally segregated from the program-matic goals, objectives, and strategies. Considering that an agency's mission cannot be achieved without its people, this is an important point. Could this be an indication that human resources management is not yet recognized as a critical contributor to agency mission accomplishment? In any case, it is clear that though there are some exceptions—as evidenced by some of the examples above—full HRM integration into agency strategic plans has not yet been realized.

The human resources issues addressed in agency plans provide insight into what aspects of human resources management are most important to agency management. In reviewing the plans, or even just by looking at the examples above, it is clear that diversity, recruitment, retention, employee development, and workforce quality are the major areas of interest. Although these could be looked at as process or output programs, when they are designed and implemented well, they lead to the ultimate result: the right people, with the right skills, in the right positions to carry out the agency mission.

Agency HRM Strategic Measures

Defining practical, meaningful measures that assess the effectiveness of agency human resources management and its support of mission accomplishment is a topic that agencies have been struggling with. It is easy to measure a process—how long does it take to complete an action? It is easy to measure productivity—how many actions were completed in any given time frame? But how do you measure the outcome of human resources management? How does an agency know if it has the right people, with the right skills, in the right positions to carry out the agency mission? Have any agencies found a way to do this? To help answer these questions, we looked to see if agencies are including HRM measures in their strategic plans, and what types of measures they have identified.

Not surprisingly, 71 percent of the plans did not identify any HRM measures. Moreover, the meaningfulness and practicality of the 29 percent of agency identified measures could be stronger. About one-third of the 29 percent contain measures that are not really measures. They are lists of activities or projects that, when completed, will help to reach the goal. In other words, they are strategies labeled as measures. The other two-thirds of that 29 percent have fairly good measures that are tied to specific mission or support goals and provide seemingly relevant information. However, even these fairly good measures tend to focus on HR processes (outputs) rather than intended outcomes. For example, some agencies measure the average number of employee training hours to measure workforce skill levels, rather than what skills are actually gained through the training or what skills the workforce actually possesses. See the following chart for some examples of the better HRM measures we saw in agency strategic plans.

HR Involvement in Agency Strategic Planning

Now that we have seen what types of goals, objectives, strategies, measures, and other forms of HRM integration are present in agency strategic plans, we should look briefly at how these were developed. The legitimacy and ultimate value of these pieces of the plan will depend substantially on where they came from.

Historically, members of the HR community have remarked on the difficulty they have had "getting to the table" with top agency management. Rather than being involved in agency planning from the beginning, HR is commonly consulted after decisions have been made in order to help implement any major changes. Considering the invaluable perspective HR has on how decisions will impact agency resources, HR professionals have been frustrated that they are not involved sooner in the planning process.

Therefore, it was surprising when 79 percent of the agencies we talked to indicated that they do play a role in the overall agency strategic planning process. The roles vary from a peripheral consultant who reviews and comments on preliminary products to an integrated team member who actively helps to identify not only HRM agency strategic goals and objectives, but programmatic goals as well. Two or three of the responding agencies fall in the former category, a handful in the latter, and the rest somewhere in between. Later, we will discuss how some HR officials are able to elevate themselves to agency strategic partner, while most are still struggling to achieve this.

When it comes to defining actual HRM goals, strategies, and measures, the roles also vary. In general, agencywide HRM-related goals, strategies, and measures are identified by the agency leader or other senior managers with HR collaboration. They decide what is most important to the agency based on the challenges the agency will face in years to come. Some use a more elaborate collaboration approach that involves agency management, HR officials, and other stakeholders, as is demonstrated in the presented examples from the Department of Commerce's Patent and Trademark Office (PTO) and the Department of Veterans Affairs (VA). Then there are the agencies that use the functional strategic planning approach where the HR office is tasked with coming up with the goals, strategies, and measures itself. In these cases, HR generally uses some type of feedback from customers to identify what is important to the agency and should be included in the plan.

Patent and Trademark Office (PTO): HR's Involvement in Strategic Planning

The PTO's planning process tracks closely with the diagram presented on page 6: the Commissioner identifies the main strategic themes; top management adds to the perspective through offsite retreats; the three business lines develop and rank their specific initiatives; and finally, representatives from all the three business lines come together to rank all of the initiatives and talk about how the budget impacts those initiatives. HR, as well as the other administrative functions, is integrally involved in and present during all aspects of planning—the top management discussions, business line planning, and overall ranking and budgetary discussions. The administrative functions serve several purposes: to inform managers what resources are available to them; to determine what resources managers will need; and to discuss the impact program initiatives will have on the agency.

Department of Veterans Affairs Collaborative Approach

The Department of Veterans Affairs (VA) Office of Human Resources Management was integrally involved in the Department's strategic planning process. Although the program offices were the drivers for the strategic goals, the administrative functions were integrally involved in establishing how resources can be attained, retained, and utilized to support the programs that deliver services to their customer, the veterans. The HR staff worked with program planners and line managers in an iterative and interactive series of meetings that provided HR with information on the Department's current and future business and corresponding human resource needs. The HR staff was able to translate this information into specific objectives with supporting strategies and performance goals that were incorporated into the VA strategic plan.

To further refine its priorities, HR held a conference attended by approximately 300 people representing its key stakeholder groups departmentwide including: HR professionals, political appointees, headquarters executives, field line managers, staff offices, unions, and veterans. A "real time" strategic planning process that included facilitation, formal presentations, and inter-active discussions led to the identification and prioritization of four critical human resources "strategic opportunities" that must be dealt with if VA is to successfully accomplish its mission. Top management at the conference committed to supporting the pursuit of these strategic oppor-tunities, and, subsequently, teams including field and headquarters, line and staff representatives were formed around these opportunities.

Agency Annual Performance Plans

In addition to reviewing strategic plans, we also reviewed 28 agency annual performance plans to see how HRM is addressed. As mentioned earlier, performance plans are the yearly operational plans defining what the agency will accomplish in that fiscal year that will contribute to the longer-term strategic goals, and how they will measure accomplishment of these performance goals. Seventy-five percent of the reviewed plans contain both HRM performance goals and measures. This is not surprising because these operational plans tend to be more process and budget focused than strategic plans and therefore contain more detail about the resources needed to accomplish the performance goals. Therefore, administrative functions, in general, are represented more fully than in the strategic plan.

The development of the performance plan is invariably more functional than overall strategic planning. At most agencies, each program and administrative function is responsible for defining its own goals and measures which it then forwards to the planning office for coordination into the annual performance plan. As with the strategic plans, the HRM goals, strategies, and measures identified by HR offices tend to focus more on processes or activities than on overall outcomes. These process measures can be helpful, but because operational goals, strategies, and measures help determine achievement of mission goals, they should focus more on whether or not the intended outcome of the activity was achieved.

The Health Care Financing Administration's Human Resources Management Strategic Plan

The Health Care Financing Administration (HCFA) has developed a very noteworthy approach to aligning human resources management with mission accomplish-ment. HCFA's Human Resources Management Group (HRMG), Learning Resources Group (LRG), and Office of Equal Opportunity and Civil Rights (OEOCR) collaborated to develop a draft Human Resources Strategic Plan that goes beyond each of these individual organi-zation's human resources responsibilities and instead addresses the entire sub-component's human resources management responsibilities. It assigns accountability for specific HRM goals to HRMG, LRG, OEOCR, senior leadership, line managers, employees, the union, and/or other non-HR stakeholders. The HRMG, LRG, and OEOCR worked very closely with the HCFA strategic planning and evaluation office to tie the plan to HCFA's strategic plan.

Specifically, the plan includes challenges that HCFA will face in the future, HRM goals that will support HCFA in meeting those challenges, potential performance indicators and strategies for each goal, the roles and responsibilities of HRMG, LRG, OEOCR, managers, employees, and other stakeholders, and finally how to implement and assess its results.

HR Strategic Plans

Approximately half of the agencies we talked to have developed separate Human Resources strategic plans. These plans generally serve one of two purposes. Either they provide direction for those agencies that have not integrated HRM into the agency strategic plan, or they are used as implementation plans which support agencywide HRM goals, strategies, and measures.

These plans are particularly important to those agencies that do not integrate HRM into the agencywide plan because it helps them map out where they want the HR program to go. They seem less important to many of the agencies that have thoroughly integrated HRM into the agency plan. For example, the Social Security Administration (SSA) has not developed a specific HR strategic plan because HR's goals and measures are part of the agencywide approach. Then, there are some agencies that integrate HR extensively into the agency plan, but still prefer to have a separate HR operational plan supporting the agencywide plan, as is often done by other corporate functions such as information technology and financial management.

Most of these plans focus on internal HR office program activities, rather than on agencywide accountability for the effective use of human resources in accomplishing the mission. Therefore, ownership of the plan belongs to the HR office, not the agency. The Health Care Financing Administration (a sub-component of the Department of Health and Human Services) is an interesting exception to this, as seen in the inset.

As with agency strategic plans, the measures identified in HR strategic plans are typically process-oriented and tend to address what steps have been taken to achieve a goal, rather than whether the intended outcome of the goal has been achieved. A little over half of the agencies use management input in developing these plans, generally in the form of previous customer satisfaction surveys.

Strategic Implementation

Strategic planning allows agencies to put down on paper where they are, where they want to go, and how they plan to get there. But the best planning in the world does nothing for an agency if it does not act on those plans. Strategic implementation of human resources management means performing activities that support agency mission accomplishment and measuring how well those activities contribute to achieving agency strategic goals.

Strategic HRM Activities

When we talk about HRM activities, we tend to focus on what the HR office, itself, is doing even though we recognize that supervisors would bear the responsibility of HR decisions in an ideal world. After all, NPR advocated deregulation and delegation and the downsizing and outsourcing of HR office activities so that human resources management could take place at the line level, making it more responsive to mission-related needs. Additionally, the HR staff would be able to devote more time to broader organizational issues, thereby improving its contribution to mission accomplishment.

Unfortunately, deregulation and delegation, as reported in OPM's 1997 special study, Deregulation and Delegation of Human Resources Management Authority in the Federal Government, have not taken hold as quickly or thoroughly as was hoped. HR is still doing most of the HR-related work and is the nerve center for HRM activities. That is why the focus of this section is on the HR office and what it does to support mission accomplishment.

So what are HR's contributions toward mission accomplishment? Although most line managers we interviewed cannot describe precisely which HR activities support specific agency strategic goals, they recognize that they could not accomplish their mission without HR's help. Ironically, the areas most often mentioned by managers as HR's most valued contributions are also the areas they feel need the most improvement: recruitment and staffing, employee development, and employee relations. They would like to see HR become more involved and innovative in these areas, but they also admit that it would be extremely difficult for them to get their jobs done without the help HR already provides. An interesting example of innovative staffing is the Federal Emergency Management Agency's Automated Disaster Deployment System described on the following page.

The Federal Emergency Management Agency: Staffing our Disasters

The Federal Emergency Management Agency's (FEMA) HR staff is an integral part of achieving the agency mission. FEMA employs approximately 2,200 permanent employees, but can surge to 7,000 or higher with any given disaster. With these highly fluctuating and extremely vital staffing needs, FEMA's mission is more directly dependent on its staffing function than most other Federal agencies. In response to this need, HR has implemented the Automated Disaster Deployment System. This automated system allows HR to track employee credentialing (including knowledge and experience levels and performance ratings), availability, past and present assignment locations, dates of employment, and other vital employee data. With this system, HR can immediately identify available deployment candidates for selection as soon as disasters are declared. Additionally, the system allows HR to better identify employee training and promotion needs, match employee expertise with specific disaster site victim needs, and create a selection routine that rotates available employees, thereby avoiding employee burnout.

Clearly, staffing, development, and employee relations are important HR activities that make a difference to agency goal accomplishment. However, there are other areas in which HR offices contribute to and align with mission accomplishment, such as the few described below.

Agency Reorganizations

Because of all of the downsizing, streamlining, and budget cuts that have been occurring in recent years, many agencies and sub-components have had to redefine their missions and restructure the program areas that support those missions. Human resources staffs play key roles in some of these redesign efforts. Managers at the Federal Emergency Management Agency and the Department of Labor's Occupational Safety and Health Administration were particularly complimentary of all of the work the HR staffs did to redeploy and retrain the workforce, provide guidance on organizational development issues, and redesign performance standards.

Workforce Planning

In this time of budget cuts, downsizing, and an aging Federal workforce, workforce planning becomes extremely important to increasing agencies' overall ability to achieve their missions. Although few agencies have strong workforce planning systems in place, some are beginning to take steps in this direction. The Department of the Army has an automated civilian forecasting system that uses 15-year workforce data trends to project future employment patterns, up to 7 years. This is part of a developing workforce planning initiative. SSA has developed a methodology to predict the number of actual retirements and is developing a workforce transition plan that will identify current and future required skill sets, determine how the workforce can obtain these skills, and set action plan milestones. Additionally, OPM is in the process of developing a workforce planning model that will assist agencies in this area.

Linking Performance Management to NASA: Mission Accomplishment

When managers and employees are interviewed, they almost always cite the performance management system as a way they are held accountable for meeting agency goals. So, does this mean performance management systems are aligned with agency strategic goals? In most agencies. the answer is "not yet"—at least not fully. Recently published research has identified over a dozen agencies and agency sub-components that have started to fomulate systematic approaches to aligning performance management to strategic goals. Most are starting by linking top management performance plans and contracts to agency goals and rating and rewarding executives based on achievement of those goals. Many of those agencies are planning to cascade the alignment down to the employee level. OPM's 1999 publication, A Handbook for Measurin Employee Performance: Aligning employee Performance with Organizational Goals, is a very useful tool to help agencies link employee performance to the goals of the organization and measure employee accomplishments.

A couple of agencies actually mandate the linkage of employee level plans to agency goals, while others are using team-based performance management approaches that include performance targets, informal team assessments, and awards that are linked to mission goals. The National Aeronautics and Space Administration (NASA), as shown in the inset, actually has an automated system that assists in the linkage. Nevertheless, as the General Accounting Office (GAO) concluded in its study, Performance Management: Aligning Employee Performance with Agency Goals at Six Results Act Pilots, aligning performance management systems with organizational missions and goals is still a "work in progress."

HR Self-Assessment

A handful of agency and sub-component HR offices are actually assessing how well their programs align with agency mission accomplishment as part of recently established HR self-assessment programs. These assessment programs focus on the compliance of HR activities with law as well as how effectively HR programs are achieving their objectives in support of mission accomplishment. Because these assessment programs are fairly new or are in the process of being revamped, it is too soon to tell the success they will have in measuring HR's impact on organizational mission accomplishment.

HRM Measurement

In the end, HR can only determine its value to the organization by measuring it. Earlier in this report, we saw that most agencies had at least defined HR output measures in agency strategic plans, annual performance plans, and/or HR strategic plans. This is an encouraging trend, but we need to look further at whether these measures are actually being tracked and used for decision-making. The best measures in the world are meaningless if not used.

HRM measures in the strategic and annual performance plans are usually tracked by the HR office and forwarded to the planning office for distribution and sharing of the information. A few agencies, such as NASA, SSA, and Education, report actually using the information for decision-making and tracking whether goals are being met. NASA even posts the information on its web page. However, we found that most agencies look at available data without really evaluating how the information can be used to enhance goal attainment.

HR staffs find that measures from HR strategic plans tend to be more useful than those in the agency strategic or annual plans, at least at the functional level. As discussed earlier, HR strategic plan measures tend to focus on internal HR programs, policies, and processes, and can therefore point to deficiencies in these areas. HR officials can then use this information to make improvements to the problem areas. From an organizational perspective, however, the measures are generally not very helpful in determining achievement of HR goals because they are process rather than outcome oriented.

Few agencies have implemented elaborate systems to track HRM goals and measures. Nonetheless, there are quite a few interesting approaches some agencies are using to measure their HRM performance.

Benchmarking is a systematic process of measuring an organization's products, services, and practices against those of a like organization that is a recognized leader in the studied area. Many Federal HR offices are using this practice to identify ways to improve service and align with business results. The most common benchmarking effort Federal HR offices have participated in is the National Academy of Public Administration-Hackett Group HR Benchmarking Study. There are at least 19 Government agencies involved in the benchmarking of 22 HR processes within four areas: administration, risk management, employee development, and decision support. The study also helps to gauge HR alignment through decision support categories such as resource planning, organizational planning, and strategic HR planning. Most participating agencies see the value in the information but have not devised strategies for how to use it.

The Balanced Scorecard is a framework many agencies are using to translate strategy into operational terms by measuring a full range of perspectives: financial, customer, internal, and learning and growth. Vice President Gore advocated the use of this type of balanced set of results to evaluate agency performance at the Global Forum on Reinventing Government, January 1999. The scorecard is generally used at the business unit level, as with the Veterans Benefits Administration (see insert). To date, most agencies are in the beginning stages of implementing balanced measurement approaches.

Activity Based Costing (ABC) is a method of cost management that determines the true cost, including overhead, for a service or product. Finding the true cost allows agencies to discover cost improvement opportunities, prepare and actualize strategic and operational plans, and improve strategic decision-making. This cost management methodology involves identifying activities, determining activity costs, determining cost drivers, collecting activity data, and calculating the service cost.

Veterans Benefits Administration's New York Regional Office: The Balanced Scorecard in Action

The Veterans Benefits Administration's New York Regional Office implemented a balanced scorecard that uses outcome measures linked to organizational goals at the team, core group, and division-wide levels. The purpose is to determine how successful its operations are and where improvements are needed. This "balanced scorecard" measures five performance areas: customer satisfaction, speed, accuracy, cost-perclaim, and employee development. For each element in the balanced scorecard, teams are awarded points based on how well they are performing, and the scorecard is aligned with individual employee assessments and incentive pay. Veterans' expectations are used to define customer performance targets, and employee measures are derived from climate surveys, team development data, and technical skills inventories.

HR has played an important role in designing the balanced scorecard, including developing measures, peer assessments, and other tools, as well as helping managers understand the approach and how to manage under it.

ABC is being explored by a number of agencies. The Patent and Trademark Office is using ABC agencywide, and the General Services Administration is using it to determine HR costs, as described on the following page.

The Malcolm Baldrige and the President's Quality Award Criteria are each based on a set of core values and concepts that integrate key business requirements into a results-oriented framework. Using the criteria as a framework for management practices and measurement can help agencies to improve performance, facilitate communication and best practice sharing, and serve as a tool for managing performance, planning, training, and assessment. HR measures are 15 percent of the total Baldrige framework score.4 Several agencies, most notably the Department of Navy's Inspector General's Office, have successfully used the criteria to assess agency mission programs.

Measuring True Cost and How to Use It

Both the General Services Administration (GSA) and the Department of Commerce's Patent and Trademark Office (PTO) have successfully used Activity Based Costing (ABC) to determine the true cost of human resources management services.

The General Services Administration began tracking HR costs due to customer complaints that services were too expensive. The problem was that no one, including HR, knew the actual cost of HR services. By using Activity Based Costing, GSA was able to compute the HR activity costs and make comparisons to other Government and private sector organi-zations using the Hackett Benchmarking Study data. HR demonstrated to managers that its costs were actually relatively low, and it had the data to prove it.

The Patent and Trademark Office (PTO) has engaged in agencywide Activity Based Costing. All senior managers were trained in the process, and each functional area, including HR, formed teams to identify activities, activity-based drivers, and primary products. PTO has used the information to close out fiscal year 1998 financial activities and to plan the fiscal year 2000 budget. ABC has helped determine the full cost of agency activities, the proper distribution of costs, and has even influenced service rates. An additional benefit to the system is that it has encouraged strategic thinking. Managers see how much a function, such as HR, costs and starts asking what value that function really adds to the program. This challenges HR to show its value and return on investment.

Strategic Relationships

The lynchpin that holds all of this planning and implementation together is the relationship between HR executives and staffs and agency management. In the past, there was often much contention between the two groups because of HR's role as "gatekeeper," enforcing the laws, rules, and regulations. Now, with the role of the human resources staff shifting toward achieving organizational results, HR and management need to work together to further HRM's ability to have an impact on agency decisions and achievement of goals. So, let's take a look at how well these relationships have been fostered thus far.

Corporate HR and Top Agency Management

The relationship between corporate HR and top agency management varies greatly by agency. A few agencies, like SSA, NASA, Air Force, and GSA, have been able to develop strong working relationships with management in which HR is a full member of the agency decision-making body. Most other agency HR executives have not been so fortunate. They are generally brought into the agency decision-making process during the implementation phase rather than being consulted in the beginning on how decisions may impact agency human resources or vice versa.

For some agencies, it has been a hard road "getting to the table." For others, it has been more of a natural transition. In exploring how to elevate HR's role to management partner, agencies where this has been achieved attribute their success to a combination of the following factors:

- Reporting relationships—In agencies where there is a direct reporting relationship between the head of HR and the head of the agency, HR generally has a more visible role in agency decision-making.

- Management advocates—In agencies where there is a strong HR advocate in senior management, HR enjoys more involvement in the agency decision-making.

- Credibility—HR representatives who are formerly program managers tend to earn more credibility from the other managers. This type of individual knows, first hand, what the program concerns are and how HR decisions will impact the program, and can speak the same programmatic language.

- Culture—In some agencies, the recognition that its people are its most important asset has traditionally been part of the culture. Therefore, it is natural for the HR leader to have a voice in agency decisions.

- Value—In all cases, HR has to bring value to the discussion in order to be considered a member of the management team. If you have little or nothing to offer, you will not keep your seat at the table.

Because HR executives have little control over agency reporting relationships, management advocacy, executive appointments, and agency culture, they need to focus their efforts on providing value to agency business discussions. But what kind of calue can HR bring to the agency decision-making table? Other corporate functions have no problem demonstrating their value. The Chief Fnancial officer has the money. The Chief Information officer has the technology. Without money and technology, an organization is severly hindered. But HR has the people, and without the people, the organization has no one to do the work. So why has HR not been able to capitalize on this strength? We are able to idetify two reasons.

First, HR has not historically had the statistics or data that can excite management and show how HRM influences agency success. Second, HR has focused on internal operations rather than activities that impact the entire agency. These facts are recognized by the Strategic Human Resources Roundtable, an OPM-sponsored working group of Governmentwide HR Directors that meets periodically to discuss HR's role in GPRA. This group acknowledges that to address these shortcomings, HR needs to ask itself what are the HRM concerns that will gain management's attention, and does HR have the data that can help address those concerns? SSA has done this, as is demonstrated in the above inset.

Now that we have explored the relationship between HR executives and top agency managers, we need to look at how the HR office interacts with its line managers and if there has been any movement toward a more cooperative, consultative relationship. HR's role is changing, but is HR changing with it? As discussed earlier, NPR advocated HR delegating, downsizing, and outsourcing so that it could start concentrating on broader organizational issues rather than transactional processes. As we have seen, this is beginning to occur at the corporate level, but what about the line level?

The problem is that delegation to managers has not taken hold very quickly, but HR offices have already been downsized. Therefore, HR is still expected to do the transactional work it did before, while also focusing on broader organizational issues, and doing all of this with an average of 20 percent less staff.5 It is not hard to understand why agency HR offices are struggling to redefine their role to strategic partner. Just how far have they gotten?

HR as Consultant

Most agency managers we interviewed acknowledge that their HR office has become more consultative. Rather than telling a manager he/she can or cannot do something, HR professionals are more helpful in finding solutions to HR issues.

HR as Contributor to Mission Accomplishment

These same managers also recognize the importance of the HR office to mission accomplishment. There is so much that HR does for managers in terms of recruitment and staffing, employee development, and employee relations that managers would have difficulty doing it on their own. However, HR does have its limitations, particularly the size of the staff in relation to the amount of work it has to do, its knowledge of the mission, and skill gaps resulting from downsizing.

HR as Strategic Partner

Few, if any, agency managers feel that their HR office is a true strategic partner. Few HR offices are included in business planning from the beginning, generally being brought in to implement a decision that has already been made. For HR to become more involved in line-level decision-making, managers would like the office to:

- have greater knowledge of the organizational mission, and
- get more involved and innovative in broad, organizational HR issues that impact most on the organization, such as recruitment and workforce and succession planning.

HR has made some headway, as demonstrated in the following NASA example, but clearly has some distance to go in being involved in line management decision-making. Now let's look at the other side of the coin—how managers are involved in making decisions about HR programs. Most line HR offices involve managers at least at an informal level, generally through satisfaction surveys or informal discussions. A few have HR/management councils that get together periodically to discuss human resources issues. This is as close as agencies get to real integration of managers into the HR program decision-making process. Generally, managers do not feel that they have a large impact on the direction of HR programs and therefore feel little ownership for them.

NASA's Centers Working Together

NASA has 10 field centers, and each of these centers maintains a strong sense of its own identity and purpose and a strong enthusiasm for its mission. At the same time, each center can identify the linkage to the agency mission. This sense of empowerment appears to help motivate the center HR staffs to actively support that identity and purpose. Personnel officers generally participate in deliberations on center affairs. HR staffs are proactive in their work by making site visits, attending line staff meetings, asking managers for input on HR issues, and briefing managers about changes in HR programs. Managers are impressed with HR's availability, knowledge, and resourcefulness. This symbiosis is portrayed well in results from various employee surveys, data trends from the Central Personnel Data File, and third party evaluations of the HR program.

Accountability

With the developing relationship between HR and management, both at the top and line levels, along with NPR and GPRA mandates, accountability should become a shared responsibility. Managers are making more and more HRM decisions while the HR staff is becoming more involved in broader organizational issues. This means that both the HR staff and managers are ultimately accountable for effective, legally compliant HRM.

Is this shared accountability occurring in Federal agencies? Approximately half of the respond-ing agencies agree that HRM accountability is shared between the HR staff and managers. Managers are accountable for the business results achieved through good human resources management, the HR staff is accountable for HR compliance, and both are accountable for the overall effectiveness of the agency HRM program. However, the other half still feels that the ultimate accountability falls on the HR staff. They are the ones responsible if actions are found non-compliant, and little attention is given to whether managers' HRM decisions are an effective use of resources. OPM's HRM Accountability System Development Guide goes into quite a bit of detail on shared accountability and can assist agencies in understanding the concept, determining who is accountable for what, and devising strategies for how to hold them accountable.

Where do We Go From Here?

Strategic alignment of human resources management has come farther than we expected to find when we embarked on this study. There is definitely a trend toward integrating HR into the business planning process, measuring aspects of human resources management and its contribution to the organizational bottom line, and establishing a collaborative working environment between HR and management. Nevertheless, there are several indications that human resources management is not yet recognized as a critical contributor to agency mission accomplishment. HRM alignment is still evolving, and there are several steps agencies can take to help it along.

Fully Integrate Human Resources Management into the Business Planning Process

Although many more agencies than expected include HR representatives in the agency planning process and integrate human resources goals, objectives, and strategies into agency strategic plans, most are still struggling in this area. Agency executives need to recognize the value that HR can impart to discussions about agency activities, priorities, and goals. In turn, HR leaders need to understand agency mission needs and be able to contribute substantive, creative solutions to meet these needs. Once these realizations occur, HR will no longer be segregated out as a support function but will become an integral, contributing factor to agency planning and success.

Focus on Organizational Activities that Assist in Agency Decision-Making

Because of NPR mandates to downsize, streamline, and improve customer service, HR's recent improvement efforts have focused on the efficiency and effectiveness of traditional HR programs and processes. These are important endeavors. However, in response to GPRA's call to measure performance and demonstrate value, it is time to start concentrating efforts outside of the traditional realm of HR and on to broader organizational issues. When HR demonstrates that it can have an impact on agency direction, then it will gain credibility with agency executives and earn a seat at the table. To generate that type of impact, HR needs to develop strategies based on actual business needs, which will require involving management in the planning process. In addition, it must address Governmentwide concerns about the workforce capabilities of the future, such as workforce planning, succession planning, training needs assessments, skill gap analyses, etc.

Measure HRM Outcomes

HR's role is evolving. Therefore, HRM measures need to evolve as well. As HR becomes more involved in broader organizational activities, HRM measures should evaluate the impact these activities have on the organization as a whole. At this point, measures typically focus on outputs and processes and are generally internalized to the HR function or office. The data are used mostly to make improvements to HR-specific policies and procedures. While this kind of measurement is important, measures should also focus on organizational outcomes. Information from these measures should then be used to inform agencywide decisions and find solutions to agencywide concerns.

Advance the Collaborative Working Environment between HR and Management

To facilitate all of the changes recommended above, HR has to have a strong, collaborative working relationship with top agency and line management. Since there is no tradition in most agencies of HR as strategic partner, much depends on personal relationships established by HR officials with top managers and key line managers. Meanwhile, HR and agency management need each other more than ever. Authorities are being delegated to line managers, HR staffs are being downsized, and top agency management is being asked to show how its resources are being used to support mission accomplishment. HR must be able to make the case that everyone in the agency, from the agency leader down to the HR function, must share accountability for ensuring that the use of human resources not only complies with Federal laws, rules, and regulations, but adds to the success of the agency.

This shared accountability is beginning to occur. HR management is beginning to earn a seat at the table. HR line offices are becoming more consultative and involved in day to day management activities. Nevertheless, there is still a long way to go in becoming strategic partners. First, HR needs to build its own internal competencies to deal with organizational issues, change, and strategizing.

Further, it needs to educate itself on agency and program missions in order to understand what is important to those organizations and be able to offer creative and innovative alternatives and solutions to organizationwide issues. Finally, it must continually assert the absolute criticality of effective HRM to organizational success.

Conclusion

This all looks so easy on paper. Do this, do that, and you will be aligned with the mission and able to demonstrate your contribution toward it. Obviously, it is not that easy. Private sector, public sector, and some Federal entities have been struggling with this issue even before GPRA was enacted—and that works to our advantage. There is a wealth of information out there that can help—hundreds of articles, books, and studies have been written, numerous tools have been created, and many organizations have already tested a number of approaches. We can learn from all of these successes and failures.

But the only way to begin is to begin. To help start you on this path, we have included a rather extensive, though certainly not all-inclusive, bibliography in the appendix of this report. In support of its program to foster development of agency accountability systems, OPM will also offer assistance to individual agencies in developing strategies for strategic alignment and has created a Governmentwide clearinghouse that will provide information on additional real life, successful approaches that agencies are employing (currently available on the OPM web page). It is in all of our interests to ensure that Government establishes and maintains a highly skilled workforce that can handle the demands of the 21st century. To achieve this goal, we must all work together.

Appendix A: Non-Federal Findings

For some reason, people tend to think that the Federal Government has fallen far behind the private sector, and even other public sector entities, when it comes to aligning human resources management with agency mission accomplishment. Although we did not talk directly with private or non-Federal public sector representatives, we conducted a fairly in-depth literature search that tells a somewhat different story.

Private Sector

There are many conflicting views on where the private sector is in regard to HRM alignment. For instance, the Conference Board recently conducted a poll of 155 private sector HR executives, and 63 percent responded that HR is "never, rarely, or only sometimes" a major player in the companies' strategic process. A Price-waterhouse-Coopers poll indicates that although 75 percent of the responding 70 companies reported that HR's effectiveness is measured by its contribution to business results, only 27 percent include HR from the beginning of the business planning cycle. Further, 43 percent rated HR's planning and policy effectiveness as only average while a mere 6 percent rated it as excellent.6

Other private sector surveys and studies over the past few years, however, have found that HR has been integrated into the strategic planning process, HR executives and top company management are strategic planning partners, HR is recognized for the importance of its role in implementing organizational change, and HR is viewed as critical to the success of the business. Clearly, there are many private sector organizations that exemplify "best-in-class" alignment strategies. They have implemented such alignment approaches as the Balanced Scorecard, Return on Investment, Activity Based Costing, Malcolm Baldrige Award-type criteria, and more. They recognize the importance of their employees to business results, and HR is considered a valued strategic partner. However, even with a number of "best practices" out there, the research agrees that HR alignment, even in the private sector, is still a work in progress.

Non-Federal Public Sector

According to recent research, the non-Federal public sector is in much the same boat as the Federal sector. As the Government Performance Project pointed out in its recent study, State governments run into many of the same HR problems as the Federal Government—rigid rules, lack of strategic management decisions, absence of statewide HR data, lack of workforce planning or the ability to plan for the future, etc. State governments have begun making HR reforms, such as reducing job classifications and streamlining hiring procedures. However, as with the Federal Government, States are focusing more on the efficiency and effectiveness of programs than how they support the bottom line.

That is not to say that local, State, and even foreign governments have not been able to align themselves with mission accomplishment. A few cases can be most instructive for Federal agencies as they ponder this issue. The City of Hampton, Virginia HR staff has played a large role in increasing the performance of government services through improvements to work environment, organizational structure, work design, employee behaviors and organizational systems. The state of Washington is developing and enhancing HR information systems in support of mission accomplishment, is using personnel data to identify improvement initiatives, and includes the Director of Personnel in the Governor's Cabinet. The

Canadian Treasury Board and HR Council of the Federal Government of Canada are developing approaches to measuring HR efficiency, effectiveness, and mission contribution. There are many other examples of how the public sector is moving toward aligning HR with mission accomplishment. Nonetheless, the research indicates that the non-Federal public sector, too, is only in the beginning stages of this transformation.

Appendix B: Hrm Alignment Bibliography

Anfuso, Dawn. "Colgate's Global HR Unites Under One Strategy." Personnel Journal, October 1995, pp. 44–48.

Anfuso, Dawn. "Kodak Employees Bring a Department into the Black." Personnel Journal, September 1994, pp. 104–112.

Bechet, Thomas P., and James W. Walker. "Aligning Staffing with Business Strategy." Human Resources Planning, 1993, pp. 1–16.

Condrey, Stephen E. Handbook of Human Resource Management in Government. San Francisco: Jossey-Bass Publishers, 1998.

Connolly, Thomas R., et al. "Transforming Human Resources." Management Review, June 1997, pp. 10–16.

Corporate Leadership Council. Corporate Executive Board. Aligning Human Resources, Business Units, and Corporate Strategy. Washington, DC: October 1997.

Corporate Leadership Council. Corporate Executive Board. Aligning HR Strategy with Corporate Strategy. Washington, DC: March 1998.

Corporate Leadership Council. Corporate Executive Board. Assessing Employee Readiness for Strategic Initiatives. Washington, DC: December 1998.

Corporate Leadership Council. Corporate Executive Board. Developing A Strategic HR Function: Aligning Individual Competencies. Washington, DC: January 1997.

Corporate Leadership Council. Corporate Executive Board. Long-Range Strategic Planning Processes. Washington, DC: November 1997.

Corporate Leadership Council. Corporate Executive Board. The Role of Human Resources as a Strategic Business Partner. Washington, DC: August 1997.

Eisenstat, Russell A. "What Corporate Human Resources Brings to the Picnic: Four Models for Functional Management." Organizational Dynamics, Autumn 1996, pp. 6–14.

Galpin, Timothy J., and Patrick Murray. "Connect Human Resource Strategy to the Business, Plan." HR Magazine, March 1997, pp. 99–104.

Gonzalez, Maria. "Synchronized Strategies." Journal of Business Strategy, May/June 1997, pp. 9–11.

Government Performance Project. "Grading the States." Governing, February 1999.

Government Performance Project. "Stacking Up: The Government Performance Project Rates How Well Agencies are Managed." Govern ment Executive, Februa ry 1999.

Gratton, Lynda. "The New Rules of HR Strategy." HR Focus, June 1998, pp. 13–14.

Guban, Edward L. and James J. Dale. "Improving Business Results Through People." Benefits & Compensation International, April 1998, pp. 14–16.

Heuerman, Allan D. "Using Performance Management to Energize the Results Act." The Public Manager, Fall 1997, pp. 17–20.

"HR News Capsules." HR Focus, January 1999.

Human Resources Council and Treasury Board of Canada Secretariat. Performance Measurement for the Human Resources Function: A Discussion Paper, Evergreen Edition #1. Ottawa, Canada: December 1998.

Kaplan, Robert S., and David P. Norton. "The Balanced Scorecard—Measures that Drive Performance." Harvard Business Review, Volume 70, Number 1, January/ February 1992, pp. 47–54.

Laabs, Jennifer J. "Hewlett Packard's Core Values Drive HR Strategy." Personnel Journal, December 1993, pp. 38–48.

Laabs, Jennifer J. "HR's Vital Role at Levi Strauss." Personnel Journal, December 1992, pp. 34–46.

McIlvaine, Andrew. "Window of Opportunity." Human Resource Executive, June 5, 1998, pp. 36–38.

National Academy of Public Administration. Alliance for Redesigning Government. Creating High Performance Government Organizations: A Practical Guide for Public Managers. San Francisco: Jossey-Bass Publishers, 1998, pp. 143–160.

National Academy of Public Administration. A Guide for Effective Strategic Management of Human Resources. Washington, DC: June 1996.

National Academy of Public Administration. Helpful Practices in Improving Government Performance. Washington, DC: 1998.

National Academy of Public Administration. Innovative Approaches to Human Resources Management. Washington, DC: August 1995.

National Academy of Public Administration. Measuring for Results: Successful Human Resources Management. Washington, DC: August 1997.

National Academy of Public Administration. New Options, New Talent: The Government Guide to the Flexible Workforce. Washington, DC: August 1998.

National Performance Review. Federal Benchmarking Consortium. Serving the American Public: Best Practices in Customer-Driven Strategic Planning. Washington, DC: February 1997.

National Performance Review. Serving the American Public: Best Practices in Performance Measurement. Washington, DC: June 1997.

Overman, Stephanie. "Big Bang Change: Re-engineering HR." HRMagazine, June 1994, pp. 50–53.

Perry, James L., and Debra J. Mesch. "Strategic Human Resource Management." Public Personnel Management: Current Concerns, Future Challenges. Second Edition. Eds. Carolyn Ban and Norma M. Riccucci. New York: Longman, 1997, pp. 21–34.

Plevel, Martin J., et al. "AT&T Global Business Communications Systems: Linking HR with Business Strategy." Organizational Dynamics, Winter 1994, pp. 59–72.

Powers, Vicki J. "Benchmarking in the Federal Government: A Lesson in Customer-Focused Improvements." Benchmarking in Practice, American Productivity & Quality Center, August/September 1997, pp. 1–8.

Rubino, Alan L. " Repositioning the Human Resource Function at Hoffman-LaRoche." Human Resource Planning, 1994, pp. 45–58.

Simons, Robert, and Antonio Davila. "How High is Your Return on Management?" Harvard Business Review, January-February 1998, pp. 71–80.

Smith, Lia. "Aligning Human Resources to Business Objectives." Continuous Journey. American Productivity & Quality Center: January 1995.

Thronburg, Linda. "HFC Declares Employees the Key to Success." HRMagazine, August 1994, pp. 60–61.

Ulrich, Dave. Human Resource Champions: The Next Agenda for Adding Value and Delivering Results. Boston, MA: Harvard Business School Press, 1997.

Ulrich, David. "Measuring Human Resources: An Overview of Practice and a Prescription for Results." Human Resource Management, Fall 1997, pp. 303–320.

Ulrich, Dave. "A New Mandate for Human Resources." Harvard Business Review, January-February 1998, pp. 124–134.

Congress. Government Performance and Results Act of 1993. Washington, DC: 1993.

Department of the Navy. "Assessment and Evaluation of Civilian Human Resources Management (HRM) and Equal Employment Opportunity (EEO)." SECNAV Instruction 12273.1. Washington, DC: 1998.

General Accounting Office. HCFA Management: Agency Faces Multiple Challenges in Managing Its Transition to the 21st Century. GAO/T-HEHS-99-58. Washington, DC: February 1999.

General Accounting Office. Major Management Challenges and Program Risks: A Governmentwide Perspective. GAO/OCG-99-1. Washington, DC: January 1999.

General Accounting Office. Management Reform: Agencies' Initial Efforts to Restructure Personnel Operations. GAO/GGD-98-93. Washington, DC: July 1998.

General Accounting Office. Performance Management: Aligning Employee Performance with Agency Goals at Six Results Act Pilots. GAO/GGD-98-162. Washington, DC: September 1998.

Merit Systems Protection Board. "Director's Perspective: Federal HRM and Strategic Planning—Hit or Miss." Issues of Merit, May 1998, pp. 1–2.

Merit Systems Protection Board. Federal Personnel Offices: Time for Change? Washington, DC: April 1993.

Merit Systems Protection Board. Federal Supervisors and Strategic Human Resources Management. Washington, DC: June 1998.

Office of Management and Budget. "Overview of Strategic Plans and Annual Performance Plan." OMB Circular A-11. Washington, DC: 1997.

Office of Personnel Management. Human Resource Flexibilities and Authorities in the Federal Government. Washington, DC: 1998.

Office of Personnel Management. The President's Quality Award Program 1999 Application and Information. Washington, DC: 1998.

Office of Personnel Management. Strategic Human Resources Management: Discussion of Key Terms and Concepts. Washington, DC: 1999.

Office of Personnel Management. Strategic Human Resources Management: Summary Report of a Roundtable Discussion, October 22, 1998. Washington, DC: 1998.

Walters, Jonathan. "Who Needs Civil Service?" Governing, August 1997, pp. 17–21.

Wintermantel, Richard E., and Karen L. Mattimore. "In the Changing World of Human Resources: Matching Measures to Mission." Human Resource Management, Fall 1997, pp. 337–342.

Yeung, Arthur K., and Bob Berman. "Adding Value Through Human Resources: Reorienting Human Resource Measurement to Drive Business Performance." Human Resource Management, Fall 1997, pp. 321–335.

Yeung, Arthur, Patricia Woolcock and John Sullivan. "Identifying and Developing HR Competencies for the Future: Keys to Sustaining the Transformation of HR Functions." Human Resource Planning, 1996, pp. 48–58.

Internet Sites

Federal

General Accounting Office, www.gao.gov

GPRA/Strategic/annual plans, www.financenet.gov

National Partnership for Reinventing Government, www.npr.gov

Office of Management and Budget, www.whitehouse.gov/WH/EOP/omb

Office of Personnel Management, www.opm.gov

Speaker of the House, www.freedom.gov

Non-Federal

The Conference Board, www.conference-board.org

Corporate Leadership Council, www.clc.executiveboard.com

Governing Magazing, www.governing.com

Government Executive, www.govexec.com

The Hackett Group, www.thgi.com

International Personnel Management Association, www.ipma-hr.org

National Academy of Public Administration, www.napawash.org

Saratoga Institute, www.sarains.com

The Society of Human Resources Management, www.shrm.org

What Impact do Global Health Initiatives have on Human Resources for Antiretroviral Treatment Roll-Out? A Qualitative Policy Analysis of Implementation Processes in Zambia

Johanna Hanefeld and Maurice Musheke

ABSTRACT

Background

Since the beginning of the 21st century, development assistance for HIV/ AIDS has increasingly been provided through Global Health Initiatives, specifically the United States Presidential Emergency Plan for AIDS Relief, the Global Fund to Fight HIV, TB and Malaria and the World Bank Multi-country AIDS Programme. Zambia, like many of the countries heavily affected by HIV/AIDS in southern Africa, also faces a shortage of human resources for health. The country receives significant amounts of funding from GHIs for the large-scale provision of antiretroviral treatment through the public and private sector. This paper examines the impact of GHIs on human resources for ART roll-out in Zambia, at national level, in one province and two districts.

Methods

It is a qualitative policy analysis relying on in-depth interviews with more than 90 policy-makers and implementers at all levels.

Results

Findings show that while GHIs do not provide significant funding for additional human resources, their interventions have significant impact on human resources for health at all levels. While GHIs successfully retrain a large number of health workers, evidence suggests that GHIs actively deplete the pool of skilled human resources for health by recruiting public sector staff to work for GHI-funded nongovernmental implementing agencies. The secondment of GHI staff into public sector facilities may help alleviate immediate staff shortages, but this practice risks undermining sustainability of programmes. GHI-supported programmes and initiatives add significantly to the workload of existing public sector staff at all levels, while incentives including salary top-ups and overtime payments mean that ART programmes are more popular among staff than services for non-focal diseases.

Conclusion

Research findings suggest that GHIs need to actively mediate against the potentially negative consequences of their funding on human resources for health. Evidence presented highlights the need for new strategies that integrate retraining of existing staff with longer-term staff development to ensure staff retention. The study results show that GHIs must provide significant new and longer-term funding for additional human resources to avoid negative consequences on the overall provision of health care services and to ensure sustainability and quality of programmes they support.

Background

There is a shortage of human resources for health (HRH) throughout sub-Saharan Africa [1]. Many countries in the region are also experiencing significant HIV epidemics, with an estimated 2.12 million persons needing antiretroviral medicines [2]. The lack of adequate human resources for health directly affects countries' ability to provide antiretroviral treatment to their population [3]. The disease burden of HIV and HIV-related mortality among health sector staff has further reduced human resources [4], at a time when the introduction of antiretroviral treatment in the public health system has substantively increased the workload of staff [5] and created an urgent need for additional human resources [6,7].

Strategies to address human resource deficits have centred around staff retention (through incentives such as allowances, salary top-ups, and better working conditions) and retraining, including shifting as many tasks as possible away from doctors, nurses and pharmacists to non-clinical staff, enabling clinical staff to concentrate on their specific areas of expertise [3,5,7]. In Malawi for example, where special attention has focused on addressing the shortage of human resources for health, all health sector workers have received a salary top-up to increase staff motivation, financed by funding provided to the Malawian Ministry of Health [8].

Many of the countries heavily affected by HIV and AIDS, which are facing a human resource crisis, are receiving large amounts of donor funding, including support for the large-scale provision of antiretroviral treatment through the public sector and private sector. Since the beginning of the 21st century, development assistance for HIV and AIDS has increasingly been provided through partnerships and Global Health Initiatives (GHIs), specifically the United States Presidential Emergency Plan for AIDS Relief (PEPFAR), the Global Fund to Fight HIV, TB and Malaria and the World Bank Multi-country AIDS Programme [9].

Evidence of the impact of GHI programmes on human resources at country level, especially at subnational level, is limited. However, some studies have examined their impact in Ethiopia [10], and in Uganda, Mozambique and Zambia [11,12], and research findings are forthcoming from studies in Malawi and other countries[13].

This paper examines the impact of GHIs on human resources for ART roll-out in Zambia, at national, province and at micro level in two districts. The focus is on GHI's ability to contribute to retain and retrain staff, and also on unintended consequences of their programmes on human resources for health.

Methods

The paper draws on more than 90 in-depth interviews with policy-makers and implementers at national and subnational level, engaged in processes governing the implementation of ART roll-out. Actors interviewed include national, provincial and district representatives from government institutions; the donor community; governmental and nongovernmental service providers; doctors and nurses; NGOs supporting the roll-out; programme managers; community workers; and networks of people living with HIV/AIDS.

Interviews were conducted in Zambia between August and December 2007, as part of wider, comparative research on policy processes relating to the implementation of ARV roll-out at national, provincial and district level. Interviews were conducted at national level, as well as at provincial level in one province, and district-level research was conducted in two districts within the focus province. Interviewees were selected based on a "snowballing" process originating from an in-country advisory panel, made up of academics, representatives of nongovernmental organizations, a Zambian clinician and a representative of a network of people living with HIV/AIDS.

Interviews were semistructured and used an interview guide that was tested and revised in consultation with the in-country advisory panel. Actors were interviewed about their perception of implementation processes relating to ART roll-out, as well as their role and personal history in relation to these processes. Where permission was granted, interviews were recorded and transcribed; otherwise extensive notes were taken.

A subset of 32 interviews was selected for this paper in which interview content focused on both GHIs and human resources. Interviews were analysed to identify five key themes identified: training, "top-ups," mentoring, coordination and recruitment of staff.

The research conducted is qualitative, so relies on, and is limited to, the perceptions of persons interviewed at national level, in one province and two districts, who are working in the ART roll-out and interacting with GHIs regularly in their work. To better understand the perceptions of actors at different levels, the results and discussion section highlight at which level—national, province or district—interviewees operate.

Where possible, the paper draws on available secondary research and data on human resources obtained by the authors during the research, allowing for validation of data collected. Given the recent, unfolding nature of the ART roll-out, and the limited secondary data available, this paper provides an empirical, contemporary spotlight on an underresearched and changing area. The research for this paper was conducted as part of a "twinning" project between a Zambian researcher and a UK researcher. Ethical clearance for the research was granted by the ethics committees of the University of Zambia and the London School of Hygiene and Tropical Medicine.

Results and Discussion

Human Resources for Health in Zambia

Zambia faces a severe shortage in human resources, exacerbated by the country's HIV epidemic—an estimated 1.2 million (17%) Zambians are currently living with the virus—with less than a third of the recommended doctor-patient ratio [14] to treat the population. But the shortage of human resources for health is not limited to doctors, nor are they in the shortest supply. The greatest need is for laboratory technicians, followed by pharmacists, doctors, nurses and data monitors [interview, national level, November 2007].

Other problems have also been identified. For example, there is a rapid turnover of staff, high staff absenteeism [15] and an unequal distribution of staff between rural and urban areas [16,17]. Ministry of Health data revealed that in 2006, 368 staff members joined the public health sector, while 380 left the sector, highlighting a continued loss [15]. The main causes of attrition of health workers in 2004 were death and resignation of workers from the health service [16]. High vacancy rates of health posts throughout the public sector are well documented [14,15].

The human resource crisis is particularly urgent in relation to the ART rollout, given the complexity of ART. Medicines need to be taken daily for the remainder of a person's life, and patients need to be initiated on the medication and reviewed on a regular basis by a doctor. Patients are also counselled by either a lay counsellor or a nurse on the importance of adherence to the treatment regime and a healthy lifestyle, while drugs need to be ordered and administered by a pharmacist. Despite the constraints, Zambia has had remarkable success in scaling up access to ART in the public sector. Between 2003 and the end of 2007, more than 130,000 persons were initiated on antiretrovirals out of 250,000 to 300,000 who are estimated to need such medication [interview, national level; October 2007].

To address the shortfalls in human resources, the Zambian government developed a specific human resources strategy in 2005, which has since received support from different donors. At the time this research was conducted, however, the only targeted human resource intervention receiving donor support, including through PEPFAR funding, was the rural retention scheme. This includes incentives to attract doctors into rural areas, including better housing, a car and a cash allowance [14].

GHIs in Zambia

Zambia receives significant amounts of funding for its HIV programme from three Global Health Initiatives: the United States Presidential Emergency Plan

For AIDS Relief (PEPFAR); the Global Fund to Fight AIDS, TB and Malaria; and the World Bank Multi-country AIDS Programme (MAP). In 2006 PEPFAR money alone made up 63% of all funding for HIV in Zambia [18]. This was in addition to resources for HIV from the World Bank MAP and the Global Fund.

However, mapping the flow of funding provided by individual GHIs in support of the public ART treatment programme is difficult[19]. This is in part because much of the funding supporting public sector programmes is channelled through NGOs or other private institutions and not directly to the government. For example, a recent study revealed that less than 5% of all PEPFAR funding for Zambia in 2005 was received by the government [19]. In some cases it is difficult to differentiate expenditure between intervention areas, such as treatment, prevention or care. Data on actual expenditure, i.e. funding disbursed to recipients at the country level, is also not easy to obtain, since PEPFAR and the World Bank MAP, for example, do not publicly share this information [18].

Despite the limitations in detailed information, broad information on funding was obtained. Interviews with key stakeholders confirmed that the preponderance of funding for treatment roll-out in the public sector is through GHIs, even if this is provided in the form of technical support and not direct funding to the government. Through consulting recent planning documents, a Ministry of Health official responsible for planning the ART roll-out for 2008–2009 expected "50% to 52% of funding from PEPFAR, 34% from the Global Fund and 10% to 15% or so from other sources" [interview, national level, November 2007].

PEPFAR funding is not allocated through the Ministry of Health but instead to US and national subrecipients, who then provide a range of support for prevention, care and treatment to facility, district and provincial level. PEPFAR subrecipients are mainly NGOs, (but also academic, private sector and government institutions) and, as they essentially implement the PEPFAR programme, they are also referred to as PEPFAR implementers. The impact and forms of this support concerning human resources, specifically support provided for treatment roll-out, are explored later.

The World Bank MAP grant, while in part envisaged to support the Ministry of Health's procurement of ART [20], in practice supported other elements of the programme, including laboratory supplies [interview, national level, November 2007] [18]. Global Fund resources are directly received by the Ministry of Health and at the time of conducting this research were paying for the actual ARV medication.

The Study Focus Province and District

The shortage of human resources for health was evident in the two study districts. At the time of conducting this research, six public sector clinics in one of the focus districts provided treatment to a population of 363,734 (GRZ 2000) with a staff of three doctors, one pharmacist and a changing number of technical (also called clinical) officers and nurses. In the second focus district, with a population of about 450,000, two doctors rotated between five clinics providing ART. Since 2004 more than 4000 people have started ART in each of the two districts, in clinics run by the district, with no additional staff provided by the Ministry of Health for these services.

In the study focus districts and province, public sector roll-out of ART was supported by one PEPFAR implementing agency, while additional PEPFAR support was provided for a private hospital in one of the districts. Funding to the Ministry of Health for actual medication and laboratory equipment aside, World Bank MAP and Global Fund support in the study districts and province focused on non-clinical interventions. In terms of supporting the clinical treatment roll-out at subnational level, PEPFAR implementers emerged as the most visible presence during the period of this research.

GHI's Addressing the Human Resources for Health Shortage

While GHIs do not provide direct financial support for additional human resources in the public sector, their programmes address the shortage in human resources through training for health care workers and volunteers in all aspects required to support the treatment programmes. They also provide allowances such as overtime payments, "top-ups," or payments of expenses, especially for volunteer counsellors or treatment support workers.

PEPFAR-funded programmes also provide ongoing mentoring or technical support in health facilities. This refers to clinical staff employed by a PEPFAR implementing organization who support health facilities, such as clinics or hospitals, on a regular basis (for example, through visits about once a week) to discuss issues relating to the treatment programme. They assist with questions relating to clinical management of patients. The exact models for technical support vary. Some PEPFAR organizations have staff based at provincial level, others send support teams from the capital on a regular basis.

In addition, PEPFAR implementers pay for, or second, data entry clerks in health facilities they support. These clerks record the number of persons who receive ART. Data are reported to both the Ministry of Health and PEPFAR. Similarly, clinical care specialists have been employed by a PEPFAR-funded organization and seconded to the provincial health directorates in each of Zambia's nine provinces.

While each of these interventions aims to alleviate the human resource shortage in relation to ART, examining their impact at district and provincial level in detail suggests possible negative, unintended consequences. The following discusses each of these interventions in turn, based on the evidence emerging from interviews with key stakeholders.

"Top-Ups": The Impact of Incentives for Health Workers in ART Delivery

PEPFAR-implementing organizations provide "top-ups" to public health care workers and community volunteers working on the ART programmes they support. "Top-ups" are either overtime payments for shifts worked in the ART clinic or transport costs for meetings for those working on PEPFAR-funded health programmes. These incentives go a long way in motivating public health workers to work in the ART clinic. All nurses interviewed as part of this research confirmed that among their colleagues the ART clinic is the most popular [interviews, district level, October and November 2007], and their enthusiasm was echoed by the observations of policy-makers that ARV clinics or programmes are liked by staff.

While this suggests that "top ups" are successful in motivating staff to work on the ART programme, it raises concerns about possible unintended consequences. A recent study conducted among health care workers in three Zambian districts found that on average only 7% of health workers who had delivered non-HIV services had received incentives, underlining the clear financial benefits arising from involvement in ART delivery and causing imbalances between different parts of the service [11].

Some interviewees were concerned about the distorting effect of such payments, diverting attention and resources from non-focal diseases [interview, national level, October 2007]. Evidence collected was not clear on whether or not this is the case in the day-to-day delivery of services at health facility level.

However, policy-makers and planners interviewed at national level felt strongly that their work had focused largely on HIV and related diseases, to the neglect of other equally urgent health issues. This may possibly be a reflection of the time and attention devoted at that level to coordination of these activities. One senior Ministry of Health official observed, "HIV, TB and malaria have taken almost 90% of our time, not to mention that they have also taken most of our budgetary money to the extent that we have actually neglected what we call noncommunicable diseases" [interview, national level, October 2007].

The provision of short-term incentives such as top-ups may also have implications for sustainability, including quality of care. Speaking about the effect on the quality of care in the longer term, a senior Ministry of Health official explained: "They [donors] support short-term incentives ...but those are highly unsustainable because they are applied for a year. You put so many people on treatment because you are providing services to the health worker, then the following year there is nothing ..." [interview, national level, November 2007].

What this official points to is the effect of the one-year funding cycle of PEP-FAR, which means that incentives cannot be guaranteed beyond that time frame, which may create resentment among existing staff members, who narrowly miss out on receiving top-ups or change their performance from year to year. There may also be a negative impact on long-term quality of care if top-ups are withdrawn after a year, and this underlines concerns about sustainability of the programmes. An advisor to the Ministry of Health said: "They [GHIs] are going to leave everything flat when they leave" [interview, national level, November 2007].

This suggests that while top-ups or incentives are successful in motivating existing health care workers to work in the ARV clinics, they may have negative immediate consequences on attention paid to the quality of care provided to non-focal diseases. This echoes findings on the impact of top-ups by Ooman et al. [12]. As top-ups are not sustainable beyond the period funded by a GHI, it also raises concerns about the ability to sustain quality of care for patients in the longer term.

Training and Mentoring of Health Care Workers for ART Provision in Zambia

One of the key GHI elements of support is training for health care workers. As a clinician from a PEPFAR implementing organization described their strategy: "We put money into doing additional training for clinical officers, medical officers...and if their sites are growing rapidly and they need additional training, the team goes and assesses the needed training" [interview, national level, October 2007].

The training helps build capacity of health care workers involved at different levels in the provision of ART. However, health care workers often leave the public sector or their position once they are trained. All PEPFAR implementing agencies supporting the ART roll-out in Zambia described this as a common experience and a key challenge. A senior district health official replied, when asked about the greatest challenge faced in implementing the ART roll-out: "human resources ...you train people to provide this and within a short time they have left. So you need to find people to continue providing the service. That has been a major challenge in terms of implementing..." [interview, district level, September 2007]. The very fast turnover of staff once trained suggests that external training, in isolation from increased resources to enable career progression and longer-term incentives in the public sector, has little effect in alleviating the shortages of skilled health care workers to support the provision of ART.

In addition, training, especially the per diems provided during such training, are part of the reasons that attract health workers to work on the ART programme, adding to the potentially distorting effects of top-ups. A further consequence of training, when externally conducted, means that these are short-term, intensive courses that take clinicians out of their clinic, imposing a further strain on the day-to-day running of the ART programme.

Mentoring and the Secondment of GHI Staff to the Public Sector

In addition to training, the PEPFAR implementing organizations in Zambia supporting ART roll-out provide ongoing technical support through mentoring of health care workers. This involves visiting ART sites and attending to patients together with health care staff, to monitor the quality of services and assist with difficult clinical cases. Some organizations have teams of specialists, ranging from clinical care to pharmacy, nursing and logistical support, who visit the clinics and hospitals supported by their organization on a monthly or weekly basis.

In some cases, technical support is provided by staff recruited and employed by a PEPFAR implementing agency and seconded to the public health sector, where they work alongside their public sector colleagues. An example of this practice is the PEPFAR-funded Health Services and Systems Programme (HSSP), aimed at providing technical support to the Ministry of Health. It focuses on aspects relating to the health systems and human resources.

As part of its support, HSSP recruited and seconded clinical care specialists to each of Zambia's nine provincial health directorates, to provide technical support to the districts and hospitals in the delivery of ART services [Abt Associates, 2007]. These clinical care specialists work in the provincial health directorate alongside a clinical care specialist employed by the Ministry of Health, but receive a higher salary. While part of the provincial health team, they also have access to a small operational budget for training and ongoing support [interview, national level, October 2007]. All nine clinical care specialists employed by HSSP are physicians, whereas the government's counterparts are nurses or technical or clinical officers (holders of a three-year, diploma-certified degree that in Zambia allows clinical practice).

While these clinical care specialists are in addition to the provincial team and undoubtedly contribute through their skills and commitment, given the salary level and remit, these posts are not sustainable beyond HSSP funding. In addition, their relative seniority compared to the government's clinical care specialists raises questions about working (and status) relationships that may affect, both positively and negatively, the implementation of services. Some national actors reported that the clinical care specialists had led to an increase in capacity, while implementers at provincial and district level reported that their engagement may have led to demotivation of government staff. In addition, interviews suggested that nurses and technical officers at district level referred to the MoH clinical care specialist, whereas doctors worked with the HSSP-employed clinical care specialist.

Increasing Workload Through Coordination

Despite efforts at national level to coordinate activities between the different implementing partners and the Zambian government through a range of bodies, including technical committees that determine a geographical and skills-based division of labour, policy-makers interviewed mentioned that coordination with individual organizations remained problematic. A senior official at the Ministry of Health said: "In Lusaka alone there are close to 236 partners working on HIV... to track what they are doing is a challenge" [interview, national level, November 2007]. When describing the coordination, another Ministry of Health official said: "...it is overwhelming, there is a lot that needs to be done and sometimes I feel as if am doing injustice to some of the activities" [interview, national level, November 2007].

There is clear evidence, from the data collected and other research focusing on human resources and ART, that the workload for staff has increased since the introduction of ART [4]. In one study district, the same number of doctors and nurses as in 2004 (before district provision of ART) were providing treatment and care to more than 4000 patients on ART by the end of 2007 [interview, district level, October 2007]. As previously highlighted, the district staffing levels at the time of conducting this research were two and three doctors in clinical care, respectively, in the focus districts, and approximately 10 members of staff at the provincial health administration. Health care workers interviewed said that their workload had not only increased due to a greater number of patients, but also due to coordination of activities funded or implemented by GHIs.

At province and district level, the coordination with PEPFAR implementers posed an additional workload for health sector staff, due to funding requirements. Districts supported by PEPFAR in their roll-out were required to provide monthly reports to the provincial office of the PEPFAR implementer. These were in addition to quarterly reports that form part of the Ministry of Health processes and the MoH's twice-annual performance reviews.

To streamline the process and avoid confusion, each district in the province had appointed a focal person to interact with PEPFAR implementers [interview, district level, October and November 2007]. Focal persons were drawn from among doctors, nurses and clinical officers working at the district level.

PEPFAR implementers held quarterly meetings with supported districts to review activities. In addition, PEPFAR implementers supported the district teams to have further regular meetings, to either coordinate with other stakeholders, such as NGOs, or to discuss issues of clinical management.

While PEPFAR implementers provided resources for these meetings, their organization and arrangements are the responsibility of the district focal person, in addition to his or her clinical workload. The rationale for making this a district responsibility was to ensure that the district managed the programmes in an integrated way. However, there were opportunity costs to district staff—such as time. Meetings tended to last a whole working day. As one district staff pointed out: "Our work has increased, like when it comes to meetings, I have to write the memos, to contact people...we have about three meetings in a month clinical meeting, quarterly review meeting and the quarterly referral meeting—which usually take the whole day..." [interview, district level, November 2007].

Many new initiatives instigated and supported by GHIs, including through financial resources for training and materials, must be implemented at existing staff level. An example of this is the introduction of ART site accreditation, introduced with the technical assistance of a local PEPFAR implementer who helped develop a standard set of indicators against which to assess sites' readiness to be accredited to have minimum requirements in place, for the provision of ART. The Zambian Medical Council has been designated to oversee the process, receiving a minimal budget for overseeing and facilitating the accreditation process, by use of existing funds for monitoring and evaluation [interview, national level, November 2008].

At provincial level, the accreditation of sites, which involves a site visit and assessment, is conducted through teams that draw on existing provincial health administration staff (10 persons) and medical practitioners from the provincial hospitals. By mid 2007, more than 30 sites were already providing ART in the focus province, and as accreditation of sites was introduced several years after the start of the public sector ART programme, these sites needed to be assessed. This was in addition to any new sites for ART roll-out [interview, district level, October 2007].

Accreditation requires a site visit and assessment. Given staffing levels, with no additional human resources available for the accreditation processes these were understandably delayed [interview, national level, November 2008]. While site accreditation is undoubtedly an important element of quality assurance, the way in which this was introduced, and its implementation envisaged, shows the limitations of such initiatives in the absence of additional funding for human resources.

This suggests that support by GHIs, particularly PEPFAR implementers, is provided in the form of training and financial support for materials and meetings, for many new initiatives that may improve the ART programme and ensure greater quality of care and treatment. Despite the clear benefits of the intended outcomes, the lack of funding for additional human resources within the health sector adds significantly to the workload of already stretched human resources for health, risking further burnout and ultimately contributing to making programme efforts less sustainable.

GHI Recruiting

A further impact of GHIs on human resources for health is the actual recruitment of health workers from within the public sector, by the various implementing agencies of GHIs, especially those funded through PEPFAR. This is particularly apparent in the support provided for a clinical intervention, such as the provision of ART roll-out, where assistance, including training and mentoring, requires clinicians familiar with the Zambian health system.

Of 15 health workers (including doctors, nurses and pharmacists) currently working for GHIs or their implementers who were interviewed for this study, nine had recently been recruited from the public sector. One senior Ministry of Health official described how PEPFAR agencies recruit government employees once they have gained experience, and then describe the government as lacking capacity: "It [PEPFAR] is strategically weakening government efforts....What is happening is that we are training people ...next you will hear that he has been taken ...next you will hear that government, you have no capacity" [interview, national level, December 2007].

Of the health workers involved in the two public sector sites that started ART in Zambia in 2002 (University Teaching Hospital, Lusaka, and Ndola Central Hospital), including the doctors leading these programmes, the majority have now left the public sector to work for GHI-funded organizations that support the roll-out of ART [interviews, national level; September-November 2007]. It appears that GHIs, by recruiting local health care workers to provide the technical support for ART, are drawing precisely from, and depleting the pool of, the most-qualified health workers in Zambia. These findings corroborate the practices observed in a three-country study by Ooman et al. [12].

Conclusion

Global Health Initiatives have vastly expanded access to life-saving treatment for thousands of people in Zambia, yet they are not effectively addressing the human resources for health shortages in their programmes supporting ART roll-out. Given the overall amount of their resources aimed at supporting ART programmes, comparatively little is being done to address the health worker shortage. While some of their interventions, such as top-ups for staff working on ART, secondment and training appear to alleviate staff shortages in the short term, and succeed in giving many health sector staff the opportunity to improve their knowledge and skills on HIV/AIDS through short term training, workshops and on-the job training, they appear less successful at staff retention. This echoes similar findings from three further districts in Zambia recently published [11].

GHIs' programmes have increased the workload of already-stretched managers and health care providers. As the majority of GHIs, particularly PEPFAR, support treatment through individual organizations, such as NGOs, there is a significant added workload for public sector health staff who have to coordinate these support activities. This appears to be the case at all levels from national to district level, adding to potential problems of staff burnout. The recruitment by GHIs of public sector health workers to work for GHI-funded nongovernment implementers that support public sector roll-out further reduces the human resources for health in the public sector in Zambia. It also raises concerns about the ethical dimension of this assistance, where instead of providing much-needed resources to the government to increase human resources for health, development agencies use aid money to hire public sector workers to provide external assistance to the ART programme.

When recommending and supporting new policies, such as site accreditation for ART, GHIs should conduct a human resource impact assessment and address the human resource needs created by such interventions through additional funding that will allow the government to recruit the staff required to implement them through the public sector.

By not providing resources for the MoH to employ further human resources, but seconding them, as in the case of additional provincial clinical care specialists, additional capacity remains external and limited to the period of GHI funding available. The more Zambia's treatment programme relies on mentoring and seconded staff, the less sustainable it becomes in the long term, creating greater dependence on GHIs to continuously fill these gaps in capacity. Different approaches, such as the model followed in Malawi, should be explored to avoid creating further dependence [8].

Similarly, as training is provided through external partners and not integrated into a longer-term strategy for developing the human resources and allowing individuals to progress professionally within the health system, there are limited incentives for health professionals to remain within the public health care system.

The impact of top-ups increases staff motivation and interest in the ART programmes, but may have a distorting effect on health services overall. There is concern that as staff move vertically towards the ART programme, quality of services for non-focal diseases may suffer. In addition, the short-term nature of funding cycles may mean a drop in quality of care for patients on ART, once these payments are discontinued. More research is needed to assess the impact of top-ups for disease-specific programmes on the overall provision of health care services.

These interventions, aimed at addressing the shortages in human resources for health, including top-ups, mentoring, secondment of staff and training, all appear "surgical" in that they are not genuinely interwoven into the Zambian health system at all levels. They could be removed or abandoned, leaving a nearly hollowed-out treatment programme behind.

The evidence discussed in this paper—from interviews with Zambian health workers at all levels from the national Ministry of Health to districts and clinics—suggests that GHIs need to rethink the impact of their overall programmes, policies and conduct in relation to human resources for health. They need to address the long-term effect on quality of care and health systems of interventions targeted at alleviating staff shortages to avoid creating an ever-growing dependency of the Zambian treatment programme on external actors.

Competing Interests

The authors declare that they have no competing interests.

Authors' Contributions

JH conceived the study and its design. MM and JH conducted interviews jointly, and worked together on transcribing and analysing data collected. They jointly developed an outline for the paper and wrote the initial draft, which they revised following comments from reviewers. All authors have read and approved the final manuscript.

Authors' Information

Johanna Hanefeld is a PhD candidate at the London School of Hygiene and Tropical Medicine, researching policy implementation processes relating to ART roll-out in Zambia and South Africa. Maurice Musheke is a social scientist based at Zambart. This article is the result of a "twinning" between the two researchers.

Acknowledgements

The authors acknowledge the contribution of Virginia Bond, Gill Walt and Lucy Gilson. Research collaboration was supported by the Evidence for Action research consortium at the London School of Hygiene and Tropical Medicine, with funding from the Department for International Development (DFID), United Kingdom.

References

1. Chen L, Evans T, Anand S, Boufford JI, Brown H, Chowdhury M, Cueto M, Dare L, Dussault G, Elzinga G, et al.: Human resources for health: overcoming the crisis. The Lancet 2004, 364:1984-1990.

2. UNAIDS W, UNICEF: Towards Universal Access 2008. UNAIDS ed. Geneva; 2008.

3. WHO: Treat, Train, Retain—The AIDS and health workforce plan. Report on the Consultation on AIDS and Human Resources for Health, WHO, Geneva, 11–12 May, 2006. Geneva 2006.

4. Dieleman M, Biemba G, Mphuka S, Sichinga-Sichali K, Sissolak D, Kwaak A, Wilt G-J: 'We are also dying like any other people, we are also people': perceptions of the impact of HIV/AIDS on health workers in two districts in Zambia. Health Policy Plan 2007, 22:139-148.

5. Van Damme W, Kober K, Kegels G: Scaling-up antiretroviral treatment in Southern African countries with human resource shortage: How will health systems adapt? Social Science & Medicine 2008, 66:2108-2121.

6. Hirschhorn L, Oguda L, Fullem A, Dreesch N, Wilson P: Estimating health workforce needs for antiretroviral therapy in resource-limited settings. Human Resources for Health 2006, 4:1.

7. MSF: Help Wanted. Confronting the health worker crisis to expand access to HIV/AIDS treatment: MSF experience in southern Africa. Johannesburg 2007.

8. Mangham L: Addressing the Human Resource Crisis in Malawi's Health Sector: Employment preferences of public sector registered nurses. ESAU Working Paper 18 ODI ed. London; 2007.

9. Bennett S, Boerma JT, Brugha R: Scaling up HIV/AIDS evaluation. The Lancet 2006, 367:79-82.

10. Schott WSK, Bennett S: Effects of the Global Fund on reproductive health in Ethiopia and Malawi: baseline findings. In The System-wide effects of the Fund (SWEF) Network. Abt Associates PfHRP ed. Bethesda, Maryland; 2005.

11. Ndubani: Global HIV/AIDS Initiatives in Zambia: Issues of Scale up and Health Systems Capacity; Interim District Report. GHIN; 2008.

12. Ooman N, Bernstein M, Rosenzweig S: Seizing the opportunity on AIDS and health systems. In HIV/AIDS Monitor. Development CfG ed. Washington, DC; 2008.

13. Global Health Initiative Network [http://www.ghinet.org]

14. Schatz JJ: Zambia's health-worker crisis. The Lancet 2008, 371:638-639.

15. Picanzo OKS: The State of Human Resources for Health in Zambia; Findings from the Public Expenditure Tracking and Quality of Service Delivery Surevy 2005/06. In Human Resources for Health Research Conference. Mulungushi International Conference Center, Lusaka, Zambia; 2007.

16. Kombe G: Human Resources for Health challenges in dealing with HIV/AIDS in Sub-Saharan Africa. In Pan American Health Organization, World Health Week. Project PfHR ed. Washington, DC; 2006.

17. GRZ MoH-: 2005 Annual Report. Health Mo; 2006.

18. Ooman N, Bernstein M, Rosenzweig S: Following the Funding for HIV/AIDS. HIV/AIDS Monitor. Washington, DC 2007.

19. Ooman N, Bernstein M, Rosenzweig S: The Numbers Behind the Stories. In HIV/AIDS Monitor. Development CfG ed. Washington, DC; 2008.

20. Worldbank: ZANARA. In Edited by: Bank W. 2001.

Biting the Hand that Feeds: Social Identity and Resistance in Restaurant Teams

James Richards and Abigail Marks

ABSTRACT

The aim of this paper is to engage with, and develop the literature on teamwork and employee resistance by examining the use of teamwork as a means of work organisation and as a distinctive forum for employee resistance. We emphasise how employees, at times of heightened conflict, first of all re-evaluate their group memberships and group loyalties (including membership of teams and other competing groups and sub-groups), and second, take action in line with the groups most suitable to helping them attain beneficial outcomes. Drawing on an ethnographical mode of inquiry, we explored what turned out to be an incompatible application of teamworking to counter the typically busy and chaotic nature of front-line hotel restaurant employment. The resistance that emerged varied from individual forms of resistance and misbehaviour to overt collective forms involving the joined up efforts of team

*members and team leaders. Subsequent analysis confirmed the value of using
a social identity approach as a means to explain workplace behaviour. However, additional work is required in considering a broader range of research
methods and team-related variables in order to verify these insights and develop knowledge on teams and resistance.*

Keywords: social identity approach, labour process, resistance, teamwork,
ethnography, hotel and catering

Introduction

Groups and teams have been a major focal point of psychological and sociological theory and research. An understanding of groups is necessary for almost every
analysis of social behaviour, including, leadership, majority-minority relations,
status, role differentiation and socialisation (Levine and Moreland, 1998). Furthermore, small groups provide important contexts within which other behaviour
occurs e.g. attraction, aggression and altruism (Geen 1998; Batson 1998). At a
functional level, people spend much of their lives in collectives of some kind; e.g.
families, school classes and sports teams, and these groups provide members with
vital material and psychological resources.

Yet, the formal use of teams within organisations is a relatively recent phenomenon. Traditional work arrangements attempted to remove the power of the
informal team and preferred a more individualised form of work organisation.
Indeed, Cohen, Ledford and Spreitzer (1996) reported that nearly half of US
organisations used self-managed work teams for at least some proportion of their
workforce. Similarly, within the UK, the 1998 Workplace Employee Relations
Survey (WERS) indicates that 65 per cent of workplaces report that they use
some form of teamwork (Cully, Woodland, O'Reilly and Dix, 1999) and a review
undertaken by the Institute of Work Psychology found team based working operating within 70 per cent of the organisations examined (Waterson, Clegg and
Axtell, 1997).

The expansion in interest in teamwork has been seen as a response to increased
competitive pressures, specifically as a mechanism for improving flexibility, re-
sponsiveness and quality (Lloyd and Newell 2000). Groups and teams have been
at the core of programmes to reform routine work within manufacturing—partly
as a response to Human Relations theory in the 1930s, sociotechnical systems
theory in the 1950s and Japanization and lean production in the 1980s. Indeed,
managerialist and psychological accounts view teamwork as the answer to all organisational ills, as it not only enhances productivity, flexibility and efficiency, but

also improves employee satisfaction, motivation and commitment to the organi-sation (e.g. Jackson, Sprigg and Parker, 2000; Wall and Jackson, 1995). More-over, organisations such as call centres, where the work is organised in a manner that would not logically adapt to teamwork are, nevertheless adopting teams and teamwork (van den Broek, Callaghan and Thompson, 2004). This has in part led to more critical writers viewing teamworking as the latest in a succession of management fads or as covert mechanism by which management intensify their control over labour (e.g. Barker, 1993; Sinclair, 1992).

Accordingly, one of the mainstays of the labour process debate, the counter-ing of managerial control by resistance behaviour (Edwards, 1986) has only been given limited analysis at a team level (e.g. Bacon and Blyton, 2005; Barker, 1993; McKinlay and Taylor, 1996a and 1996b). The very nature of the team system, which cultivates patterns of commonality and mutual support, provides the ideal domain for employees to contextualised and reinterpret managerial interventions. In one sense the team is providing employees with organisational resources that can be used to develop resistance behaviour (Vallas, 2003).

We suggest that in order to further detail resistance within teams it is of value to take account of, at least some of the principles of the social identity approach (Haslam, 2004). Social identity theory (SIT) purposely examines the methods by which collections of individuals interpret and behave towards their own group and other important groups (Tyler and Blader, 2001; Turner and Oakes, 1997; van Knippenberg and van Schie, 2000). Importantly, SIT not only recognises that dimensions of identity derive from self-enhancement strategies, but also from the groups that we belong to and the significance that we place on those groups. In-deed, the emphasis of SIT is on the processes through which groups chose to what extent they wish to share beliefs regarding their self-definitions, i.e. SIT is likely to aid our understating on how the relationship within the group and between the group and the organisation or management body will impact on resistance behaviour.

As such, the main aim of this article is to demonstrate that by using a social identity approach we can begin to explain how the processes within teams and between the team and the organisation lead to resistance behaviour. We draw on empirical evidence from a detailed ethnographic study of the restaurant in Hotelcorp—a branch of a large hotel chain, to illustrate and further explain the relationships between team identity and resistance. We start by looking at some of the existing work on resistance and specifically resistance within teams. Our following discussion concerns the social identity approach. However, the social identity approach is considerable (see Haslam, 2004 for a review) and only some dimensions are relevant to the current discussion. Following a summary of the social identity approach, we present our research methods and then examine the interplay between identity and resistance for the teams within our sample. We conclude this paper with a more detailed evaluation of how this work contributes to existing theorising within the area and make suggestions for further study.

Teamwork and Employee Resistance

Edwards and Scullion (1982) refer to resistance as overt action taken to express recognition of conflict. As such, resistance equates first and foremost with attempts to subvert management demands. The basis for understanding resistance, however, is far more contentious. Despite having some noteworthy strengths and many supporters at both management and governmental level; both a unitary and a pluralist approach are viewed as being inadequate analyses for the basis of industrial conflict (Edwards, 1986). Moreover, whilst the Marxist perspective emphasises the central importance of the division between those who own the means of production and those who merely have their labour to sell, many Marxist concepts have often proven to be somewhat blunt instruments for analysts seeking to understand the nature of employment relations within different work contexts (Blyton and Turnbull, 2004). Indeed, a further dilemma is put forward by Foucauldian writers (e.g. Jermier, Knights and Nord, 1994) who believe that the most prevalent way of analysing resistance—a reactive process where agents embedded in power relations actively oppose initiatives by other agents—is associated with an overly simplistic view of who resists and how and why they do so. This is despite the fact that actual accounts of resistance can rarely be found in such studies (Ackroyd and Thompson, 1999).

This work is not for the purpose of taking sides in the orthodox versus Foucauldian labour process debate—in particular, the rather adversarial debates over 'subjectivity' or 'self-identity.' In actuality, we are responding to an inherent problem in labour process theory outlined by Thompson (1989). That is the limited focus within existing work on the role of individual and social identity within the conceptual structure for explaining the labour process. Following Thompson (1989) and Thompson and McHugh (2002), we make the case for (and ultimately wish to demonstrate) the use of a critical psychology to inform our understandings of the labour process. Namely, how resistance is engendered as much by the indeterminate social identity of employees as it is by the subjectivity associated with dominating forms of work organisation.

However, for this particular analysis of team-related resistance, we correspond with the materialist approach advocated by Edwards (1986). This is because an analysis based on Edward's position, where an omnipresent 'structured antagonism' leads to the subjection of workers to the authority of management and the need to plan production with the needs of a capitalist market, is likely to be accepted in principle by people committed to the capitalist system, yet at the same time allow us to develop genuinely objective concepts of resistance.

Indeed, many of the first accounts of teams as a potential source of resistance centred very much on Edward's materialist approach and established that resistance could actually flourish in what many believed to be inhospitable circumstances. For example, McKinlay and Taylor (1996a and 1996b) gave detailed accounts of informal team-based peer review processes and how tacit trading of scoring team members were said to nullify its disciplinary content. There were also chronicles of other ways in which teams gradually withdrew from their disciplinary role, 'silent strikes,' and, a three-week go-slow. Moreover, Palmer (1996) reported on young employees who turned out to be far less malleable than initially imagined to be by management. This was evidenced in poor attendance and high turnover that persisted despite threats of disciplinary action. As a result, management was forced into making formal and informal concessions to their lowest level and least skilled workers. However, not all reports of team activity pointed towards spirited expressions of conflict and unplanned management accommodation. For instance, Delbridge (1995) suggested that whilst worker resistance and 'misbehaviour' may persist in such circumstances, it would be in ways that are increasingly fragmentary and marginal. Similarly, Knights and McCabe (1998 and 2000) outlined arguably weak and typically individual forms of team-based resistance. These included call operatives 'mouthing words' as a means to have a rest and engaging in fiddles to avoid being disciplined.

Other research on team based resistance has focused on more detailed accounts of the process. For instance, Griffiths (1998) suggest that team-based resistance (mostly in the form of humour) can be attributed to leadership styles. More specifically, humour allowed team members to put pressure on the team leader to listen more carefully to their concerns. What is more, a series of articles lead by Kirkman (i.e. Kirkman and Shapiro, 1997; Kirkman, Jones and Shapiro, 2000; Kirkman and Shapiro, 2001) suggested 'cultural values' were a problematic reality when implementing teams as a new form of work organis ation. In effect, enduring cultural values were said to seriously conflict with the main objectives of self-managed work teams—setting goals, self-monitoring, self-evaluation, self-reward and self-punishment. It was also suggested that low levels of trust, low tolerance of change, or even a disdain for making sacrifices for others were key determinates in team-based resistance.

Recent work has started to move towards more detailed explanations of the micro-social processes that lead to resistance in teams, or at least points to why this level of analysis is necessary. For example, Vallas (2003) outlines why teams could be said to be a particularly suitable forum for resistance. Despite his admission that teamworking clearly heightened lateral tensions between team members, he argued that 'team systems' fostered new ways of resistance by providing workers with a rhetorical framework that enables them to negotiate boundaries of managerial authority. Teams are also said to enable workers to contest or recast managerial initiatives. Teams provide workers with organisational resources that can be used to claim discretionary powers that may have been previously been denied, the contradictions of control and reality of teams (essentially a re-engineered) authoritarian practices rekindled oppositional consciousness amongst workers, and, team systems essentially encourage collectivism in an environment where unions may fail to do so. However, Vallas point to a need for further research to disentangle the micro-social processes involved in team systems, yet other than the apparently paradoxical features of teamworking philosophies and teamworking realities, what are the more explicit or localised conditions that cause team members to bite the hand that feeds?

Applying a Social Identity Approach

This section is essentially guided by what we view as being the most appropriate method or theoretical framework for unravelling the micro-social processes implicated in team level resistance. Whilst a labour process perspective (e.g. Bain and Taylor, 2000) provides a sophisticated socioeconomic explanation of the structural causes of resistance, it fails to 'get to grips' with the actual phenomenon that occurs in terms of the interactions within a group that lead to and promote resistance behaviour. On the other hand, by adopting a traditional psychological approach to team resistance (e.g. Kirkman and Shapiro, 1997; Kirkman, Jones and Shapiro, 2000), the focus on the minutiae of variations in personality profiles, team size and diversity perversely ignores any impact of structure or broader context on the resistance process. In effect, we are rejecting what is commonly referred to as 'methodological individualism' (Jenkins, 1999) For these reasons, there needs to be a focus on the social psychological processes that not only explain the course of resistance within the team, but also what triggers the responses that lead to that resistance occurring.

Hence, it is proposed that by adopting a social identity approach (Tajfel, 1978; Haslam, 2004), it is possible to start to explain and refine understandings of the experience of team level resistance. Indeed, SIT has been described as being a concept that lies at the intersection of social psychology, sociology and political science, and is rapidly gaining prominence within all these fields (Sanchez-Mazas and Klein, 2003). Although SIT (e.g. Turner, 1978) was established as a distinct theory as opposed to a theoretical perspective or paradigm, it has been argued by Haslam (2001: 26) that SIT can 'lay the foundation for an alternative way of approaching' the study of behaviour within organisations, in that the psychology of the individual can not be separated from the psychological and social reality of the groups. Social identity therefore affords a mechanism for examining behaviour at both an individual and group level.

An examination of identity enables the understanding of how social interaction is bound up with individuals' social identities, i.e. their definition of themselves in terms of group memberships, as opposed to just studying individuals as individual (Haslam, 2001). Specifically, this perspective not only recognises how dimensions of the self and identity derive from individual self-enhancement strategies, but also from membership of groups and the relationship between these groups and other groups. The weight that social identity theory puts on the process by which team members acquire shared beliefs, assist in the understanding of why some groups will resist organisational control, whilst other groups subscribe to the company's ideology.

Importantly, we need to understand the interplay between social identity processes and organisational control mechanisms and how this leads to a collective notion of resistance within a team. Let us start with the knowledge that even when placed within a team, individuals do not always operate as a collective. This is accepted within the social identity approach in terms of opposite poles of social behaviour (Tajfel, 1974). At one extreme can be found interactions that are wholly determined by interpersonal relations and individual characteristics and not by the groups and categories to which they belong (Deschamps and Devos, 1998). At the opposite pole are interactions between groups of individuals that are entirely determined by their respective membership of different groups and are not affected by inter individual relations among the relevant persons (Tajfel and Turner, 1979).

These extremes of behaviour are in practice hypothetical, as membership of a social group or social category always plays some role in shaping interaction. Tajfel (1974) alleged that social identity processes start to be performed; the further behaviour is defined at the intergroup extreme of this continuum. Namely, individuals define themselves in terms of their group membership when the context in which they find themselves is defined along group-based lines. For instance, if two departments within an organisation merge, each employee is more likely to define themselves in terms of one department or the other rather than as an individual.

Consequently, Tajfel (1978) developed an important premise, that the more that behaviour becomes defined in intergroup terms, the more that members of the group would react in a similar way to members of the outgroup. A number of other writers have supported this premise, specifically that heightened group salience is associated with an increase in perceptions that of homogeneity of the group and heterogeneity of the outgroup (Haslam, Turner, Oakes, McGarty and Reynolds, 1998). David and Turner (1999) found the extreme ingroup members were more likely to influence more moderate group members in an intergroup situation as opposed to an intragroup situation. Similarly, Abrams, Marques, Brown and Henson (2000), suggested that intergroup context is an important mechanism for conveying that the ingroup is distinct from the outgroup. Other group members evaluate group members that deviate from the group norm more negatively. This premise concurs precisely with traditional psychological theory, that individuals are attracted to people who hold similar views and beliefs (Horowitz and Bordens, 1995). Moreover, recent research has found that teams where members perceive themselves as 'being similar,' have highly salient social identities regardless of whether there is the perception of the existence of an outgroup or not (Marks, 2005).

However, from an organisational perspective, there is one factor missing from the ingroup/outgroup equation. There is an assumption from SIT that by making the ingroup/outgroup comparison that there is some congruity in terms of size and structure between the two groups (Haslam, 2004). That is the ingroup and outgroup are two departments within the same organisation or two teams working within the same plant. The reality however, could be very different. The organisation itself could be viewed as the outgroup and the team the ingroup. Moreover, if this is the case, there is evidence from some writers that a highly salient team social identity is not always the product of viewing the outgroup as fundamentally different to the ingroup, it may also be a product of viewing the outgroup as similar to the team or ingroup. Jenkins (2000) argues that if an external body, such as an organisation is viewed as being legitimate in the eyes of a group, that this implies some shared beliefs and understandings of authority. As such, there will be a strong identification with both the organisation and the team. That is, if the role of the team is seen as being legitimate and team members accept the structures of control within the organisation the team will have a highly salient identity as a team or members of a team. However, Jenkins (2000) also argues that if the definition as a team results from an imposition of power or that the form of control that the organisation has or uses is not seem as legitimate the members of the team (or in Jenkins' terms the categorised) will resist.

Yet, this resistance and striving for autonomy of self-identification may in itself lead to an internalisation of the notion of the team and paradoxically, in this case, we may also find a highly salient team social identity. This notion is compatible with the work of Bacon and Blyton (2005), who explore how workers respond to teamworking and look at employee attributions of management motives for teamworking. Bacon and Blyton classify employee views of management by four main types: economic, political, institutional and cultural. What this reveals is not so much directly related to resistance strategies, it relates to the idea that workers are very much attuned with management motives for teamworking.

Crucially, the evidence from this research suggests that these workers were able to distinguish both unfavourable and beneficial aspects of new methods of organising work and at the same time scrutinise every motive management had in implementing them. As such they make informed decisions as to whether they accept teamwork both in terms of their day to day work activities and the control mechanisms associated with it.

However, as per the norm, the story is not that straightforward. It is important to understand why a highly salient team identity will embrace group members into resisting a team rather than exiting from a situation that they feel dissatisfied with. Tajfel (1975), believed that one of the fundamental components of the social identity perspective, are an individual's belief structures which also lie on a continuum from a philosophy of social mobility on the one hand to social change on the other. As long as membership of a group enhances one's self-esteem, one will remain a member of that group. But, Tajfel argues (1978), if the group fails to satisfy this requirement, the individual may try to change the structure of the group (social change); seek a new way of comparison which would favour his/her group, and hence, reinforce his/her social identity (social creativity); or leave/abandon the group with the desire to join the 'better' one (social mobility). For those with high social change beliefs, and hence high social identity salience, there is the belief that the only way to improve negative conditions lies in group action. Within an organisation, this may relate to forms of collective action such as through trade union membership, which actively presses forward for the cause of the ingroup. Hence, strong identity salience is underpinned by a supposition that that is not possible to escape one's group for self-advancement (in part due to the benefits of team membership to individual's self-esteem). In this case we are likely to see collective examples of resistance as a means of improving unfavourable conditions. On the other hand, social mobility beliefs are likely to result in individual action as individual team members sense they are free to move between groups in order to improve or maintain their social standing. In short, we argue that in a situation where a team could be said to have a strong social identity, we are likely to witness social change beliefs as the key to explaining resistance strategies. In the absence of a strong social identity salience, it is doubtful whether resistance will take a collective form.

Methods

Hotelrest was the subject of 12 weeks of intensive data collection. The methodologies used are essentially ethnographic by nature and supplemented by recognition of company documentation. Unobtrusive participant observation was considered to be the most appropriate method of investigating this form of organisational behaviour (Analoui, 1995; Analoui and Kakabadse, 1989). The data collection was undertaken by the lead author who accessed Hotelcorp by gaining paid employment and assuming the dual role of employee and research data collector.

This method of data collection has been undertaken by many other researchers (e.g. Roy, 1952; Bradney, 1957; Analoui and Kakabadse, 1989; Graham, 1995; Calvey, 2000) and helps overcomes the unwillingness of management to let academics research the phenomenon as well as the reluctance of employees to divulge information regarding the trend under investigation. Observations are efficient because it reveals behaviour that people usually prefer not to report and the researcher has greater opportunity to identify manifestations without attempts to conceal or distort them. Furthermore, longitudinal studies may reveal causal relationships. Other than documentary information in the form of corporate literature, the vast majority of data was collected in the form of daily journal entries based on observed activities, guided discussions and regular reflective accounts of emerging patterns in team activity. To demonstrate this point and commitment to the research method, the final diary of events at Hotelrest was comprised of over 30,000 words.

The daily journal entries and company data were then analysed for keywords and phrases and themes. Both authors coded data independently. They then conferred before determining final categories and codes. This is a form of content analysis, a technique social psychologists have traditionally used to deal with qualitative data (Holsti, 1968; Babbie, 2001). Although the generation of categories and themes implicit in content analysis may not be ideal for understanding some of the subtleties of the discourse in the interviews, for analysing diary data the method provides an effective portrayal of the broader culture and work structures in the organisation. Descriptions of the work process are based on the report and experience of the researcher, who only worked the day shift. Extracts from the diary are inserted when appropriate.

Unsurprisingly, the method chosen to research the reality of teamworking in the hospitality industry comes with a range of limitations and ethical issues. For instance, commenting on unobtrusive participation observation Analoui and Kakabadse (1989) believe such methods can be a 'long, laborious and often dangerous process, with the danger of "getting sacked," one's cover "being blown" or being made "redundant" ever present' (1989, p. 13). Beyond the practicalities, however, lies a range of procedural obstacles. Indeed, it is believed that the nature of being "hidden" increases the chances of the researcher becoming passive to what is going on around him or herself (Riecken, 1967) and being (hypothetically) less free than an overt observer decreases the chances of access to wider social interaction (Dean, Eichhorn and Dean, 1967). What is more, a further consideration is of knowing when to withdraw from the research site (Viditch, 1969).

Whilst it is necessary to point out that covert data collection is a surprisingly common and efficient research method (Reynolds, 1979), we cannot ignore the lack of informed consent that comes with unobtrusive methods (Bulmer, 1982). Indeed, as the British Sociological Association (2004) points out, covert methods should only be considered, 'where it is impossible to use other methods to obtain essential data' (2004, p. 5). We believe the nature of what is being researched—the reality of social interaction in a busy and highly conflictual environment combined with management unlikely to grant full access to an outsider in such situations—does not allow the use of open methods of collecting data. More importantly though, we also believe no other method is likely to allow the researcher to gain acceptance from both co-workers and management (Hodson and Sullivan, 1990).

Hotelrest and Hotelcorp

Hotelrest is the catering facility of a Hotel which is part of the Hotelcorp chain. Hotelcorp describes itself as a 'global hotel' and employs over 10,000 people in the UK alone. Its most recent management initiative is the introduction of '[Service] Standards,' or in Hotelcorp's own words: 'maintaining corporate standards through brand identity, brand position supported by behaviour, attitude, product consistency and performance.' Service Standards involve the regulation and routinisation of all dimensions of work which are clearly documented and disseminated to employees through formal documentation, team meetings and training sessions.

At the research site, Hotelcorp employs around 250 employees. The hotel's restaurant takes up to 230 'covers' a day. However, there are significant retention problems for the 60 employees that work in Hotelrest. The aggregate turnover at Hotelrest is over 50 per cent despite Hotelcorp's strategy of compulsory training and development programme focusing on 'Job-related Skills' (anonymised and JRS for short). The JRS programme has a strong emphasis on teamwork. Completing JRS training can, supposedly, be up-dated to a nationally recognised vocational qualification (NVQ level II for waiting staff and level III for supervisory staff). Moreover, completion of training entitles each employee to what Hotelcorp promotes as being a lucrative hotel-related package of benefits. This includes greatly reduced admission to the adjacent health club and highly discounted room rates throughout Hotelcorp's chain of hotels. However, JRS was not viewed as particularly effective at either engendering loyalty or retaining employees. One full time member of the waiting staff, James, explained how it had taken nearly a year to complete the JRS training and nearly two years later he was still awaiting his health club membership. Some members of staff had been with the company over a month and had, to date, received no JRS training. At team meetings employees frequently complained about waiting for their card entitling them to the benefits package. Although one employee, when commenting on the discounted room rates noted, 'you get the smallest and smelliest room that they probably couldn't sell anyway.'

Hotelrest serving staff work in groups of approximately 10 employees. The composition of the shift varies day to day dependant on scheduling. Each shift team is frequently augmented with agency workers. As well as the serving staff there are about 10 individuals working in the kitchen as chefs and kitchen porters. The hotel classifies both serving and kitchen staff as members of the Hotelrest team, however there is a clear separation between the waiting and kitchen staff. Importantly, as the fieldwork was carried out in the restaurant rather than the kitchen this is the main focus of the research.

The Hotelrest serving staff are an even mixture of waiters and waitresses, the rest are supervisors, 'hosts' or team leaders (six), two assistant managers, and one restaurant manager. All supervisory staff and assistant managers have been promoted from within; quite rapidly in some cases. However, the restaurant manager was recruited from outwith the company. There is also a dedicated trainer who works approximately 25-30 hours per week. Pay for waiting is low with those aged 22 and over receiving an hourly rate on a par with the national minimum wage (NMW). Waiters and waitresses aged 21 years or below (the majority of the waiting group) earn less than their older counterparts, but higher than the NMW for this category. Supervisors earn about ten per cent over the NMW.

Hotelrest and Teamworking

Hotelcorp presents the face of an organisation with a generous commitment to teamwork. This commitment is most acute for those who are front-line staff in the restaurant. For instance, potential Hotelrest employees are subjected to a mock team-based selling exercise during the selection procedure. During the day-long induction, new recruits are provided with an induction handbook with significant reference to the principles of teamworking. The most explicit representation to the devotion to teamworking is the compulsory and lengthy monthly team meeting. Furthermore, the upholding of Service Standards included in JRS training are based on teamworking and team communication processes, a typical eight-hour shift involves a minimum of three team briefings—immediately before serving starts, after serving ends and before re-organising restaurant for next setting, and prior to start of second period of service. As a final point, indiscipline is often confronted with team-based chastisements such as widely broadcast humiliations, e.g. team leaders regularly admonish front-line employees for neglecting their team-based loyalties and responsibilities. The lengths that Hotelrest go to in attempting to infuse a teamworking attitude amongst waiters and waitresses are epitomised during the monthly team meeting. The first team meeting during the research period lasted for just over three hours and included a presentation on teamworking as means of increasing sales.

Superficially at least, Hotelcorp looked as if its policy on the promotion of team based work was functioning effectively. When the hotel was closed or during quiet periods, and when the number of waiting staff exceeded the requirement of the number of guests dining, employees appeared to cooperate with one another and with team leaders. During these periods, this co-operation was interjected by relatively open, yet playful acts of what Ackroyd and Thompson (1999) call misbehaviour or irresponsible autonomy. These acts included waiting staff engaging in a variety of horseplay, flirting rituals and playful humour. Nevertheless, this did not tend to be at the expense of the achievement of allocated work to an acceptable standard.

Yet, the reality of teamwork for most employees was inconsistent with the rhetoric presented by the organisation. Teamwork was only really implemented as a managerial ideology aimed at tightly controlling and determining a wide range of employee behaviour and activity. Despite a clear rationale by management for teamwork—as a mechanism to implement good customer service in the guise of Service Standards—the Taylorised nature of Service Standards made the performance of any teamwork behaviour, especially under stressful conditions, impracticable. Whilst the catering group were defined as a team for the undertaking of work, there was no joint nature to the technical division of work and no collective responsibility or indeed flexibility in terms of work organisation. This is demonstrated clearly in the following sections.

Teams, Collective and Individual Resistance Strategies

As with the current work, other research on teams in the service sector found tight control, high commitment management and low value incentives (e.g. Kinnie, Hutchinson and Purcell, 2000). We also found teamwork to be unworkable due to the size and nature of supervision of the team. Teams were so poorly defined that this form of work organisation ultimately caused great conflict between groups of employees rather than harmony. The size and structure of the teams fashioned a situation which was entirely in opposition to the unitarist ideology espoused by the firm. Even the weak or diluted form of teamwork identified by other researchers failed to materialise (e.g. Batt, 1999; van den Broek, Callaghan,

Thompson, 2004). There was no indication of collective learning or problem solving (apart from the odd example of employee resistance) and the only true function of teamwork appeared to be as a structure of control over employees and Service Standards.

Any authority with the objectives of teamwork was really only apparent in times of calm when employees had a high degree of control over their work. Consent broke down under a number of specific circumstances; work intensification, mobilisation of friendship groups and endorsement of individualised strategies of resistance by management.

The diary entries detailed below demonstrate the emergence of chaos and the collapse of teamworking initiatives and other formal working policies and practices, when work conditions suddenly intensify.

> *The shift itself was a bit of a disaster, i.e. from the views of the customer and the employees. For example, the use of Service Standards broke down with tables used and not re-set, remains of meals were left on tables, long queues developed, and few if any guests got their orders on time. The team suddenly appeared to lack a will to co-operate and waiters and waitresses just looked after their own immediate concerns. This was despite the close presence of two assistant managers who were themselves put under enormous strain at this particular time of the working day. It was also apparent that Hotelcorp-employed waiters made even less effort to help the agency staff brought into deal with staff shortages (Field notes, 18 September).*

> *Today was a living nightmare. We were stretched well beyond our limits with over 370 guests for breakfast in a restaurant that has a capacity of 230, and therefore requires around 140 resets. The support I had at the beginning of the shift soon dissipated as the queue lengthened by the minute and the disquiet amongst the queuing customers increased (Field notes, 14 October).*

With no holds barred, consent and compliance with team-based values and Service Standards collapsed the moment the pace of work intensified. An increase in pace triggered a widespread inability to cope with the pressures of carrying work out in a strict and arguably unsustainable style, which occurred on an almost daily basis, but always at the weekend when customer levels were nearly always close to or at hotel capacity. It also transpired when staffing levels dropped due to unauthorised absence and high turnover of labour. When consent broke down the behaviour that ensued varied quite dramatically. Some waiters and waitresses worked on regardless and did whatever they could to satisfy the typically understanding and tolerant customers, whilst an equal number of waiters and waitresses avoided work to some degree as a result of these pressures. Importantly, under times of work pressure, friendship groups began to mobilise and perform collective forms of resistance. For outgroup members—those not included in friendship cliques—there was an almost automatic default to individualistic forms of resistance strategies.

Field notes suggested that many individual acts of resistance were, in fact, undertaken with the tacit support of the team (these included pilfering of food, unsolicited smoking breaks, stretching the time for room service request, disposal or deliberate damage of company materials such as crockery or cutlery, and unauthorised absenteeism). In contrast, far more overt examples of collective resistance included waiters and waitresses making their fellow team members aware that they suspect a mystery guest had arrived on the premises. Waiters and waitresses increasingly shunned agency staff sent to 'help' them, and there was evidence of an organised slow down once customers left the restaurant or the next shift was imminent. Further examples of this order included a broad-based boycott of the new incentive scheme introduced at the beginning of the research, and waiting staff stopping work at their official finishing time even when offered discretionary incentives, the chance to be praised at the next team briefing or even team meeting or threatened with disciplinary action.

Informal teams or friendship groups—sub-sections of a larger team—were largely often difficult for management to identify, although the use of teamworking was certainly applied as a measure to divide these informal loyalties. Mostly as a result of the ignorance of informal activity and potent commercial and operational pressures, management could only make superficial attempts to unmake these collectives. In the example below, management made an explicit attempt to counteract the 'subversive' potential of friendship groups.

Michelle [assistant manager] was setting up for the event. She had used the £40 or so tips from the last coach trippers to pay for large amounts of sweets, crisps, soft drinks, and some wine, etc. The meeting was in the McDonald suite and was set out with tables around the outside. The refreshments were in a small room to the side. From a quick head count there were about 25 waiters and six supervisors or management staff. As people came in, whether they were on duty or not, they sat with their friends. The supervisory staff sat on a table at the front of the room and looked like a panel. Dismayed that the room had been split up into cliques, Peter [one of the restaurant's 'hosts'] re-organised the waiters and waitresses in a random fashion in preparation for team activities (Field notes, 16 September).

On the other hand, many of the explicitly individualised examples of resistance were undertaken by established members of the organisation and were at least tacitly endorsed by management. For example, long tenure waiters or waitresses were allowed to 'opt out' of specific team roles or obligations, such as specialising in one favourable aspect of restaurant work when form rules disallowed this. There was also open collusion or authorisation over activities that clearly breached Service Standards.

Contradictions in Practice

We would argue that the discussion above, in part, demonstrates cynicism towards the principles of teamwork. Although Hotelrest placed a strong emphasis on the team and the notion of teamwork, the nature of the work (highly individualised) and the nature of the teams (composed of core and peripheral members) contradict the principles of teamwork and this was picked up by team members, not only in terms of behaviour, but in the way that they reacted to the formal team briefing and team training sessions. Examples of this are provided in the two diary extracts below:

After the final presentation and the room began to quiet down Jeanette [trainer] asked the team as a whole what they thought the task was really about. No one responded to this. However, Jeanette ignored the silence and went on talk about how it was a 'way of expressing yourself...exchanging ideas...working together...to give you more confidence...so you can pull together as a team'. She also asked the question 'do you think you could have done the task on your own?' In reply, a few tamely said no. Jeanette finished on the words 'we can't do it on our own', which is a phrase that I had already become increasingly familiar with (Field notes, 16 September).

The feedback session was by far the most interesting section and lasted for approximately one hour and forty minutes. I have no doubt it would have gone on much longer as after 100 minutes we had only heard from about a third of the group as other waiters and waitresses kept interjecting and upsetting the round-the-table process. Of particular note was how the session started with most staff remaining silent or failing to say much if they were asked their opinion. However, when Susan [waitress on a working holiday from Australia] began to speak out the tone of the event quickly changed. Specifically, most waiters and waitresses had clearly felt restrained until that point. Furthermore, her comments not only provoked others into action, the issues then on became increasingly critical of and specific to management (Field notes, 16 September).

It would seem that despite a high profile commitment to incorporating teamworking into the Hotelcorp's business and human resource strategy, the management at Hotelrest clearly has problems convincing the majority of restaurant employees of its merits. This was certainly the case when management arranged the opportunity for team-based feedback, i.e. the situation quickly turned from being a team bonding exercise into a forum for a range of responses that included passive silence and participation to a barrage of criticism.

However, this contradiction was unbearable for many and compelled many employees to leave Hotelcorp, in terms of the practice of what Thompson (2003) labels the externalisation of resistance. In other words, the high turnover of team members appears to be in part a result of the length that team members are prepared to tolerate both work intensification and incongruity in practice and policy. Whilst long term team members were less inclined to undertake informal resistance behaviour and sought solitude in favourable terms and conditions afforded by management, the behaviour was different for lower tenure employees. In the absence of robust forms of collectivism either in terms of the formal team or trade union representation, Hotelrest was typified by 'micro-collectivism' or cliques that were capable of transcending formal group boundaries and formal group hierarchies.

Teare, Ingram, Scheuing and Armistead (1997) noted that teams in the hospitality industry are characterised by inter-group conflict. This was confirmed by the findings of the current study. Not only were there tensions between young and old (the older members of staff thought that the younger employees were lazy), but also between the kitchen and the restaurant staff. On the 7th September the diary entry noted how there was a break time discussion about inter-group rivalry. One member of the waiting staff said 'chefs don't like us but we don't like them either.' This is a theme that was common in the field notes. Tensions arose when kitchen staff thought that waiting staff were not clearing up after themselves and therefore creating more work for the kitchen.

This division was re-enforced by kitchen staff not being invited to team meetings. Indeed, team meetings provided an arena for many other tensions in the group to be played out. This is illustrated in a diary entry dated 2nd of October:

> *It is becoming obvious that the ideas of teamwork in the restaurant do not bring cohesion between waiters and supervisors/managers. What's more, it is clear and fair to say that the 'team' is in fact at least two groups (if not more), with team-working limited to manageable tasks performed under ideal circumstances that are not typical to restaurant work. Where such occupational groups come together as a team appears to be on the basis of resisting higher-level commands and not concerning what the team should be doing (Fieldnotes, 2 October).*

The disloyalty to the team, however, is not surprising as during the three months of research in the restaurant there was only one explicit attempt at a teambuilding exercise and even this was focused on customer relations and sales. Employees were placed into groups in a team meeting and asked to sell a number of items to other members of the meeting—these items included a high chair, a soup bowl, a toast rack, tomato juice and salt and pepper sachets. No one in the room appeared to take the exercise seriously apart from management.

Yet, despite very modest training activities and supervisors being on hand to reinforce team ideals, employees complained bitterly in the wider work setting that they never received help from other team members and one noted that 'it's not my problem' or 'I've not been told to do that' were phrases that were commonly heard on the shopfloor. Indeed, further conflicts between employees were mentioned in the diary on a daily basis. On the 2nd of October, one employee threatened to 'kick the butt' of another team member over the issue of re-using dirty dishes and cutlery. The more experienced of the two then started to quote teamworking propaganda to his colleague. His tirade was based on the ideas presented in the JRS handbook—focusing on the notion of 'letting other team members down' when an employee does not pull their weight. Despite being indoctrinated with teamwork principles and ideals, normative values of being a team player and cultural on cohesion were rarely put into practice. On the 17th October, one employee even stated, 'teamworking is really every man for himself.'

In a wider sense, it was not only teamworking that made employees cynical. For instance, most employees appeared unhappy with their work, as shown in this diary entry from 23rd September.

> *I spoke to a woman who started at the same time as I did. She came out of her way to say hello and asked me what I though of the job so far. I asked her and she said 'I'd rather be stacking shelves in Tesco' (Field notes, 23 September).*

Comments such as this were common. However, there were a few employees who appeared a little happier with the work. This was often based on the advantage of the benefits package to them. A couple of female employees liked to travel round the country so made good use of the reduced rate hotel rooms. Another employee (28th October) spent a great deal of time explaining how pleased she was with her reward club membership. Although one of her colleagues stated, 'I see you are now a fully paid up member of the brainwashed club.'

A Re-Evaluation of Team Resistance Using a Social Identity Approach

Taking a very superficial analysis of events, it would appear that our findings concur with the basic premise of SIT, that by merely placing individuals within a collective that they will identify with the group (Tajfel, 1974; Tajfel, 1979). The waiting staff, in times of quiet, demonstrated communality in their work and compliance to the guiding principles of teamwork as presented by the organisation. However, when work intensified, in the terms of the labour process debate, this compliance, or in the terms of SIT, this identification with the team, dissipated, and led to a clear division in terms of both collective and resistance behaviour. This follows Jenkins' (2000) argument that suggests that if power and control mechanisms are not seen as legitimate, this may facilitate identity work. That is an individual response to pressure, which involves coping strategies that tend to be instrumentally derived tactics and accommodation to the dominant culture as well as different types of resistance (Thompson and McHugh, 2002). Instead of necessarily being controlled by the organisation, individuals are viewed as managing in the best fashion that they can, in the given circumstances and the 'form of response being determined in subjective terms by available scripts and what appears to work' (Thompson and McHugh, 2002: 346).

In this case, it was frequently at the point where work built up to potentially unmanageable levels that we started to observe the interplay in terms of behaviour between resistance and identity strategies. What is more, employees quickly sensed what was required was unreasonable, lacked legitimacy and went on to engage in behaviour to manage this situation. A social identity approach would suggest that the group as a whole would engage in behaviour to either resist or cope with the pressure. However, in the case of Hotelrest, behaviour was not that straightforward. Instead of employees' behaving in terms of the organisationally imposed idea of the team, any collective behaviour focused on illicit inter-occupational coalitions, friendship groups and cliques. Members of the team that were not part of the friendship group either failed to engage in any resistance behaviour and continued with their work or used highly individualised methods of coping. Except to continue working in an individualistic fashion made the team less efficient and likely to make committed team members cynical of teamworking. The friendship groups, in a classical correspondence with theories of group attractiveness and SIT (e.g. Horowitz and Bordens, 1995; Tajfel and Turner, 1979) resisted collectively.

Yet, contrary to the work of David and Turner (1999), who suggest that core group members define the behaviour of the entire group, these friendship groups or extreme ingroup members did not affect the behaviour of other group members. Hence, not only was there an ingroup-outgroup separation between managers and ingroup members on formal functional duties, there was a separation within the group between the cliques or friendship groups who resisted collectively and the other team members who resisted individually. Perceptions of homogeneity or attraction caused an identity affect but not throughout teams as a whole.

These group members or cliques who had a highly salient group identity when dissatisfied with the existing situation undertook resistance or misbehaviour as a group. Being a member of a subgroup or an alternative team-nurtured group served a valuable purpose in terms of self-esteem and getting work done. As such, having multiple group memberships allows in one sense alternative paths to being capable of coping with work and retaining a sense of dignity, but in another, highlights the crucial trigger for employees who in this instance are constantly faced with being members of an inferior and sub-standard group—that is, the team. Whereas the other members of the team, took what Tajfel (1978) would classify as a combination of a social creativity and social mobility response, that is appear to abandon the group (possibly the organisation as well) but also adapt the existing situation to a point which favours the individual. It is believed that the adopted research approach allowed such acute nuances to be observed and relayed to non-organisational members.

Although on the face of it this case demonstrates that the imposition of team-working can lead to team-based forms of resistance, this is a highly simplified picture. As we have demonstrated there are some serious limitations or generalisations from the social identity approach, in the assumption that by labelling people as a group that they will behave collectively. However, one compensatory factor has been to promote and not neglect the deep-seated significance of asymmetrical employment relations in forming the basis of formal and informal group activity. Moreover, this study provides further insight into a recent trend of introducing teamworking initiatives to organisations where work at an even superficial level, is in reality highly individualised.

We moved beyond an analysis that focuses on the inappropriateness of the label and the transposition of teamwork to individualised work (e.g. van den Broek, Callaghan and Thompson, 2004). We have focused on the impact that this label the label of 'team' has had on the groups with Hotelrest. We believe that, in part, the organisation created a situation that has presented little benefit in terms of motivation or productivity but may have led to team based resistance for subgroups or cliques. For these subgroups, teamworking nurtures tacit counter collectivism, despite the fact that employees themselves were also fully aware of the contradictions that they were faced within in terms of the forced commitment to teamworking without the real opportunity to practice as a team. This conflict between ideology and practice and the reaction to it by employees was expressed most clearly within the forum of the monthly team meeting.

It could be argued that the scenarios of team based resistance within manufacturing settings which have a clearer infrastructure for collective behaviour would provide more simplified and lucid accounts of the relationship between the identity process and group level resistance (e.g. McKinlay and Taylor, 1996a and 1996b; Ezzamel and Willmott, 1998). However, the benefits of the teamwork paradox observed in this study, are that they allow for a more complex understanding of why teams fail to function as planned and why identity and resistance behaviour may grow or persist on such introductions. Moreover, further benefits of this particular case study (and methods) are that they allowed observation of behaviour that may not manifest so obviously or quickly elsewhere—that is, if the intolerable conditions at Hotelrest were apparent in a highly unionised context we may expect to see serious formal industrial action, on a regular basis, and the same time less informal resistance or group behaviour.

We suggest that this work needs to be interpreted in the context in which the data was collected. Hence, it is essential to account for, if only briefly, the strengths and weaknesses of the current study. Importantly, the work reported in this study is a single organisational case study, and as such the generalisability to other organisations maybe limited. Furthermore, one researcher using a single method collected the majority of the data. Although the method was highly rigorous and detailed there is still the potential for bias. Nevertheless, there were many interesting dynamics that have emerged from this analysis and support the propositions made earlier in the paper. This work develops existing studies and theorising regarding both SIT and resistance.

Further research is required to incorporate a greater variety of team structures, team sizes, and management approach to teams. Moreover, future research into team-related resistance must cater for unionisation, professional or occupational affiliation, or any other salient identities that are prone to manifestation in the context of the workplace. It should be acknowledged at this point, that most research on workplace identity looks at employees where occupation forms a core element of an individual's identity (e.g. Marks and Lockyer's 2005 study on software developers). It is unlikely that waiting staff embrace their occupation as a strong element of their identity, which is why friendship groups were of such importance and resistance strategies so overt. If the occupation in itself, rather than the social group in the workplace, had had a greater impact on identity we may have seen less resistance behaviour. Similarly, although we can look at tensions between formal requirements and the informal group, any examination of multiple workplace identities (e.g. the organisation and the profession) are problematic due to the weak ties with work based entities. Finally, additional work using a wider array and combinations of research methods is likely to shed further light on such strategies.

References

Abrams, D., Marques, J.M., Bown, N.J., and Henson, M. (2000). Pro-norm and anti-norm deviance within in-groups and out-groups. Journal of Personality and Social Psychology, 12(4), 906–912.

Ackroyd, S, and Thompson, P. (1999). Organizational misbehaviour. London: Sage.

Analoui, F. (1995). Workplace sabotage: Its styles, motives and management. Journal of Management Development, 14(7), 48–65.

Analoui, F, and Kakabadse, A. (1989). Defiance at work. Employee Relations, 11(3).

Babbie, E. (2001). The practice of social research. London: Wadsworth.

Bacon, N. and Blyton, P. (2005). Worker responses to teamworking: Exploring employee attributions of managerial motives. International Journal of Human Resource Management, 16(2), 238–255.

Bain, P. and Taylor, P. (2000). Entrapped by the 'electronic panopticon'? Worker resistance in the call centre. New Technology, Work and Employment, 15(1), 2–18.

Barker, J. (1993). Tightening the iron cage: Concertive control in self-managing teams. Administrative Science Quarterly, 38, 408–437.

Batson, D. (1998). Altruism and prosocial behavior. In D. Gilbert, S. Fiske & G. Lindzey (Eds.), The handbook of social psychology (pp. 282–316). Boston, MA: McGraw-Hill.

Batt, R. (1999). Work organization, technology, and performance in customer service and sales. Industrial and Labor Relations Review, 52(4), 539–564.

Blyton, P. and Turnbull, P. (2004). The dynamics of employee relations (3rd ed.). Basingstoke: Palgrave Macmillan.

Bradney, P. (1957). The joking relationship in industry. Human Relations, 10, 179–187.

British Sociological Association (2004). Statement of ethical practice for the British Sociological Association. Durham: BSA.

Bulmer, M. (1982). The merits and demerits of covert participant observation. In M. Bulmer (Ed.), Social research ethics: An examination of the merits of covert participant observation (pp. 217251). London: Macmillan.

Calvey, D. (2000). Getting in the door and staying there. A covert participant study of bouncers. In G. Lee-Treweek & S. Linkogle (Eds.), Danger in the field: Risk and ethics in social research (pp. 4360). London: Routledge.

Cohen, S., Ledford, G. and Spreitzer, G. (1996). A predictive model of self-managing work team effectiveness. Human Relations, 49, 643–676.

Cully, M., Woodland, S., O'Reilly, A. and Dix, G. (1999). Britain at work: As depicted by the 1998 Workplace Employee Relations Survey. London: Routledge.

David, B. and Turner, J. (1999). Studies in self-categorization and minority conversion: The ingroup minority in intragroup and intergroup contexts. British Journal of Social Psychology, 38, 115–134.

Dean, J.P., Eichhorn, R.L. and Dean, L.R. (1969). Limitations and advantages of unstructured methods. In G.J. McCall & J.L. Simmons (Eds.), Issues in participant observation: A text and reader (pp. 19–24). London: Addison-Wesley.

Delbridge, R. (1995). Surviving JIT: Control and resistance in a Japanese transplant. Journal of Management Studies, 32(5), 803–817.

Deschamps, J.C., and Devos, T. (1998). Regarding the relationship between social identity and personal identity. In S. Worchel, J.F. Morales, D. Paez & J.C. Deschamps (Eds.), Social identity: International perspectives (pp. 1–12). London: Sage.

Edwards, P. (1986). Conflict at work: A materialist analysis of workplace relations. Oxford: Basil Blackwell.

Edwards, P. and Scullion, H. (1982). The social organization of industrial conflict: Control and resistance in the workplace. Oxford: Basil Blackwell.

Ezzamel, M. and Willmo tt, H. (1998). Accounting for teamwork: A critical study of group-based systems of organizational control. Administrative Science Quarterly, 42(2), 358–396.

Geen, R. (1998). Aggression and antisocial behavior. In D. Gilbert, S. Fiske & G. Lindzey (Eds.), The handbook of social psychology (pp. 317–356). Boston, MA: McGraw-Hill.

Graham, L. (1995). On the line at Subaru-Isuzu. The Japanese model and the American worker. New York, NY: Cornell University Press.

Griffiths, L. (1998). Humour as resistance to professional dominance in community mental health teams. Sociology of Health and Illness, 20(6), 874–895.

Haslam, A. (2001). Psychology in organizations: The social identity approach. London: Sage.

Haslam, A. (2004). Psychology in organizations: The social identity approach (2nd ed.). London: Sage.

Haslam, A., Turner, J., Oakes, C., McGarty, C. and Reynolds, K. (1998). The groups as a basis for emergent stereotype consensus. European Review of Social Psychology, 9, 203–239.

Hodson, R. and Sullivan, T. (1990). The social organization of work. London: Wadsworth.

Holsti O.R. (1969). Content analysis for the social sciences and humanities. London: Longman.

Horowitz, I. A., and Bordens, K. S. (1995). Social psychology. Mountain View, CA: Mayfield Publishing.

Jackson, P., Sprigg. C. and Parker, S. (2000). Interdependence as a key requirement for the successful introduction of team working: A case study. In S. Proctor & F. Muelle (Eds.), Teamworking (pp. 83–102). London: Macmillan.

Jenkins, R. (1999). Social Identity. London: Routledge.

Jenkins, R. (2000). Categorization: Identity, social process and epistemology. Current Sociology, 48(3), 7–25.

Jermier, J., Knights, D. and Nord, W. (1994). Resistance and power in organizations. London: Routledge.

Kinnie, N. Hutchinson, S. and Purcell, J. (2000). Fun and surveillance: The paradox of high commitment in call centres. International Journal of Human Resource Management. 11(5), 967–985.

Kirkman, B., Jones, R. and Shapiro, D. (2000). Why do employees resist teams? Examining the 'resistance barrier' to work team effectiveness. The International Journal of Conflict Management, 11(1), 74–92.

Kirkman, B. and Shapiro, D. (1997). The impact of cultural values on employee resistance to teams: Toward a model of globalised self-managing work team effectiveness. Academy of Management Review, 22(3), 730–757.

Kirkman, B. and Shapiro, D. (2001). The impact of cultural values on job satisfaction and organizational commitment in self-managing work teams: The mediating role of employee resistance. Academy of Management Journal, 44(3), 557–569.

Knights, D. and McCabe, D. (1998). 'What happens when the phone goes wild?': Stress and spaces for escape in a BPR telephone banking system work regime. Journal of Management Studies, 35(2), 163–194.

Knights, D. and McCabe, D. (2000). 'Ain't misbehavin'? Opportunities for resistance under new forms of 'quality' management. Sociology, 34(3), 421–436.

Levine, J., and Moreland, R. (1998). Small groups. In D. Gilbert, S. Fiske & G. Lindzey (Eds.), The handbook of social psychology (pp. 415–469). Boston, MA: McGraw-Hill.

Lloyd, C., and Newell, H. (2000). Selling teams to the sales force. Teamwork in the UK pharmaceutical industry. In S. Proctor & F. Mueller (Eds.), Teamworking (pp. 183–202). London: Macmillan.

Marks, A. (2005). Reconciling competing debates within the teamwork literature. A social identity approach. PhD Thesis. University of Strathclyde.

Marks, A., and Lockyer, C. (2005). Debugging the system: The impact of location on the identity of software team members. International Journal of Human Resource Management, 16(2), 219–237.

McKinlay, A. and Taylor, P. (1996a). Commitment and conflict: Worker resistance to HRM in the microelectronics industry. In B. Towers (Ed.), The handbook of human resource management (pp. 467–487). Oxford: Blackwell.

McKinlay, A. and Taylor, P. (1996b). Power, surveillance and resistance: Inside the 'factory of the future'. In P. Ackers, C. Smith & P. Smith. (Eds.), The new workplace and trade unionism: Critical perspectives on work and organization (pp. 279–300). London: Routledge.

Palmer, G. (1996). Reviving resistance: The Japanese factory floor in Britain. Industrial Relations Journal, 27(2), 129–142.

Reynolds, P.D. (1979). Ethical dilemmas and social research. An analysis of moral issues confronting investigators in research using human participants. London, Jossey-Bass.

Riecken, H.W. (1967). The unidentified interviewer. In G.J. McCall & J.L. Simmons (Eds.), Issues in participant observation: A text and reader (pp. 39–45). London: Addison-Wesley.

Roy, D. (1952). Quota restriction and goldbricking in a machine shop. American Journal of Sociology, 57(5), 427–442.

Sanchez-Mazaz, M. and Klein, O. (2003). Social identity and citizenship: Introduction to the special issue. Psychologica Belgica, 43(1), 1–8.

Sinclair, A. (1992). The tyranny of a team ideology. Organization Studies, 13, 611–626.

Tajfel, H. (1974). Social identity and intergroup behaviour. Social Science Information, 13, 65–93.

Tajfel, H. (1975). The exit of social mobility and the voice of social change. Social Change Information, 14, 101–118.

Tajfel, H. (1978). Differentation between social Groups: Studies in the social psychological of intergroup relations. London: Academic Press.

Tajfel, H. and Turner, J. (1979). An integrative theory of intergroup conflict. In W. Austin & S. Worchel (Eds.), The social psychology of intergroup conflict (pp. 33–47). Monterey, CA: Brooks/Cole.

Teare, R., Ingram, H., Scheuing, E. and Armistead, C. (1997). Organizational team-working frameworks: evidence from UK and USA-based firms. International Journal of Service Industry Management, 8(3), 250—263.

Thompson, P. (1989). The nature of work: An introduction to the debates on the labour process (2nd ed.). London: Macmillan.

Thompson, P. (2003). Fantasy island: A labour process critique of the 'age of surveillance'. Survey and Society, 1(2), 138–151.

Thompson, P. and McHugh, D. (2002). Work Organizations (3rd ed.). London: Palgrave Macmillan.

Turner, J. (1978). Social comparison, similarity and ingroup favouritism. In H. Tajfel (Ed.), Differentiation between social groups: Studies in the social psychology of intergroup relations. European Monographs in Social Psychology 14, London: Academic Press.

Turner, J. and Oakes, P. (1997). The socially structured mind. In C. McGarty & A. Haslam (Eds.), The message of social psychology (pp. 355–373). London: Blackwell.

Tyler, T, and Blader, S. (2001). Identity and co-operative behaviour in groups. Group Processes and Intergroup Relations, 4(3), 207–226.

Vallas, S. (2003). The adventures of managerial hegemony: Teamwork, ideology, and worker resistance. Social Problems, 50(2), 204–225.

van den Broek, D., Callaghan, G. and Thompson, P. (2004). Teams without teamwork? Explaining the call centre paradox. Economic and Industrial Democracy, 25(2), 197–218.

van Knippenberg, D. and van Schie, E. (2000). Foci and correlates of organisational identification. Journal of Occupational and Organisational Psychology, 73(2), 137–147.

Viditch, A.J. (1969). Participant observation and the collection and interpretation of data in G.J. McCall, & J.L. Simmons (Eds.), Issues in participant observation: A text and reader (pp. 78–86). London: Addison-Wesley.

Wall, T, Jackson, P. (1995). New manufacturing initiatives and shopfloor job design. In A. Howard (Ed.), The changing nature of work (pp. 139–174). San Francisco, CA: Jossey Bass.

Waterson, P., Clegg, C. and Axtell, C. (1997). The dynamics of work organization, knowledge and technology during software development. International Journal Human-Computer Studies, 46, 79, 101.

An Occupation in Transition: A Comprehensive Study of the Federal Human Resources Community

United States Office of Personnel Management

Executive Summary

As the leader in human resources management for the Executive Branch, the Office of Personnel Management (OPM) is committed to partnering with Federal agencies to attract, develop and retain the Human Resources (HR) professionals required for the ever changing environment of the 21st century. Fundamental to this commitment is a comprehensive three part study of the Federal HR workforce.

Part 1 highlights the demographic makeup of the HR workforce over a span of almost 30 years. This report is the second installment of OPM's overall study. Its purpose is to provide information about "competencies" with a particular emphasis on changing HR roles, emerging structures, and various competency models. Part 3 will synthesize findings from the first two reports with original research based on interviews with current practitioners including HR Directors, management focus groups, and a survey of HR professionals.

There are a number of reasons why the issue of competencies has risen to the attention of the HR community. This report highlights the following trends that are making the case for the use of HR competencies.

- *HR has undergone dramatic changes over the last five years. These include downsizing of the HR workforce, structural reorganizations, delegations of HR authority to line managers, and an influx of technology to name a few.*

- *The business of HR is changing. Increased emphasis on the need to improve the efficiency of HR services is leading to innovative approaches to redesigning HR delivery systems. In addition, agencies are redefining the role of the HR professional to be more consultative than rules-oriented.*

- *There is growing concern over how to meet organizational needs with fewer HR professionals. Competencies help organizations to focus on the characteristics their employees must possess in order for them to be successful. Competencies also provide a way to measure employee performance and to align performance with business stra-tegies.*

- *There are a number of competency models already in existence. Thus, agencies do not have to "reinvent the wheel" since many existing models can be tailored to fit individual organizational needs.*

Introduction

Background

Janice R. Lachance, Director, U.S. Office of Personnel Management, led off the Public HR Management Conference & Expo (March 1999, Washington, DC) with the assertion that HR professionals in the Federal sector workforce are in a state of transition. "Narrowly focused specialists are being asked to grow into the new generalists' roles in the evolving workplace." She went on to note, "In addition to the technical competencies that already are required, the HR generalists of the future will have to have all the skills necessary to play an active role in charting the strategic direction of our agencies."

In his book, Human Resource Champions, Dave Ulrich challenged HR to shed its old myths, adopt new competencies, redefine roles focused on results, and evolve into a true profession that makes a difference for the organization. This challenge, among others voiced by practitioners, management officials, and professional associations over the past decade, has led to the development of "HR competency models" as a way to refocus and revitalize the HR workforce. As noted by the Editor of Public HR (April 1999): "Competencies can offer [HR practitioners] an opportunity to define excellence—and, even more importantly, demonstrate the value they bring to their organizations . . . Ultimately, HR practitioners who can demonstrate their value to their organizations will inevitably be rewarded with that ever-elusive 'seat at the table.'"

The new emphasis on competencies comes at a time of tumultuous change in HR. Once considered a stable occupation defined by precise rules and standardized procedures, it is now confronting dynamic change in uncharted territory. In 1993, the National Performance Review called for HR reform and targeted reductions in staff. In response to this call, OPM abolished 10,000 pages of personnel rules, initiated HR reform legislation and adopted regulatory changes. The downsizing of the HR workforce, which continues today, began.

HR downsizing is chronicled in-depth in the first installment of our study, Federal HR Workforce Trends. From 1991 to 1998, the HR workforce decreased by 17.5 percent. (Note: Most of this downsizing was in the Department of Defense where the HR workforce decreased by 25.5 percent as contrasted with a decrease of 11 percent across all civilian agencies). A major part of the overall decrease was achieved by the early retirement of many "seasoned personnelists." This loss of HR experience and skills may be further exacerbated because about one-third of the HR community will be eligible to retire in the next five years.

This trend was already observed in 1993, in the Merit Systems Protection Board (MSPB) report Federal Personnel Offices: Time for Change which concluded that "over half of the managers and almost half of the personnel specialists surveyed cited lack of sufficient skill in the personnel staff...." The situation appears to have worsened since then. OPM's 1997 report Deregulation and Delegation of Human Resource Management Authority in the Federal Government, suggests that supervisors and managers share a similar concern over the exodus of HR expertise from Government. As one supervisor stated, "I'm concerned over what is an apparent decrease in the knowledge level of the personnel staffs as they continue to downsize."

HR in Transition

Six years after its conception, there is ample evidence of the effects that the National Performance Review has had in shaping HR. The following are examples of how HR is changing within organizations.

Agencies are Realizing that they cannot do Business as Usual

HR responsibilities, once tasked to HR staff, slowly are being delegated to managers. Many agencies have already begun outsourcing key HR services on a temporary, recurring or permanent basis. Others have restructured their HR delivery systems in an attempt to save money, improve effectiveness and/or ward off threats of outsourcing.

For example, the Department of Defense (DoD) has undertaken HR regionalization on a grand scale. In 1994, DoD made the decision to regionalize its HR delivery system. A primary purpose of regionalization was to address existing HR structural deficiencies that prevented greater efficiency in service delivery. The DoD service ratio was then 1 HR professional for 61 employees (1:61). DoD plans ultimately to increase this ratio to 1:100 through regionalization that includes the full implementation of technological enhancements. Annually, approximately $150M dollars of personnel savings and avoided costs are expected.

Managers are Taking on a Greater Role in the HR Arena

As a direct result of the National Performance Review recommendations, managers are being given increasing delegations of authority over HR matters. In light of this, DoD's regionalization was designed to increase the availability of improved technology that facilitates HR decision-making by managers and reduces workload for HR professionals. Many agencies are relying heavily on the Internet to educate managers about existing HR flexibilities. For example, the Air Force developed the Personnel Management Information Support System (PERMISS) for managers that provides basic information and guidance on civilian human resources management. This on-line system, used in conjunction with a computer-based long distance learning system, has received positive reactions from managers.

HR is Being Restructured and Reinvented

Over the last five years, many agencies, large and small, have restructured and reinvented their HR functions. The Department of Veterans Affairs has been restructuring its HR delivery services by incorporating technology into HR operations and delegating traditional HR authorities, such as classifying positions, to managers. The Department of Education's Office of Human Resources undertook a marketing campaign to highlight the services they provided to the organization. This effort resulted in being asked to "sit at the table" in a consultative role. To prepare for this new role, they reinvented themselves as a group, bringing in new staff, hiring consultants, sponsoring training seminars and incorporating technology.

As agencies continue to streamline HR, new structures are emerging to support innovative ways to deliver HR services. While there is no one right way to deliver HR, many agencies are restructuring along similar lines. A number of agencies are reorganizing their HR workforce and delivery systems around their leading customer, the manager. Within large, multi-mission agencies, service delivery is also being aligned with major mission areas (e.g., housing or community planning and development in Housing & Urban Development; contracting or logistics in the Defense Logistics Agency). Advisory services are being established, staffed by HR generalists who provide front-line advisory and consultative services to managers. "Back room" personnel functions are being centralized into shared service centers, staffed by HR specialists who coordinate and administer a variety of HR programs and services.

HR is Relying on Technology to Get its Work Done

Technology will help to shape the work of HR professionals as they carve out new roles. Access to desktop computers and linkages to computer networks will allow HR professionals to have the latest information at their finger tips as they focus on their new roles in helping managers manage. Federal agencies are increasingly reaching out to contractors and purchasing private sector HR expert systems. Of the twenty departments contacted for input to this study, seventeen are making or evaluating major technology investments to alleviate transaction workload, improve customer service, or—in the words of one—"to try to do at least better, if not more, with less."

Many Agencies are Finding New Ways to Improve the Efficiency of HR

A number of agencies are relying on the private sector for consultant expertise and advice to improve the efficiency of HR management. However, a few pioneer Federal HR offices have ventured to franchise their own operations, charging other Federal entities for services rendered. For example, the Department of Health and Human Services (HHS) restructured their HR organization by establishing a Program Support Center (PSC) to provide support services to all Federal agencies on a competitive, "fee for service" basis. It should be noted that such franchises have come to the attention of agency components dissatisfied with their existing, traditional HR service providers. This raises the possibility of "shopping for alternative service" which, some believe, may help to improve efficiency and customer service.

Some HR Offices are Transforming their HR Roles from a Rules-Based to More of a Consultative Approach

Many HR professionals have embraced the challenge of serving in the role of business strategists and change agents for their agencies. Many Federal managers are desperate for such help from HR. In response to these opportunities and demands, new HR roles are emerging along with the identification of new competencies needed to get the job done.

Private Sector Trends

Federal HR Trends are Paralleling HR Trends in the Private Sector

The 1998 study, Human Resource Competencies for the Year 2000: The Wake-Up Call by the Society for Human Resource Management (SHRM), found that some surveyed participants assumed their roles were relatively secure. Others were either in denial over the emerging HR trends or in fear of the future viability of HR as a function. Still, many saw the current situation as an opportunity to play a more critical role in the organization. The study indicated also that most HR professionals need to build new competencies and skills immediately. Although many study participants were aware of the changing environment, the overall picture seems to be that HR in the private sector is behind the curve in preparing itself for new roles and responsibilities. In another study focusing on HR in the private sector, only 10-35 percent of the HR workforce reported having the necessary competencies to operate effectively in the new environment.

Regardless of the Competency Gap, HR Roles in the Private Sector Continue to Change Significantly

As the following table shows, HR staffs spent 22 percent of their time maintaining records in the early 1990's compared to only 15 percent in 1996. The role of HR auditing fell from 19.4 percent to 12 percent during this same period. The shift is toward the role of strategic partner (22 percent) and the development of new HR systems and practices (19 percent). These results suggest that while HR professionals will need the traditional HR competencies that have served them well in the past, they will also need new competencies to support changing roles.

Competencies and HR

In the struggle to rethink new approaches to HR, many private businesses and government entities are moving toward competencies and competency-based systems as the answer to meeting organizational needs. But what do we mean by competencies and how do they actually relate to HR? For the purpose of this study, the following definition was chosen for the word "competency": "An underlying characteristic of an employee (i.e., a motive, trait, skill, aspects of one's self-image, social role, or a body of knowledge) which results in effective and/or superior performance (Boyatzis, 1982)."

Table

Human Resources Roles Are Changing			
	1989 - 1991	1996	Difference
Maintaining Records *Collect, track and maintain data on employees*	22.2%	15.0%	Significant Decrease
Auditing/Controlling *Ensure compliance to internal operations, regulations, legal and union requirements*	19.4%	12.0%	Significant Decrease
HR Service Provider *Assist with implementation and administration of HR practices*	35.0%	31.3%	Significant Decrease
Practice Development *Develop new HR systems and practices*	14.0%	19.0%	Significant Increase
Strategic Business Partner *Member of the management team. Involved with strategic HR planning, organization design and strategic change*	11.0%	22.0%	Significant Increase

Source: Adapted from a 1996 study by the Center for Effective Organizations, University of Southern California, and the Human Resources Planning Society, as published in "WORKFORCE," May 1998.

Competencies may be grouped as follows (Tucker and Cofsky, 1994):

- skills: the demonstration of expertise (e.g., the ability to make effective presentations, or to negotiate successfully);

- knowledge: information accumulated in a particular area of expertise (e.g., accounting, human resources management);

- self-concepts: attitudes, values and self-image;

- traits: a general disposition to behave in certain ways (e.g., flexibility); and

- motives: recurrent thoughts driving behaviors (e.g., drive for achievement, affiliation).

Organizations that have used competencies tend to define these competencies in their own terms, tailored to their own unique situations. The National Park Service, for example, defines its competencies as a combination of knowledge, skills, and abilities in a particular career field which when acquired, allows a person to perform a task or function at a specifically defined level of proficiency.

Competencies can be further broken down into different categories that distinguish different purposes and/or uses:

- Essential Competencies serve as the foundation of knowledge and skills needed by everyone. (Spencer et al., 1990). These can be developed through training and are relatively easy to identify.

- Differentiating Competencies distinguish superior performance from average performance (Spencer et al., 1990). These include self-concepts, traits and motives and although hard to develop, can determine long-term success on the job. With a valid competency-development methodology, one can define, measure and reward these competencies.

- Strategic Competencies include those that are "core" competencies of the organization. These tend to focus on organizational capability and include competencies that create a competitive advantage (e.g., innovation, speed, service, technology).

Why Competencies?

Competencies can be used to Facilitate Change in Human Resources

There is recognition that the role of HR is moving from an emphasis on rules to a focus on results. To help facilitate this paradigm shift, a variety of organizations, both public and private, are identifying new competencies. Competencies are being used as a way to refocus the organization on what is really important and what it takes for the workforce to be successful. In addition, competencies provide the mechanism to zero in on the technical aspects of a particular job and devise a critical path through regulations and laws to the results desired by management. Furthermore, competency models highlight competencies needed by the organization and serve as vehicles for change.

Competencies can be used to "Raise the Bar" on Employee Performance

According to a 1996 American Compensation Association (ACA) study focusing on competency applications in HR, organizations are using competencies to integrate selection, training, appraisal, and compensation. In staffing, competencies are used to select and promote employees. In human resources development, competencies are used to identify and close the gaps in individuals' capabilities. In performance management, competencies and results are appraised to connect how a job was done to the results achieved. In compensation, pay can be based on the certified skills and competencies used on the job. Many hope that competencies will also help their organizations communicate desired behaviors, control costs and increase customer satisfaction.

Competencies are also being used in the following ways to Support the New Role of Human Resources

- as a strategy to strengthen the link with organizational culture, results, and individual performance by emphasizing competencies that are needed across occupational specialties;

- as a tool to help describe work and what is required from employees in jobs in a broader, more comprehensive way;

- as a method to align individual and team performance with organization, vision, strategies, and the external environment.

How do Competencies Relate to KSAs?

Traditionally knowledges, skills, and abilities (KSAs) have been used in the Federal Government to determine an applicant's qualifications for selection or promotion. Such KSAs serve as the foundation for competency models. Competencies can be used to assess and train employees for future needs, while KSAs focus typically on what is needed to do the job today. Competencies build upon the same KSAs used under the current Federal system but are more inclusive in that they also include traits, motives, and behaviors.

Additionally, key knowledge, skills and abilities can be clustered to form a set of competencies that determine superior, not just basic, performance. Competencies can then be linked to a set of behaviors that answer the question, "How do we know good per-formance when we see it?" And they can serve as the foundation to hire, train and develop employees and ultimately to set their pay. The ease of integrating all HR applications and communicating these linkages to stakeholders appears to be an attractive feature of competencies and serves as the compelling reason for their increasing popularity over traditional HR methods.

Knowledge, skills and abilities (KSAs) and competencies are not mutually exclusive, but can complement and build upon each other to reinforce desired behaviors.

What is a Competency Model?

New Competencies, New Roles

In his book, Human Resource Champions, David Ulrich speaks of a new vision for HR, "that it be defined not by what it does, but by what it delivers—results that enrich the organization's value to customers, investors (taxpayers), and employees." He believes HR needs to shed "Old Myths" and take on "New Realities" (Figure 2), and adopt competencies and redefine roles focused on results in order to evolve into a true profession that makes a difference for the organization.

Table

OLD MYTHS	NEW REALITIES
People go into HR because they like people.	HR departments are not designed to provide corporate therapy or social or health-and-happiness retreats. HR professionals must create the practices that make employees more competitive, not more comfortable.
Anyone can do HR.	HR activities are based on theory and research. HR professionals must master both theory and practice.
HR deals with the soft side of a business and is therefore not accountable.	The impact of HR practices on business results can and must be measured. HR professionals must learn how to translate their work into financial performance.
HR focuses on costs, which must be controlled.	HR practices must create value by increasing the intellectual capital within the firm. HR professionals must add value, not reduce costs.
HR's job is to be the policy police and the health-and-happiness patrol	The HR function does not own compliance - managers do. HR practices do not exist to make employees happy but to help them become committed. HR professionals must help managers commit employees and administer policies.
HR is full of fads.	HR practices have evolved over time. HR professionals must see their current work as part of an evolutionary chain and explain their work with less jargon and more authority.
HR is staffed by nice people.	At times, HR practices should force vigorous debates. HR professionals should be confrontational and challenging as well as supportive.
HR is HR's job	HR work is as important to line managers as are finance, strategy, and other business domains. HR professionals should join with managers in championing HR issues.

Source: Ulrich, Dave, *Human Resource Champions*, Harvard Business School Press, Boston, MA, 1997. p. 18

Ulrich's vision of the "New Realities" of HR is applicable to the Federal sector. With HR changes occurring in the Federal Government related to HR processes, structures, and delivery of HR services, Federal HR professionals are taking on new roles to perform effectively in this changing environment.

What are these new roles and what competencies are needed? The National Academy of Public Administration (NAPA) was a pioneer in identifying the Federal HR competencies needed today. In its report, A Competency Model for Human Resources Professionals, NAPA convened three groups of Federal agency HR directors, senior staff and expert level specialists to pro-vide insights and input into the development of a compe-tency model designed for the Federal HR workforce. The competency model includes 30 competencies and carves out five HR roles for the Federal HR Professional: business partner, change agent, leader, HR expert, and advocate.

HR's capability to assume new roles and increase the level of new competencies will determine the magnitude and impact HR will have on the organization in the future.

The International Personnel Management Association (IPMA) has also been active in this arena, developing its competency model based on the NAPA model. The IPMA model includes 22 competencies divided into four major HR roles: HR expert, business partner, change agent and leader. While recognizing the continued importance of the HR expert role, the IPMA model envisions a new HR professional who partners with managers to proactively devise effective solutions to organizational problems, leads and manages change, and serves as a role model to promote leadership, ethics and integrity.

The IPMA Competency Model shows the interrelationship among the four roles. The roles are carried out in the context of the work that needs to be accomplished and the organizational environment. Each role is performed separately but is closely related and often requires the same competencies. The HR expert role serves as a foundation for all other roles and competencies. The combination of technical expertise and other competencies results in superior performance.

OPM's Personnel Resources and Development Center has done extensive research on the application of competencies in the HR arena. The Human Resources Competency Model depicts a compilation of the NAPA, IPMA, and OPM research. Five HR roles are exhibited with corresponding competencies. The HR expert role serves as a foundation for all other roles and competencies. The combination of technical expertise and other competencies results in superior performance.

In addition, OPM's research was crucial to the development of a new more general competency framework based on the concept of "emotional intelligence." The Emotional Competence Framework is based on the idea that emotional intelligence may be more important than cognitive intelligence as a determinate of outstanding performance at work. The five elements (Selfawareness, Motivation, Self-regulation, Empathy, and Social Skills) reflect the way workers handle interpersonal relationships on the job. The framework also provides the corresponding skills that must be learned to achieve emotional competence.

The Department of Defense's (DoD) HR Competency Framework includes three over-arching competency components (business management, professional and technical HR) that are common in DoD's HR environment. Applicable occupations range from generalists and specialists to HR managers. The DoD HR Competency Framework recognizes the evolving role of the HR practitioner, transitioning from performing paper intensive work to becoming a strategic business partner with management. "Soft" skills (e.g., team building, customer service and problem solving) are important, as well as HR technical knowledge and skills in order for the HR professional to be effective in today's world.

Behavioral Anchors

Competency experts warn that competency models need to include "behavioral anchors," or as they are often called, "behavioral indicators." Such anchors typically include scales which measure the varying degrees of a given competency that an employee is required to display. This is critical if the competency model is to be used as a "basis of legally defensible decisions related to selection, development or compensation." (Tucker and Cofsky, 1994)

Behavioral anchors need to describe observable and specific behaviors that leave no room for interpretation or assumptions. These behaviors can be measured to determine whether or not an employee meets a defined competency. A performance management system can be tailored to tie these behaviors to results for the purpose of identifying whether these behaviors are exhibited and informing employees about why they are important. The following table is an example of a customer-service competency that includes behavioral anchors (Tucker and Cofsky, 1994).

Table

Competency: Understanding and Meeting Customer Needs Description: The demonstrated desire to work with, serve or do something helpful for customers. Includes initiative and tenacity in understanding the needs of others, including internal customers, external customers, suppliers and vendors.
BEHAVIORAL ANCHORS (from low to high level)
1. Follows up on customer issues: Follows through on customer inquiries, requests or complaints. Keeps customers updated about progress of projects or services, but does not explore customers' issues or problems.
2. Seeks to understand customer issues: Maintains clear communication with customers regarding mutual expectations. Monitors customer satisfaction. Listens and responds to customers' concerns. Is sensitive to resource concerns of customers.
3. Takes full personal responsibility for resolving issues: Personally sees that customer problems or concerns are addressed satisfactorily. Demonstrates leadership in resolving conflicts with customers. Is fully available to customers, especially during critical periods.
4. Adds value beyond customer issues: Works to add value to the customer and to make things better than the customer may expect.
5. Assesses underlying customer needs: Seeks information about the real, underlying needs of customers beyond those expressed initially and matches these needs to available or customized services. Looks for long term benefits to the customer.
6. Becomes a trusted adviser: Gets personally involved in customer activities and decisions. Develops an independent opinion on customers' current and long-term needs, problems, opportunities and alternatives for implementation. Acts on this opinion, for example, by recommending appropriate approaches that are new and different from those requested by the customer.
7. Sacrifices short-term benefits for long term benefits: Takes customers' side against the organization, as necessary, with long-term mutual benefit to customers and the organization.

Source: Hay/McBer as printed in ACA Journal, Spring 1994, Volume 3, Number 1.

Competencies and Emerging Structures

A review of the literature shows that organizations seeking to move to the new HR competency models are not sure of the best way to position HR to serve as a strategic business partner. The reality is that organizations are starting from different positions and will need to structure their HR functions in different ways based on mission. There is no "one size fits all" solution. To overcome these barriers, the literature recommends that organizations begin to ask three overarching questions:

(1) What is the optimum HR structure for the company?

(2) Does this optimum structure require different skills?

(3) Do current HR practitioners possess the new skills or must the company provide them with new tools and competencies?

Finding answers to these questions is the first step in aligning HR competencies with organizational structures. According to the California Strategic Human Resource Partnership, a consortium of senior HR business executives, the competencies needed by senior HR generalists are very different, for example, from those required of HR specialists at other parts of the organization structure. The Partnership commissioned a study that included interviews with leading HR corporate executives. Based on research and inter-views with ten leaders representing Fortune 500 companies, researchers developed and proposed an Integrative Model of HR Competencies, one that corresponds to the emerging structure of HR in the private sector.

There was consensus between HR researchers and practitioners regarding current and future HR competencies. The overall list of competencies is fairly consistent among companies from various industries, although different competencies are emphasized in different HR roles. Researchers support the value of developing a new HR competency model that is both generic (applicable to companies in different industries) and specific (i.e., highlighting the competency differences in different HR roles and structural levels).

The study also concluded that the next wave of HR competency models should be able to account for different competencies depending on where in the organizational structure HR professionals find themselves. In the public sector, the evolution of HR structures is still taking place. Once the major components are in place, organizations will be able to build structure-based competency models that can be used to tailor and operationalize the competencies needed to meet the requirements of each organizational level and the needs of various customers.

Looking to the Future

One More Piece in the Competency Puzzle

The traditional role of HR is based on the image of an HR practitioner providing services (policy, advice, technical assistance, transaction processing, etc.) to a set of customers (organizations, individuals). With the focus changing to integrating HR into organizational business planning, another dimension is added to this picture of HR service delivery. Namely, those HR professionals who are managers and supervisors must take on the emerging roles of business partner, change agent, and leader in new organizational structures different from the past. Their challenge is even more daunting as they try to model the new or expected competencies, while continuing the day-to-day operational and political management of HR.

In many environments, they must do all this with a downsized staff which does not have the expertise or abilities (competencies) needed to meet the demands. These current leaders of the HR function—advocating the new roles for HR, seeking and sometimes finding the elusive seat at the table, orchestrating the HR transformation—are setting the course for the future of the HR occupation. Are they capable of meeting all these challenges? How are we preparing them to meet these challenges? Are we preparing others for these leadership roles when current leaders retire or move on?

Preparing for the Challenges Ahead

In the years ahead, agencies will likely be given new authorities to design unique pay systems tailored to their agency mission. HR professionals will be relied upon by managers to use their HR technical competencies to help design and implement these new pay systems and to meet other challenges that arise in aligning HR systems to agency mission. In addition to HR technical expertise which will be a continuing requirement, competencies in the areas of system design, organizational culture, business strategy, change, consensus building, consultation, communication, and marketing skills will be even more important than they are now.

The development of Demonstration Projects under 5 U.S.C. 47 is one illustration of HR professionals already serving in these new roles and using the new competencies. Demonstration Projects are vehicles to test innovative approaches to HR that require waivers from title 5. A cross-functional team of HR experts and agency managers partner with OPM to design new HR systems from scratch or tailor previously tested innovations for new environments.

Based on the demonstration experience, managers will be willing to bring HR "to the table" once HR has proven its worth. The most credible HR professionals in the eyes of the managers are those who serve in the role of business partner by providing a variety of options and solutions. Instead of just saying "no" to some perhaps ill-conceived idea, HR experts say "yes" and help managers design systems tailored to their agencies within the framework of the Merit System Principles. With increased flexibility in pay, performance-based organizations and higher expectations on the part of line managers for strategic HR programs, HR will also be relied upon to a greater extent to serve in the role of change agent. That is, they will be called upon not only to design new HR systems and processes, but also to facilitate and manage the change process.

Knowing that these changes are necessary is a major step on the road to transforming HR. To begin moving forward, agencies need to know where they stand in terms of the necessary HR competencies that are required for organizational effectiveness. As mentioned earlier, the next report in this study will provide findings and insights on which competencies are currently possessed by Federal HR professionals. These will be compared to those competencies which experts in both the private and Federal sectors say are needed now and in the future. Based on this analysis, competency gaps will be identified and practical recommendations will be made so that each agency can assess its own situation, take corrective actions, and better prepare to meet the future challenges of our dynamic HR community.

References

American Compensation Association. Raising the Bar: Using Competencies to Enhance Employee Performance. May 1996.

American Compensation Association's Competencies Research Team. "The Role of Competencies in an Integrated HR Strategy." ACA Journal. Summer 1996. Pages 5–21.

Cofsky, Kathryn M. "Critical Keys to Competency-Based Pay." Compensation & Benefits Review. November-December 1993. Pages 46–52.

Corporate Leadership Council. Developing Individual Competencies for HR Professionals. April 1998. Pages. 1–13. Washington: The Advisory Board Company.

Corporate Leadership Council. Developing a Strategic HR Function: Aligning Individual Competencies. January 1997. Washington: The Advisory Board Company.

Laabs, Jennifer. "Why HR Can't Win Today." Workforce. May 1998. Pages 62–74. National Academy of Public Administration. A Competency Model for Human Resources Professionals. June 1996.

Schoonver, Stephen C., Phd. Human Resource Competencies for the Year 2000: The Wake-Up Call.

Society for Human Resource Management. 1998. Spencer, Lyle M., David C. McClelland, and Signe M. Spencer. Competency Assessment Methods: History and State of the Art. Boston: Hay/McBer Research Press. 1990.

Spencer, Lyle M., and Signe M. Spencer. Competence at Work: Models for Superior Performance. New York: J. Wiley & Sons. 1993.

Tucker, Sharon A., and Kathryn M. Cofsky. "Competency-Based Pay on a Banding Platform." ACA Journal. Spring 1994. Volume 3. Number 1.

Ulrich, Dave. "The Future Calls for Change." Workforce. January 1998. Pages 87–91.

Ulrich, Dave. Human Resource Champions. Harvard Business School. Boston, MA. 1997. Pages 1– 281.

Ulrich, Dave. "A New Mandate for Human Resources." Harvard Business Review. 1998. USDA Graduate School. Competency Based Training Task Force Report. October 1998.

U.S. Merit Systems Protection Board. Federal Personnel Offices: Time for Change? 1993.

Yeung, Arthur, Patricia Woolcock, and John Sullivan. "Identifying and Developing HR Competencies for the Future: Keys to Sustaining the Transformation of HR Functions." Human Resource Planning. 1996. Volume 19. Number 4. Pages 48–58.

The Importance of Human Resources Management in Health Care: A Global Context

Stefane M. Kabene, Carole Orchard, John M. Howard,
Mark A. Soriano and Raymond Leduc

ABSTRACT

Background

This paper addresses the health care system from a global perspective and the importance of human resources management (HRM) in improving overall patient health outcomes and delivery of health care services.

Methods

We explored the published literature and collected data through secondary sources.

Results

Various key success factors emerge that clearly affect health care practices and human resources management. This paper will reveal how human resources management is essential to any health care system and how it can improve health care models. Challenges in the health care systems in Canada, the United States of America and various developing countries are examined, with suggestions for ways to overcome these problems through the proper implementation of human resources management practices. Comparing and contrasting selected countries allowed a deeper understanding of the practical and crucial role of human resources management in health care.

Conclusion

Proper management of human resources is critical in providing a high quality of health care. A refocus on human resources management in health care and more research are needed to develop new policies. Effective human resources management strategies are greatly needed to achieve better outcomes from and access to health care around the world.

Background

Defining Human Resources in Health Care

Within many health care systems worldwide, increased attention is being focused on human resources management (HRM). Specifically, human resources are one of three principle health system inputs, with the other two major inputs being physical capital and consumables [1]. Figure 1 depicts the relationship between health system inputs, budget elements and expenditure categories.

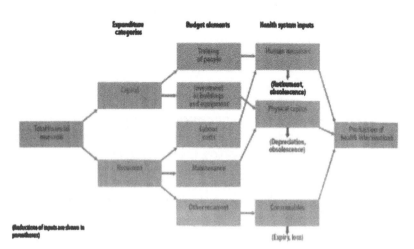

Figure 1. Relationship between health system inputs, budget elements and expenditure categories. Source: World Health Report 2000 Figure 4.1 pg.75. http://www.who.int.proxy.lib.uwo.ca:2048/whr/2000/en/whr00_ch4_en.pdf

Figure 1 identifies three principal health system inputs: human resources, physical capital and consumables. It also shows how the financial resources to purchase these inputs are of both a capital investment and a recurrent character. As in other industries, investment decisions in health are critical because they are generally irreversible: they commit large amounts of money to places and activities that are difficult, even impossible, to cancel, close or scale down [1].

Human resources, when pertaining to health care, can be defined as the different kinds of clinical and non-clinical staff responsible for public and individual health intervention [1]. As arguably the most important of the health system inputs, the performance and the benefits the system can deliver depend largely upon the knowledge, skills and motivation of those individuals responsible for delivering health services [1].

As well as the balance between the human and physical resources, it is also essential to maintain an appropriate mix between the different types of health promoters and caregivers to ensure the system's success [1]. Due to their obvious and important differences, it is imperative that human capital is handled and managed very differently from physical capital [1]. The relationship between human resources and health care is very complex, and it merits further examination and study.

Both the number and cost of health care consumables (drugs, prostheses and disposable equipment) are rising astronomically, which in turn can drastically increase the costs of health care. In publicly-funded systems, expenditures in this area can affect the ability to hire and sustain effective practitioners. In both government-funded and employer-paid systems, HRM practices must be developed in order to find the appropriate balance of workforce supply and the ability of those practitioners to practise effectively and efficiently. A practitioner without adequate tools is as inefficient as having the tools without the practitioner.

Key Questions and Issues Pertaining to Human Resources in Health Care

When examining health care systems in a global context, many general human resources issues and questions arise. Some of the issues of greatest relevance that will be discussed in further detail include the size, composition and distribution of the health care workforce, workforce training issues, the migration of health workers, the level of economic development in a particular country and sociodemographic, geographical and cultural factors.

The variation of size, distribution and composition within a county's health care workforce is of great concern. For example, the number of health workers available in a country is a key indicator of that country's capacity to provide delivery and interventions [2]. Factors to consider when determining the demand for health services in a particular country include cultural characteristics, sociodemographic characteristics and economic factors [3].

Workforce training is another important issue. It is essential that human resources personnel consider the composition of the health workforce in terms of both skill categories and training levels [2]. New options for the education and in-service training of health care workers are required to ensure that the workforce is aware of and prepared to meet a particular country's present and future needs [2]. A properly trained and competent workforce is essential to any successful health care system.

The migration of health care workers is an issue that arises when examining global health care systems. Research suggests that the movement of health care professionals closely follows the migration pattern of all professionals in that the internal movement of the workforce to urban areas is common to all countries [2]. Workforce mobility can create additional imbalances that require better workforce planning, attention to issues of pay and other rewards and improved overall management of the workforce [2]. In addition to salary incentives, developing countries use other strategies such as housing, infrastructure and opportunities for job rotation to recruit and retain health professionals [2], since many health workers in developing countries are underpaid, poorly motivated and very dissatisfied [3]. The migration of health workers is an important human resources issue that must be carefully measured and monitored.

Another issue that arises when examining global health care systems is a country's level of economic development. There is evidence of a significant positive correlation between the level of economic development in a country and its number of human resources for health [3]. Countries with higher gross domestic product (GDP) per capita spend more on health care than countries with lower GDP and they tend to have larger health workforces [3]. This is an important factor to consider when examining and attempting to implement solutions to problems in health care systems in developing countries.

Socio-demographic elements such as age distribution of the population also play a key role in a country's health care system. An ageing population leads to an increase in demand for health services and health personnel [3]. An ageing population within the health care system itself also has important implications: additional training of younger workers will be required to fill the positions of the large number of health care workers that will be retiring.

It is also essential that cultural and geographical factors be considered when examining global health care systems. Geographical factors such as climate or topography influence the ability to deliver health services; the cultural and political values of a particular nation can also affect the demand and supply of human resources for health [3]. The above are just some of the many issues that must be addressed when examining global health care and human resources that merit further consideration and study.

The Impact of Human Resources on Health Sector Reform

When examining global health care systems, it is both useful and important to explore the impact of human resources on health sector reform. While the specific health care reform process varies by country, some trends can be identified. Three of the main trends include efficiency, equity and quality objectives [3].

Various human resources initiatives have been employed in an attempt to increase efficiency. Outsourcing of services has been used to convert fixed labor expenditures into variable costs as a means of improving efficiency. Contracting-out, performance contracts and internal contracting are also examples of measures employed [3].

Many human resources initiatives for health sector reform also include attempts to increase equity or fairness. Strategies aimed at promoting equity in relation to needs require more systematic planning of health services [3]. Some of these strategies include the introduction of financial protection mechanisms, the targeting of specific needs and groups, and re-deployment services [3]. One of the goals of human resource professionals must be to use these and other measures to increase equity in their countries.

Human resources in health sector reform also seek to improve the quality of services and patients' satisfaction. Health care quality is generally defined in two ways: technical quality and sociocultural quality. Technical quality refers to the impact that the health services available can have on the health conditions of a population [3]. Sociocultural quality measures the degree of acceptability of services and the ability to satisfy patients' expectations [3].

Human resource professionals face many obstacles in their attempt to deliver high-quality health care to citizens. Some of these constraints include budgets, lack of congruence between different stakeholders' values, absenteeism rates, high rates of turnover and low morale of health personnel [3].

Better use of the spectrum of health care providers and better coordination of patient services through interdisciplinary teamwork have been recommended as part of health sector reform [4]. Since all health care is ultimately delivered by people, effective human resources management will play a vital role in the success of health sector reform.

Methods

In order to have a more global context, we examined the health care systems of Canada, the United States of America, Germany and various developing countries. The data collection was achieved through secondary sources such as the Canadian Health Coalition, the National Coalition on Health Care and the World Health Organization Regional Office for Europe. We were able to examine the main human resources issues and questions, along with the analysis of the impact of human resources on the health care system, as well as the identification of the trends in health sector reform. These trends include efficiency, equity and quality objectives.

Results

Health Care Systems

Canada

The Canadian health care system is publicly funded and consists of five general groups: the provincial and territorial governments, the federal government, physicians, nurses and allied health care professionals. The roles of these groups differ in numerous aspects. See Figure 2 for an overview of the major stakeholders in the Canadian health care system.

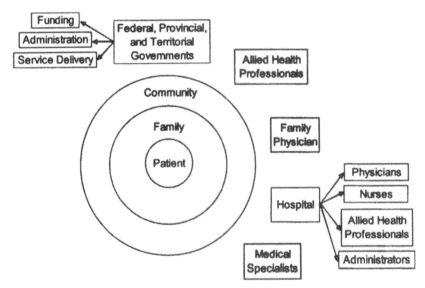

Figure 2. Overview of the major stakeholders in the Canadian health care system.

Figure 2 depicts the major stakeholders in the Canadian health care system and how they relate.

Provincial and territorial governments are responsible for managing and delivering health services, including some aspects of prescription care, as well as planning, financing, and evaluating hospital care provision and health care services [5]. For example, British Columbia has shown its commitment to its health care program by implementing an increase in funding of CAD 6.7 million in September 2003, in order to strengthen recruitment, retention and education of nurses province-wide [6]. In May 2003, it was also announced that 30 new seats would be funded to prepared nurse practitioners at the University of British Columbia and at the University of Victoria [6]. Recently the Ontario Ministry of Health and Long Term Care announced funding for additional nurse practitioner positions within communities. Furthermore, most provinces and territories in Canada have moved the academic entry requirement for registered nurses to the baccalaureate level, while increasing the length of programmes for Licensed Practice Nurses to meet the increasing complexity of patient-care needs. Several provinces and territories have also increased seats in medical schools aimed towards those students wishing to become family physicians [7].

The federal government has other responsibilities, including setting national health care standards and ensuring that standards are enforced by legislative acts such as the Canada Health Act (CHA) [5]. Constitutionally the provinces are responsible for the delivery of health care under the British North America (BNA) Act; the provinces and territories must abide by these standards if they wish to receive federal funding for their health care programs [8]. The federal government also provides direct care to certain groups, including veterans and First Nation's peoples, through the First Nationals and Inuit Health Branch (FNIHB). Another role of the federal government is to ensure disease protection and to promote health issues [5].

The federal government demonstrates its financial commitment to Canada's human resources in health care by pledging transfer funds to the provinces and direct funding for various areas. For example, in the 2003 Health Care Renewal Accord, the federal government provided provinces and territories with a three-year CAD 1.5 billion Diagnostic/Medical Equipment Fund. This was used to support specialized staff training and equipment that improved access to publicly funded services [6].

The third group – private physicians – is generally not employed by the government, but rather is self-employed and works in a private practice. They deliver publicly-funded care to Canadian citizens. Physicians will negotiate fee schedules for their services with their provincial governments and then submit their claims to the provincial health insurance plan in order to receive their reimbursement [5].

The roles of nurses consist of providing care to individuals, groups, families, communities and populations in a variety of settings. Their roles require strong, consistent and knowledgeable leaders, who inspire others and support professional nursing practice. Leadership is an essential element for high-quality professional practice environments in which nurses can provide high-quality nursing care [9].

In most Canadian health care organizations, nurses manage both patient care and patient care units within the organization. Nurses have long been recognized as the mediators between the patient and the health care organization [10]. In care situations, they generally perform a coordinating role for all services needed by patients. They must be able to manage and process nursing data, information and knowledge to support patient care delivery in diverse care-delivery settings [10]. Workplace factors most valued by nurses include autonomy and control over the work environment, ability to initiate and sustain a therapeutic relationship with patients and a collaborative relationship with physicians at the unit level [11].

In addition to doctors and nurses, there are many more professionals involved in the health care process. Allied health care professionals can consist of pharmacists, dietitians, social workers and case managers, just to name a few. While much of the focus is on doctors and nurses, there are numerous issues that affect other health care providers as well, including workplace issues, scopes of practice and the impact of changing ways of delivering services [12]. Furthermore, with health care becoming so technologically advanced, the health care system needs an increasing supply of highly specialized and skilled technicians [12]. Thus we can see the various roles played by these five groups and how they work together to form the Canadian health care system.

Canada differs from other nations such as the United States of America for numerous reasons, one of the most important being the CHA. As previously mentioned, the CHA sets national standards for health care in Canada. The CHA ensures that all Canadian citizens, regardless of their ability to pay, will have access to health care services in Canada. "The aim of the CHA is to ensure that all eligible residents of Canada have reasonable access to insured health services on a prepaid basis, without direct charges at the point of service" [6].

Two of the most significant stipulations of the CHA read: "reasonable access to medically necessary hospital and physician services by insured persons must be unimpeded by financial or other barriers" and "health services may not be withheld on the basis of income, age, health status, or gender" [5]. These two statements identify the notable differences between the Canadian and American health care systems. That is, coverage for the Canadian population is much more extensive.

Furthermore in Canada, there has been a push towards a more collaborative, interdisciplinary team approach to delivering health care; this raises many new issues, one of which will involve successful knowledge transfer within these teams [13]. Effective knowledge management, which includes knowledge transfer, is increasingly being recognized as a crucial aspect of an organization's basis for long-term, sustainable, competitive advantage [34]. Even though health care in Canada is largely not for profit, there will still be the need for effective knowledge management practices to be developed and instituted. The introduction of interdisciplinary health teams in Canadian hospitals is a relatively new phenomenon and their connection to the knowledge management policies and agendas of governments and hospital administrations raises important questions about how such teams will work and to what extent they can succeed in dealing with the more difficult aspects of knowledge management, such as the transfer of tacit knowledge.

The multidisciplinary approach tends to be focused around specific professional disciplines, with health care planning being mainly top-down and dominated by medical professionals. Typically there is a lead professional (usually a physician) who determines the care and, if necessary, directs the patient to other health care specialists and allied professionals (aides, support workers). There is generally little involvement by the patient in the direction and nature of the care. Interdisciplinary health care is a patient-centred approach in which all those involved, including the patient, have input into the decisions being made.

The literature on teamwork and research on the practices in hospitals relating to multidisciplinary teams suggests that interdisciplinary teams face enormous challenges [13], therefore multidisciplinary teamwork will continue to be a vital part of the health care system. However, the goal of this teamwork should not be to displace one health care provider with another, but rather to look at the unique skills each one brings to the team and to coordinate the deployment of these skills. Clients need to see the health worker most appropriate to deal with their problem [14].

Some of the issues regarding the Canadian public system of health have been identified in the Mazankowski Report, which was initiated by Alberta's Premier Ralph Klein in 2000. Many issues have arisen since this time and have been debated among Canadians. One of the most contentious, for example, is the possibility of introducing a two-tier medical system. One tier of the proposed new system would be entirely government-funded through tax dollars and would serve the same purpose as the current publicly-funded system. The second tier would be a private system and funded by consumers [5].

However, the CHA and the Canadian Nurses Association (CNA) are critical of any reforms that pose a threat to the public health care system. It should be noted that although Canada purports to have a one-tier system, the close proximity of private, fee-for-service health care in the United States really creates a pay-as-you-go second tier for wealthy Canadians. In addition, many health care services such as most prescriptions and dental work are largely funded by individuals and/ or private or employer paid insurance plans.

It is important to realize the differences between the proposed two-tier system and the current health care system. Presently, the public health care system covers all medically necessary procedures and the private sector provides 30% for areas such as dental care. With the new system, both public and private care would offer all services and Canadians would have the option of choosing between the two.

The proposal of the two-tier system is important because it highlights several important issues that concern many Canadians, mainly access to the system and cost reduction. Many Canadians believe the current public system is not sustainable and that a two-tiered system would force the public system to become more efficient and effective, given the competition of the private sector. However, the two-tiered system is not within the realm of consideration, since the majority of Canadians are opposed to the idea of a privatized system [5]. No proposals have come forward that show how a privately funded system would provide an equal quality of services for the same cost as the current publicly funded system.

United States of America

The health care system in the United States is currently plagued by three major challenges. These include: rapidly escalating health care costs, a large and growing number of Americans without health coverage and an epidemic of substandard care [15].

Health insurance premiums in the United States have been rising at accelerating rates. The premiums themselves, as well as the rate of increase in premiums, have increased every year since 1998; independent studies and surveys indicate that this trend is likely to continue over the next several years [15]. As a result of these increases, it is more difficult for businesses to provide health coverage to employees, with individuals and families finding it more difficult to pay their share of the cost of employer-sponsored coverage [15]. The rising trend in the cost of employer-sponsored family health coverage is illustrated in Figure 3.

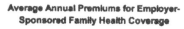

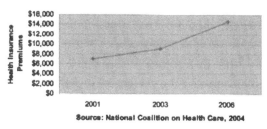

Figure 3. The trend of the cost of employer-sponsored family health care coverage in the United States. Source: National Coalition on Health Care 2004 pg.9. http://www.nchc.org/materials/studies/reform.pdf.

Figure 3 illustrates the increase in health insurance premiums since 2001. These increases are making it more difficult for businesses to continue to provide health coverage for their employees and retirees [15].

To help resolve this problem, health maintenance organizations (HMO) have been introduced, with the goal of focusing on keeping people well and out of hospitals in the hope of decreasing employer costs. HMOs are popular alternatives to traditional health care plans offered by insurance companies because they can cover a wide variety of services, usually at a significantly lower cost [16]. HMOs use "networks" of selected doctors, hospitals, clinics and other health care providers that together provide comprehensive health services to the HMOs members [16]. The overall trade-off with an ***HMO Is Reduced Choice in Exchange for Increased Affordability.***

Another problem to address regarding the American health care system is the considerable and increasing number of Americans without health coverage. Health care coverage programs such as Medicare offer a fee-for-service plan that covers many health care services and certain drugs. It also provides access to any doctor or hospital that accepts Medicare [17]. Patients with limited income and resources may qualify for Medicaid, which provide extra help paying for prescription drug costs [17]. However, according to figures from the United States Census Bureau, the number of Americans without health coverage grew to 43.6 million in 2002; it is predicted that the number of uninsured Americans will increase to between 51.2 and 53.7 million in 2006 [15].

Those Americans without health care insurance receive less care, receive care later and are, on average, less healthy and less able to function in their daily lives than those who have health care insurance. Additionally, the risk of mortality is 25% higher for the uninsured than for the insured [15].

Despite excellent care in some areas, the American health care system is experiencing an epidemic of substandard care; the system is not consistently providing high-quality care to its patients [15]. There appears to be a large discrepancy between the care patients should be receiving and the care they are actually getting. The Institute of Medicine has estimated that between 44 000 and 98 000 Americans die each year from preventable medical errors in hospitals [15].

It is also useful to examine the demographic characteristics of those Americans more likely to receive substandard care. Research shows that those Americans with little education and low income receive a lower standard of care [18]. This finding may be explained by the fact that patients who have lower education levels tend to have more difficulty explaining their concerns to physicians, as well as eliciting a response for those concerns because health professionals often do not value their opinions [18].

Case Studies

As shown by the extensive literature, statistics and public opinion, there is a growing need for health care reform in the United States of America. There is a duty and responsibility of human resources professionals to attempt to elicit change and implement policies that will improve the health care system.

Case 1

It is informative to examine case studies in which human resources professionals have enacted positive change in a health care setting. One such case from 1995 is that of a mid-sized, private hospital in the New York metropolitan area. This case presents a model of how human resources can be an agent for change and can partner with management to build an adaptive culture to maintain strong organizational growth [19].

One of the initiatives made by human resources professionals in an attempt to improve the overall standard of care in the hospital was to examine and shape the organization's corporate culture. Steps were taken to define the values, behaviors and competences that characterized the current culture, and analyze these against the desired culture [19]. A climate survey was conducted in the organization; it became the goal of the human resources professionals to empower employees to be more creative and innovative [19]. To achieve this, a new model of care was designed that emphasized a decentralized nursing staff and a team-based approach to patient care. Nursing stations were redesigned to make them more accessible and approachable [19].

Human resources management also played an important role in investing in employee development. This was achieved by assisting employees to prepare and market themselves for internal positions and if desired, helping them pursue employment opportunities outside the organization [19]. This case makes obvious the important roles that human resources management can play in orchestrating organizational change.

Case 2

Another case study that illustrates the importance of human resources management to the health care system is that of The University of Nebraska Medical Center in 1995. During this period, the hospital administrative staff recognized a variety of new challenges that were necessitating organizational change. Some of these challenges included intense price competition and payment reform in health care, reduced state and federal funding for education and research, and changing workforce and population demographics [20]. The organizational administrators recognized that a cultural reformation was needed to meet these new challenges. A repositioning process was enacted, resulting in a human resources strategy that supported the organization's continued success [20]. This strategy consisted of five major objectives, each with a vision statement and series of action steps.

- Staffing: Here, the vision was to integrate a series of organization-wide staffing strategies that would anticipate and meet changing workforce requirements pertaining to staff, faculty and students. To achieve this vision, corporate profiles were developed for each position to articulate the core competences and skills required [20].

- Performance management: The vision was to hold all faculty and staff accountable and to reward individual and team performance. With this strategy, managers would be able to provide feedback and coaching to employees in a more effective and timely manner [20].

- Development and learning: The vision was to have all individuals actively engaged in the learning process and responsible for their own development. Various unit-based training functions were merged into a single unit, which defined critical technical and behavioral competencies [20].

- Valuing people: The vision was to have the hospital considered as a favored employer and to be able to attract and retain the best talent. To facilitate this vision, employee services such as child care and wellness were expanded [20].

- Organizational effectiveness. The vision was to create an organization that is flexible, innovative and responsive [20]. The developments of these human resources strategies were essential to the effectiveness of the organization and to demonstrate the importance of human resources in the health care industry.

Both these case studies illustrate that effective human resources management is crucial to health care in a practical setting and that additional human resources initiatives are required if solutions are to be found for the major problems in the United States health care system.

Germany

Approximately 92% of Germany's population receives health care through the country's statutory health care insurance program, Gesetzliche Krankenversicherung (GKV). GKV designed an organizational framework for health care in Germany and has identified and constructed the roles of payers, providers and hospitals. Private, for-profit companies cover slightly less than 8% of the population. This group would include, for example, civil servants and the self-employed. It is estimated that approximately 0.2% of the population does not have health care insurance [21]. This small fragment may be divided into two categories: either the very rich, who do not require it, or the very poor, who obtain their coverage through social insurance. All Germans, regardless of their coverage, use the same health care facilities. With these policies nearly all citizens are guaranteed access to high-quality medical care [22].

While the federal government plays a major part in setting the standards for national health care policies, the system is actually run by national and regional autonomous organizations. Rather than being financed solely through taxes, the system is covered mostly by health care premiums [22]. In 2003, about 11.1% of Germany's gross domestic product (GDP) went into the health care system [23] versus the United States, with 15% [24] and Canada at 9.9% [25]. However, Germany still put about one third of its social budget towards health care [22].

The supply of physicians in Germany is high, especially compared to the United States, and this is attributed largely to the education system. If one meets the academic requirements in Germany, the possibility to study medicine is legally guaranteed [26]. This has led to a surplus of physicians and unemployment for physicians has become a serious problem. In 2001, the unemployment rate for German physicians of 2.1% led many German doctors to leave for countries such as Norway, Sweden and the United Kingdom, all of which actively recruit from Germany [27].

Germany's strong and inexpensive academic system has led the country to educate far more physicians than the United States and Canada. In 2003, Germany had 3.4 practicing physicians per 1000 inhabitants [23], versus the United States, which had 2.3 practicing physicians per 1000 inhabitants in 2002 [24] and Canada, which had 2.1 practicing physicians per 1000 inhabitants in 2003 [25]. It is also remarkable that health spending per capita in Germany (USD 2996) [23] amounted to about half of health spending per capita in the United States (USD 5635) [24], and slightly less than Canada's health spending (USD 3003) [25]. This clearly demonstrates the Germans' strength regarding cost containment.

There are several issues that physicians face in the German health care system. In a 1999 poll, 49.9% of respondents said they were very or fairly satisfied with their health care system, while 47.7% replied they were very or fairly dissatisfied with it [28]. Furthermore, the degree of competition between physicians is very high in Germany and this could lead to a reduction in physician earnings. Due to this competition, many younger physicians currently face unemployment. The German law also limits the number of specialists in certain geographical areas where there are issues of overrepresentation [22]. Thus, the oversupply of physicians in Germany leads to many challenges, including human resources management in the health care system.

In Germany a distinction is made between office-based physicians and hospital-based physicians. The income of office-based physicians is based on the number and types of services they provide, while hospital-based physicians are compensated on a salary basis. This division has created a separated workforce that German legislation is now working to eliminate by encouraging the two parties to work together, with the aim of reducing overall medical costs [22].

Developing Countries

Accessing good-quality health care services can be incredibly arduous for those living in developing countries, and more specifically, for those residing in rural areas. For many reasons, medical personnel and resources may not be available or accessible for such residents. As well, the issue of migrant health care workers is critical. Migrant health workers can be defined as professionals who have a desire and the ability to leave the country in which they were educated and migrate to another country. The workers are generally enticed to leave their birth country by generous incentive offers from the recruiting countries [29].

Developing countries struggle to find means to improve living conditions for their residents; countries such as Ghana, Kenya, South Africa and Zimbabwe are seeking human resources solutions to address their lack of medically trained professionals. Shortages in these countries are prevalent due to the migration of their highly educated and medically trained personnel.

Professionals tend to migrate to areas where they believe their work will be more thoroughly rewarded. The International Journal for Equity in Health (2003) suggested that those who work in the health care profession tend to migrate to areas that are more densely populated and where their services may be better compensated. Health care professionals look to areas that will provide their families with an abundance of amenities, including schools for their children, safe neighborhoods and relatives in close proximity. For medical professionals, the appeal of promotions also serves as an incentive for educating oneself further [30]. As one becomes more educated, the ability and opportunity to migrate increases and this can lead to a further exodus of needed health care professionals.

These compelling reasons tend to cause medical professionals to leave their less-affluent and less-developed areas and migrate to areas that can provide them with better opportunities. This has caused a surplus in some areas and a huge deficit in others. This epidemic can be seen in nations such as Nicaragua. Its capital city, Managua, holds only one fifth of the country's population, yet it employs almost 50% of the medically trained health care workers. The same situation can be found in other countries, such as Bangladesh, where almost one third of the available health personnel are employed "in four metropolitan districts where less than 15% of the population lives" [30]. Clearly this presents a problem for those living outside these metropolitan districts.

Other possible explanations put forth by Dussault and Franceschini, both of the Human Development Division of the World Bank Institute, include "management style, incentive and career structures, salary scales, recruitment, posting and retention practices" [31]. Salary scales can differ quite drastically between originating and destination countries, which are shown in Figures 4 and 5. They also state that in developing countries the earning potential one would see in more affluent or populated urban areas is much higher than one would expect to earn in rural areas.

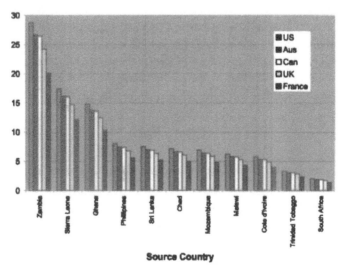

Source Country

Figure 4. Ratio of nurse wages (PPP USD), destination country to source country. Source: Vujicic M, Zurn P, Diallo K, Orvill A, Dal Poz MR 2004. http://www.human-resources-health.com/content/2/1/3.

Figure 4 shows the difference between the wage in the source country and destination country for nurses. This difference is also known as the "wage premium" [29].

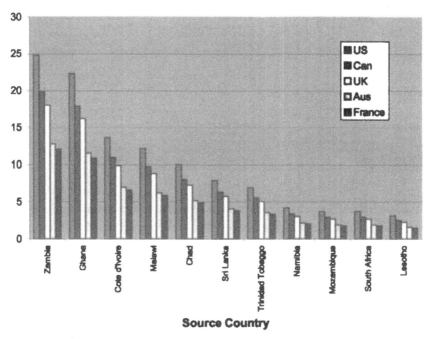

Figure 5. Ratio of physician wages (PPP USD), destination country to source country. Source: Vujicic M, Zurn P, Diallo K, Orvill A, Dal Poz MR 2004. http://www.human-resources-health.com/content/2/1/3.

Figure 5 shows the difference between the wage in the source country and destination country for physicians [29].

As more health professionals emigrate to urban areas, the workloads for those in the rural areas greatly increase. This leads to a domino effect, in that those in such dire situations look for areas where they may be able to find more satisfactory and less demanding working conditions [31]. Vujicic et al. (2004) summarizes numerous variables that influence the migration pattern and has created a formula to express their impact. It is possible to quantify the factors, and human resources professionals need to look at the costs and benefits of altering the factors so that the migration pattern is more favorable. This formula is expressed as the results shown in Table 1, which shows the different reasons for one to migrate in terms of the popularity of a given reason.

Table 1. Factors influencing health care professionals' intent to migrate, reason for migrating and willingness to remain in their home country. Source: Vujicic M, Zurn P, Diallo K, Orvill A, Dal Poz MR 2004 http://www. human-resources-health.com/content/2/1/3.

	For what reasons do you intend to leave your home country?	For what reasons did you leave your home country?	What would make you remain in your home country?
Cameroon	Upgrade qualifications (85%)	Recruited (29%)	Salary (68%)
	Gain experience (80%)	Gain experience (28%)	Continuing education (67%)
	Lack of promotion (80%)	Better pay (17%)	Working environment (64%)
	Living conditions (80%)	Living conditions (19%)	Health care system management (55%)
Ghana		Gain experience (86%)	Salary (81%)
		Lack of promotion (88%)	Work environment (64%)
		Despondency (86%)	Fringe benefits (77%)
		Living conditions, Economic decline (71%)	Resources in health sector (70%)
Senegal	Salary (89%)		Work environment (n/a)
	N/a		Salary (n/a)
	N/a		Better career path (n/a)
	N/a		Benefits (n/a)
South Africa	Gain experience (43%)		Salary (78%)
	Violence and crime (38%)		Work environment (68%)
	Heavy workload (41%)		Fringe benefits (66%)
	Declining health service (38%)		Workload (59%)
Uganda	Salary (72%)	Salary (55%)	Salary (84%)
	Living conditions (41%)	Economic decline (55%)	Fringe benefits (54%)
	Upgrade qualifications (38%)	Save money (54%)	Work environment (36%)
	Gain experience (24%)	Declining health service (53%)	Workload (30%)
Zimbabwe	All factors	All factors	All factors

There is a tendency for developed countries faced with decreasing numbers of nationally trained medical personnel to recruit already-trained individuals from other nations by enticing them with incentives. Zimbabwe has been particularly affected by this problem. In 2001, out of approximately 730 nursing graduates, more than one third (237) of them relocated to the United Kingdom [29]. This was a dramatic increase from 1997, when only 26 (approximately 6.2%) of the 422 nursing program graduates migrated to the United Kingdom [29]. This leads to the loss of skilled workers in developing countries and can be very damaging, since the education systems in developing countries are training individuals for occupations in the medical profession, yet are not able to retain them [29].

Countries that have the capacity to educate more people than necessary in order to meet their domestic demand have tried to counterbalance this problem by increasing their training quota. Vujicic et al. (2004) identify that "the Philippines has for many years trained more nurses than are required to replenish the domestic stock, in an effort to encourage migration and increase the level of remittance flowing back into the country" [29].

Developed countries attract internationally trained medical professionals for many reasons. To begin with, "political factors, concerns for security, domestic birth rates, the state of the economy and war (both at home and abroad)" [26] influence the number of people that will be allowed or recruited into a country. Also, due to the conditions of the labor market compared to the demand in developed countries, governments may make allowances to their strict policies regarding the type of and number of professionals they will allow into their country [29]. This can be seen in a Canadian example:

Canada maintains a list of occupations within which employment vacancies [are] evident. Potential immigrants working in one of these [listed] occupations would have a much higher chance of being granted entry than if they worked in a non-listed occupation [29].

Though Canada attracts internationally trained medical professionals, those employment vacancies may not always be open. Although there may be up to 10 000 international medical graduates (IMG) in Canada, many are not legally allowed to practice. Many immigrants cannot afford the costs of retraining and may be forced to find a new job in a completely unrelated field, leaving their skills to go to waste [32]. In 2004, Ontario had between 2000 and 4000 IMGs looking for work in medical fields related to their training and background [33]. That year, IMG Ontario accepted 165 IMGs into assessment and training positions, which was a 50% increase over the last year, and a 600% increase from the 24 positions in 1999 [33].

Another appeal for developed countries with regard to foreign trained health care professionals is that they may be less of a financial burden to the host country than those trained domestically. This is because educational costs and the resources necessary for training are already taken care of by the international medical schools and governments [29]. Though these reasons may make recruiting foreign medical professionals seem appealing, there are still ongoing debates as to whether those trained outside the host country are equally qualified and culturally sensitive to the country to which they migrate. Developing countries are addressing these concerns by establishing health professional training programs similar to those in developed countries [29]. These practices can be seen in, "the majority of nursing programs in Bangladesh, the Philippines and South Africa [which] are based on curricula from United Kingdom or USA nursing schools" [29]. Because of these actions, those who are trained may be more likely to leave and use their skills where they will be recognized and more highly rewarded.

There are also ethical considerations when examining the practice of recruiting health care professionals, particularly if they are recruited from regions or countries where health care shortages already exist. The rights of individuals to move as they see fit may need to be balanced against the idea of the greater good of those left behind.

Due to the shortages, it has been found the level of health service in rural or poor areas has decreased, leading to lower quality and productivity of health services, closure of hospital wards, increased waiting times, reduced numbers of available beds for inpatients, diversion of emergency department patients and underuse of remaining personnel or substitution with persons lacking the required skills for performing critical interventions [30].

The article "Not enough here, too many there: understanding geographical imbalances in the distribution of the health workforce" (2003), states that a reduced number of health care workers in a given area has a direct effect on the life expectancy of its residents. For example, in the rural areas of Mexico, life expectancy is 55 years, compared to 71 years in the urban areas. Additionally, in "the wealthier, northern part of the country, infant mortality is 20/1000 as compared to more than 50/1000 in the poorer southern states" [31].

Globalization—A Common Thread

While the issues raised in this article are common to many countries, the approaches taken to address them may not be the same in each country. Factors affecting the approaches that can be taken, some of which have been raised, include demographics, resources and philosophical and political perspectives. However, an overarching issue that affects not only health care but many other areas is that of globalization itself.

Different countries have traditionally had different perspectives on health care that have influenced their approaches to health care delivery. In Canada for example, health care is considered a right; its delivery is defined by the five main principles of the Canada Health Act, which officially precludes a significant role for private delivery of essential services. In the United States, health care is treated more as another service that, while it should be accessible, is not considered a right. Therefore there is a much larger private presence in health care delivery the United States than there is in Canada. In other parts of the world, the approach to health care falls between these perspectives.

As the move towards globalization for many goods and services increases, countries will have to consider how this will affect their approaches to health care delivery. As mentioned earlier, there is already a degree of labor mobility within a country that affects the quality and availability of health care services. There is also already a degree of international mobility of health care workers, as shown by the number of workers recruited developed countries.

While the international mobility of labor is generally not as unencumbered as that for goods and capital, that may be changing as more and more regional free trade agreements are considered. Canada, the United States and Mexico have NAFTA (North American Free Trade Agreement), Europe has the EU (European Union) and talks are under way to consider expanding the NAFTA agreement to include Central and South America, to expand EU membership and to consider an Asian trading bloc including China and India.

If health care becomes a part of these new trade agreements, countries will be obliged to treat health care delivery according to the rules of the agreement.

Using the NAFTA as an example, if health care is included, governments could not treat domestic providers more favorably than foreign firms wanting to deliver services. In Canada the concern is that it would mean the end of the Canada Health Act, since NAFTA would allow private, for-profit American or Mexican firms to open.

All five issues raised in this research would be affected by the increase in international trade agreements that included health care. Therefore, governments, health care providers and human resources professionals cannot ignore this important consideration and trend when examining solutions to the issues. Depending upon their relative negotiation strengths and positions, some countries may not benefit as much as others with these agreements.

For example, it is more likely that countries with well-developed private, for-profit, health care expertise, such as the United States, would expand into developing countries rather than the other way around. If there is an increased ability for labor mobility, then it is likely that health care professionals in the poorer, developing countries would move to where the opportunities are better. We already see this internally in the move from rural to urban centers; this would likely continue if the health care professionals had the opportunity to move out of country to where they could have greater financial rewards for their expertise.

When considering the countries examined in this paper, it is likely that Canada and the United States would initially be the two most likely to move towards a more integrated approach to health care delivery. There is already a trade agreement in place, many of the factors influencing health care are similar (demographics, training, level of economic development, geography, cultural factors) and they are currently each other's largest trading partners. While the current agreement, which includes Mexico, does not cover health care, there is pressure to broaden the agreement to include areas not currently covered. If this happens, human resources professionals will have to increase their understanding of what the new health care delivery realities could be. For example, if the move is more towards the Canadian example of a largely not-for-profit, mainly publicly-funded health care delivery system, then it will be more of an adjustment for the American professionals.

However, the likelihood of the Canadian approach to health care's being adopted in the United States is very slim. During the presidency of Bill Clinton, the government attempted to introduce a more universal health care delivery system, which failed completely. Even though there are over 40 million Americans with no health care coverage, the idea of a universal, publicly-funded system went nowhere. Also, within Canada there is increasing pressure to consider a more active role for private health care delivery. Therefore, it is more likely that Canadian health care and human resource professionals will have to adapt to a style more like the American, privately delivered, for-profit approach.

If this is the direction of change, human resources professionals in Canada will need to adjust how they approach the challenges and new realities. For instance, there would likely be an increased role for insurance companies and health maintenance organizations (HMO) as they move towards the managed care model of the United States. With an HMO approach, financial as well as health needs of the patients are considered when making medical decisions. An insured patient would select from the range of services and providers that his/her policy covers and approves. Human resources professionals would need to work with a new level of administration, the HMO, which currently does not exist to any significant degree in Canada.

As mentioned earlier, it is likely that developing countries would be receiving health care models and approaches from developed countries rather than the other way around. In particular, a country such as the United States that has a strong, private, for-profit approach already in place would likely be the source from which the health care models would be drawn. Therefore, health care, as well as human resources professionals in those countries, would also need to adapt to these new realities.

In Germany, where there is currently an oversupply of physicians, a move towards a more global approach to health care delivery, through increased trade agreements, could result in even more German health care professionals' leaving the country. The challenge to be addressed by human resource professionals within the German health care system in this situation would be to prevent, or slow, the loss of the best professionals to other countries. Spending public resources in educating professionals only to have significant numbers of them leave the country is not a financially desirable or sustainable situation for a country.

Discussion

While examining health care systems in various countries, we have found significant differences pertaining to human resources management and health care practices. It is evident that in Canada, CHA legislation influences human resources management within the health care sector. Furthermore, the result of the debate on Canada's one-tier versus two-tier system may have drastic impacts on the management of human resources in health care. Additionally, due to a lack of Canadian trained health professionals, we have found that Canada and the United States have a tendency to recruit from developing countries such as South Africa and Ghana, in order to meet demand.

Examination of the relationship between health care in the United States and human resources management reveals three major problems: rapidly escalating health care costs, a growing number of Americans without health care coverage and an epidemic regarding the standard of care. These problems each have significant consequences for the well-being of individual Americans and will have devastating affects on the physical and psychological health and well-being of the nation as a whole.

The physical health of many Americans is compromised because these factors make it difficult for individuals to receive proper consultation and treatment from physicians. This can have detrimental effects on the mental state of the patient and can lead to large amounts of undue stress, which may further aggravate the physical situation.

Examining case studies makes it evident that human resources management can and does play an essential role in the health care system. The practices, policies and philosophies of human resources professionals are imperative in developing and improving American health care. The implication is that further research and studies must be conducted in order to determine additional resource practices that can be beneficial to all organizations and patients.

Compared to the United States, Canada and developing countries, Germany is in a special situation, given its surplus of trained physicians. Due to this surplus, the nation has found itself with a high unemployment rate in the physician population group. This is a human resources issue that can be resolved through legislation. Through imposing greater restrictive admissions criteria for medical schools in Germany, they can reduce the number of physicians trained. Accompanying the surplus problem is the legislative restriction limiting the number of specialists allowed to practice in geographical areas. These are two issues that are pushing German-trained physicians out of the country and thus not allowing the country to take full advantage of its national investment in training these professionals.

Developing countries also face the problem of investing in the training of health care professionals, thus using precious national resources, but losing many of their trained professionals to other areas of the world that are able to provide them with more opportunities and benefits. Human resources professionals face the task of attempting to find and/or retain workers in areas that are most severely affected by the loss of valuable workers.

Human resources management plays a significant role in the distribution of health care workers. With those in more developed countries offering amenities otherwise unavailable, chances are that professionals will be more enticed to relocate, thus increasing shortages in all areas of health care. Due to an increase in globalization, resources are now being shared more than ever, though not always distributed equally.

Human Resources Implications of the Factors

While collectively the five main areas addressed in the article represent health care issues affecting and affected by human resources practices, they are not all equal in terms of their influence in each country. For instance, in Canada there are fewer health care issues surrounding the level of economic development or migration of health workers, whereas these issues are much more significant in developing countries. In the United States, the level of economic development is not a significant issue, but the accessibility of health care based upon an individual's financial situation certainly is, as evidenced by the more than 40 million Americans who have no health care coverage. Germany's issues with the size of its health care worker base have to do with too many physicians, whereas in Canada one of the issues is having too few physicians. Table 2 summarizes some of the implications for health care professionals with regard to the five main issues raised in the article. One of the main implications of this paper, as shown in Table 2, is that HRP will have a vital role in addressing all the factors identified. Solutions to health care issues are not just medical in nature.

Table 2. Human resources implications of the factors

	Countries			
Factors	Canada	United States	Germany	Developing countries
Number, composition and distribution of health care workers				
Workforce training issues				
Migration of health workers				
Level of economic development in a country				
Sociodemographic, geographical and cultural				

Policy Approaches in a Global Approach to Health Care Delivery

As mentioned at the start of this paper, there are three main health system inputs: human resources, physical capital and consumables. Given that with sufficient resources any country can obtain the same physical capital and consumables, it is clear that the main differentiating input is the human resources. This is the input that is the most difficult to develop, manage, motivate, maintain and retain, and this is why the role of the human resources professional is so critical.

The case studies described earlier showed how human resources initiatives aimed at improving organizational culture had a significant and positive effect on the efficiency and effectiveness of the hospitals studied. Ultimately all health care is delivered by people, so health care management can really be considered people management; this is where human resources professionals must make a positive contribution.

Human resource professionals understand the importance of developing a culture that can enable an organization to meet its challenges. They understand how communities of practice can form around common goals and interests, and the importance of aligning these to the goals and interests of the organization.

Given the significant changes that globalization of health care can introduce, it is important that human resources professionals be involved at the highest level of strategic planning, and not merely be positioned at the more functional, managerial levels. By being actively involved at the strategic levels, they can ensure that the HR issues are raised, considered and properly addressed.

Therefore, human resources professionals will also need to have an understanding not only of the HR area, but of all areas of an organization, including strategy, finance, operations, etc. This need will have an impact on the educational preparation as well as the possible need to have work experience in these other functional areas.

Conclusion

We have found that the relationship between human resources management and health care is extremely complex, particularly when examined from a global perspective. Our research and analysis have indicated that several key questions must be addressed and that human resources management can and must play an essential role in health care sector reform.

The various functions of human resources management in health care systems of Canada, the United States of America, Germany and various developing countries have been briefly examined. The goals and motivations of the main stakeholders in the Canadian health care system, including provincial governments, the federal government, physicians, nurses and allied health care professionals, have been reviewed. The possibility of a major change in the structure of Canadian health care was also explored, specifically with regard to the creation of a two-tier system. The American health care system is currently challenged by several issues; various American case studies were examined that displayed the role of human resources management in a practical setting. In Germany, the health care situation also has issues due to a surplus of physicians; some of the human resources implications of this issue were addressed. In developing countries, the migration of health workers to more affluent regions and/or countries is a major problem, resulting in citizens in rural areas of developing countries experiencing difficulties receiving adequate medical care.

Since all health care is ultimately delivered by and to people, a strong understanding of the human resources management issues is required to ensure the success of any health care program. Further human resources initiatives are required in many health care systems, and more extensive research must be conducted to bring about new human resources policies and practices that will benefit individuals around the world.

Competing Interests

The author(s) declare that they have no competing interests.

Authors' Contributions

SK conceived the paper, worked on research design, did data analysis and led the writing of the paper. CO, JH, MS and RL all actively participated in data analysis, manuscript writing and review. All authors read and approved the final manuscript.

Acknowledgements

The authors are grateful to Valerie Sloby from PCHealthcare for her editorial assistance and helping in reviewing the manuscript.

References

1. World Health Organization: [http://www.who.int.proxy.lib.uwo.ca:2048/whr/2000/en/whr00_ch4_en.pdf] World Health Report 2000. Health Systems: Improving Performance. Geneva. 2000.

2. World Health Organization: [http://www.who.int.proxy.lib.uwo.ca:2048/whr/2003/en/Chapter7-en.pdf] World Health Report 2003: Shaping the Future. Geneva. 2003.

3. Zurn P, Dal Poz MR, Stilwell B, Adams O: Imbalance in the health workforce. Human Resources for Health 2004, 2:13.

4. Kirby MJL: The health of Canadians – the federal role. In The Senate of the Government of Canada. Volume 6. Ottawa, ON: Government of Canada; 2002:78.

5. Makarenko J: [http://www.mapleleafweb.com/features/medicare/mazankowski/index.html.] The Mazankowski Report: A Diagnosis of Health Care in Canada. Edmonton, AB: Government of the Province of Alberta; 2002.

6. Dosanjh U: [http://www.hcsc.gc.ca/medicare/Documents/CHAAR%202003-04.pdf] Canada Health Act Report 2003–2004. Ottawa: Government of Canada; 2004.

7. Ministry of Health and Long term Care: [http:/ / www.health.gov.on.ca/ english/ public/ pub/ ministry_reports/ nurseprac03/ exec_summ.pdf] Report on the Integration of Primary and Health Care Nurse Practitioners into the Province of Ontario. Toronto, ON; 2005.

8. Canadian Health Coalition: [http://www.healthcoalition.ca/history.html] The History of Medicare Shows that Canadians Can Do It. Ottawa, ON;

9. Canadian Nurses Association: Succession Planning for Nursing Leadership. [http://www.cna-nurses.ca/CNA/practice/leadership/default_e.aspx] Ottawa, ON; 2006.

10. Hannah KJ: Health informatics and nursing in Canada. [http://hcccinc.qualitygroup.com/hcccinc2/pdf/Vol_XIX_No_3/Vol_XIX_No_3_7.pdf] Healthcare Information Management and Communications Canada 2005, 14:3.

11. Manojlovich M, Ketefian S: The effects of organizational culture on nursing professionalism: Implications for health resource planning. The Canadian Journal of Nursing Research 2002, 33:15–34.

12. Health Canada: [http://www.hc-sc.gc.ca/english/pdf/romanow/pdfs/HCC_Chapter_4.pdf] Investing in Health Care Providers. Ottawa, ON; 2003.

13. Romanow RJ: Building on Values: The Future of Health Care in Canada. Commission on the Future of Health Care in Canada. Ottawa, ON; 2002.

14. Kirby MJL: The Health of Canadians – The Federal Role. Volume 4. The Senate of the Government of Canada. Ottawa, ON: Government of Canada; 2002:111.

15. National Coalition on Health Care: [http://www.nchc.org/materials/studies/reform.pdf] Building a Better Health Care System: Specifications for Reform. Report from the National Coalition on Health Care. Washington, DC. 2004, 5–12.

16. The Texas Department of Insurance: [http://www.tdi.state.tx.us/consumer/cbo69.html] Health Maintenance Organizations. Austin, TX; 2005.

17. Centers for Medicare and Medicaid Services: [http://www.medicare.gov/publications/pubs/pdf/10050.pdf] Medicare and You. Baltimore, Maryland; 2006.

18. Malat J: Social distance and patient's ratings of health care providers. Journal of Health and Social Behavior 2001, 42:360–72. Publisher Full Text

19. Anson BR: Taking charge in a volatile health care marketplace. Human Resource Planning 2003, 23(4):21–34.

20. Jones DA: Repositioning human resources: a case study. Human Resources Planning 1996, 19(1):51–54.

21. World Health Organization Regional Office for Europe: [http://www.euro.who.int/eprise/main/who/progs/chhdeu/system/20050311_1] Highlights on Health. Germany. Copenhagen. 2004.

22. The Library of Congress: [http://lcweb2.loc.gov/frd/cs/detoc.html] A Country Study: Germany. Washington, DC. 1995.

23. Organization for Economic Co-operation and Development: [http://www.oecd.org/dataoecd/16/6/34970073.pdf] OECD Health Data 2005. How Does Germany Compare. Paris. 2005.

24. Organization for Economic Co-operation and Development: [http://www.oecd.org/dataoecd/15/23/34970246.pdf] OECD Health Data 2005. How Does the United States Compare. Paris. 2005.

25. Organization for Economic Co-operation and Development: [http://www.oecd.org/dataoecd/16/9/34969633.pdf] OECD Health Data 2005. How Does Canada Compare. Paris. 2005.

26. Bundesministerium für Gesundheit: [http:/ / www.bmg.bund.de/ cln_041/ nn_617014/ EN/ Health/ health-node,param=.html_nnn=true] Information on Medical Training in the Federal Republic of Germany. Kohn, GDR; 2005.

27. Medknowledge: [http://www.medknowledge.de/germany/] Working Formalities for Foreign Physicians in Germany. Munster. 2000.

28. National Coalition on Health Care: [http://www.nchc.org/facts/Germany.pdf] Health Care in Germany. Washington, DC. 1999.

29. Vujicic M, Zurn P, Diallo K, Orvill A, Dal Poz MR: The role of wages in the migration of health care professionals from developing countries. [http://www.

human-resources-health.com/content/2/1/3] Human Resources for Health 2004, 2:3.

30. Gupta N, Zurn P, Diallo K, Dal Poz MR: Uses of population census data for monitoring geographical imbalance in the health workforce: snapshots from three developing countries. [http://www.equityhealthj.com/content/2/1/11] International Journal for Equity in Health 2003, 2:11.

31. Dussault G, Franceschini M: Not enough here, too many there: understanding geographical imbalances in the distribution of the health workforce. [http://www.lachsr.org/ observatorio/ eng/ pdfs/ Geographical Imbalances05-13-03. pdf] Washington, DC: The World Bank Institute 2003.

32. Findlay J: [http://www.fims.uwo.ca/newmedia2005/default.asp?id=166] Doctors with Borders: Struggles Facing Foreign Physicians in Canada. New Media Journalism. University of Western Ontario. London, ON; 2005.

33. Findlay J: [http://www.fims.uwo.ca/newmedia2005/default.asp?id=175] Facts on Foreign Doctors. New Media Journalism, University of Western Ontario. London, ON; 2005.

34. Barney J: Gaining and Sustaining Competitive Advantage. Reading, MASS: Addison-Wesley Publishing Co.; 1997.

Copyrights

Index

For Product Safety Concerns and Information please contact our EU
representative GPSR@taylorandfrancis.com Taylor & Francis Verlag GmbH,
Kaufingerstraße 24, 80331 München, Germany

Printed and bound by CPI Group (UK) Ltd, Croydon, CR0 4YY
08/05/2025
01864407-0001